RETHINKING THE MEDIA AUDIENCE

The New Agenda

Edited by Pertti Alasuutari

SAGE Publications

London • Thousand Oaks • New Delhi

First published 1999

 SAGE Publications Ltd
6 Bonhill Street
London EC2A 4PU

SAGE Publications Inc
2455 Teller Road
Thousand Oaks, California 91320

SAGE Publications India Pvt Ltd
32, M-Block Market
Greater Kailash – I
New Delhi 110 048

British Library Cataloguing in Publication data

A catalogue record for this book is
available from the British Library

ISBN 0–7619–5070–2
ISBN 0–7619–5071–0 (pbk) ✓

Library of Congress catalog card number   98–61885

Typeset by M Rules
Printed in Great Britain by Biddles Ltd, Guildford, Surrey

CONTENTS

NOTES ON CONTRIBUTORS

Pertti Alasuutari is Professor of Sociology at the University of Tampere and an editor of the *European Journal of Cultural Studies*. His areas of interest are cultural and media studies and qualitative methods, and his publications include *Desire and Craving: A Cultural Theory of Alcoholism* (1992), *Researching Culture: Qualitative Method and Cultural Studies* (1995) and *An Invitation to Social Research* (1998).

Ann Gray is Head of the Department of Cultural Studies and Sociology at the University of Birmingham and an editor of the *European Journal of Cultural Studies*. Her publications include *Video Playtime: The Gendering of a Leisure Technology* (1992), *Studying Culture* (1993, 1997) and *Turning it On: A Reader in Women and Media* (1996). She is currently writing a book on ethnographic research methods in cultural studies and is researching consumption and citizenship.

Ingunn Hagen is Associate Professor in Media and Communication Psychology at Department of Psychology, the Norwegian University of Science and Technology, NUST, in Trondheim, Norway. She is the author of *News Viewing Ideals and Everyday Practices: The Ambivalences of Watching Dagsrevyen* (1992), and has published a number of articles related to audience reception and political communication. Her recent work includes popular culture media products – like *Blind Date* and Disney – and also information and communication technology.

Heikki Hellman, Ph.D., is Arts & Literature Editor of *Helsingin Sanomat*, Helsinki, Finland. His publications include *From Companions to Competitors: The Changing Broadcasting Markets and Television Programming in Finland* (1999) and articles on public service television, television programming, the video and phonogram market, as well as media and cultural policy.

Joke Hermes is Lecturer in Television, Culture and Media Studies at the University of Amsterdam. Her research concentrates on popular culture and cultural citizenship. Her publications include *Reading Women's Magazines* (1995) and (as co-editor) *The Media in Question: Popular Cultures* *and Public Interests* (1998). She is an editor of the *European Journal of Cultural Studies*.

Birgitta Höijer is Professor in Mass Communication at the Department of Media and Communication, University of Oslo, Norway. She has published books and several articles about audiences. She is co-editor of *Cultural Cognition: New Perspectives in Audience Theory* (1998), and author of *Det hörde vi allihop* (1998) – a book on the role and meaning of radio and television in the lives of people during 75 years of broadcasting in Sweden.

David Morley is Professor of Communications, Goldsmiths College, University of London. He is the author of *The Nationwide Audience* (1980), *Family Television* (1986) and *Television, Audiences and Cultural Studies* (1992).

Kim Christian Schrøder is Professor in the Department of Communication, Roskilde University, Denmark. He is co-author of *The Language of Advertising* (1985) and *Medier og Kultur* (1996), and co-editor of *Media Cultures: Reappraising Transnational Media* (1992). His published work includes a cross-cultural study of DYNASTY audiences and a qualitative study of media use and democracy in Denmark.

John Tulloch is professor of Media Communication at Cardiff University, Wales; and was formerly Professor of Cultural Studies and Director of the Centre for Cultural Risk Research at Charles Sturt University, Australia. He is the author of 11 books in media, film and literary theory, with a recent emphasis on audience theory. These include: *Television Drama: Agency, Audience and Myth* (1990), *Science Fiction Audiences: Watching Doctor Who and Star Trek* (1995; with Henry Jenkins), *Television, AIDS and Risk* (1997; with Deborah Lupton) and *Performing Culture: Stories of Expertise and the Everyday* (forthcoming).

ACKNOWLEDGEMENTS

Over the course of the more than four years that putting together this book has taken, I have incurred a great debt to many people. First of all, I want to thank Stephen Barr at Sage, who was very supportive from the very beginning but also made me further develop the book proposal before it was even sent out for review. I am also grateful to all the authors of this book for kindly fulfilling my request to write a piece for this collection. I have learned a lot about media studies in our correspondence about the contents of each chapter. I want especially to thank Ann Gray and Joke Hermes, who during these four years also became my close friends and colleagues as editors of the *European Journal of Cultural Studies*. Their knowledgeable, critical but always constructive comments have greatly improved my own contribution. Finally I want to collectively thank all the people with whom I have discussed the past and future of cultural media studies.

Pertti Alasuutari

PART I

THE SHAPE OF AUDIENCE RESEARCH

1

INTRODUCTION
Three Phases of Reception Studies

Pertti Alasuutari

The key idea of this book is to argue that a 'third generation' of reception studies and audience ethnography is presently taking shape and will establish itself in the near future. However, the division of the development of reception studies and audience research into three 'generations' outlined in this introductory chapter must not be taken matter-of-factly. Rather,. the outline of the suggested division should be seen as a way of pointing out an emergent trend, a direction audience research could take. There are elements in the present research that already lead the way to the new agenda that future research should, in my view, address, but a solid body of research tackling the new field of research is yet to be done. I hope that with the book at hand we can help to address the new questions and outline the basic dimensions of the new field.

The role of this book, in other words, is to act as a midwife: to suggest a 'story line' in cultural media research, a way to read its history in such a way that it points to the emergent trend outlined here and illustrated, developed and discussed in the chapters of this book. This of course means that the history of the 'three generations' told here is a retrospective view, a history of the present (as Foucault says histories always are) or of an anticipated future. Because media audience and reception research has been a rich and many-faceted field, there would be many other ways to tell its history. Other stories would take up other aspects in the development of the field, and would thus imply different worthwhile future trends. The future is always open, and there will most probably be several future trends in the field. As long as future developments are solutions to problems per- ceived in past and present research, they will affect history-writing.

The 'three generations' talked about here must be understood metaphorically also in the sense that the tradition of cultural media research is at most a loose 'school' and has throughout the years since its inception incorporated research undertaken in other fields as influential parts of the 'tradition'. In that sense, its histories can only be told retro- spectively, from the viewpoint of the present and future rather than the perspective of the motives of the researchers counted as part of that 'tra- dition'. The influences of James Lull's (1980a, 1980b) and Janice Radway's (1984) studies serve as good examples of this.

To recapitulate, the history of cultural media research told here is not the only possible line of development that could be discerned in the field. However, that does not mean that it is totally unsubstantiated. Instead, I argue that many researchers in the field perceive the history in the way it is outlined here. The 'inscribed audience' trend of media research is taking its shape. To draw an outline of the emergent agenda, of the questions addressed within it, let us first discuss the three phases of cultural media research.

The first generation: reception research

The birth of reception studies in mass communication research is typically dated back to Stuart Hall's (1974) *Encoding and Decoding in the Television Discourse*, which in its earliest version came out as a 'Stencilled Occasional Paper,' No. 7 in the Media Series of the Centre for Contemporary Cultural Studies. What became known as reception research in media studies was from the very beginning associated with cultural studies and the Birmingham Centre, although it has later been pointed out that reception theory also has other roots. First, in a sense it carried on and readdressed the themes already raised in what was known as the 'uses and gratifica- tions' paradigm. Second, reception studies in mass communication research was historically preceded and later influenced by German recep- tion theory developed in late 1960s literary criticism.[1]

Despite other roots and influences, Hall's encoding/decoding article laid the foundation for and articulated the problems to be addressed in the 'reception paradigm' of what became known as 'media studies'. Media studies was understood as a branch of the broader intellectual movement called cultural studies. Hall's article really presents a fairly simple model, but it was partly just because of its elegant simplicity that it gained a rep- utation as a key text.

When compared to earlier communication models (e.g. Gerbner, 1956; Lasswell, 1948; Shannon and Weaver, 1963), Hall's encoding/decoding model is actually not a very radical change. Like the older models, it approaches (mass) communication as a process whereby certain messages are sent and then received with certain effects. For instance, it does not approach television and other mass media in themselves as part of modern society and its structures, and neither does it address the fact that the media are constitutive of or at least affect the communicated events. However, the reception paradigm Hall promoted did involve a shift from a technical to a semiotic approach to messages. A message was no longer understood as some kind of a package or a ball that the sender throws to the receiver. Instead, the idea that a message is encoded by a programme producer and then decoded (and made sense of) by the receivers means that the sent and received messages are not necessarily identical, and different audiences may also decode a programme differently. Hall does not altogether dismiss the assumption that a message may have an effect, but the semiotic framework he introduces means that one moves away from a behaviouristic stimulus–response model to an interpretive framework, where all effects depend on an interpretation of media messages.

> At a certain point [. . .] the broadcasting structures must yield an encoded message in the form of a meaningful discourse. The institution–societal relations of production must pass into and through the modes of a language for its products to be 'realized'. This initiates a further differentiated moment, in which the formal rules of discourse and language operate. Before this message can have an 'effect' (however defined), or satisfy a 'need' or be put to a 'use', it must first be perceived as a meaningful discourse and meaningfully de-coded. It is this set of de-coded meanings which 'have an effect', influence, entertain, instruct or persuade, with very complex perceptual, cognitive, emotional, ideological or behavioural consequences. (Hall, 1974: 3)

With this linguistic or semiotic turn that Hall proposes, the arguments about effects are effectively swallowed up or at least made dependent upon people's interpretations or thought processes. This turn could have led directly to a kind of radical phenomenology where everything – including, say, the 'structures of production' Hall talks about – is conceived as a social and linguistic construct. Instead of such a big leap, Hall concentrates on applying the semiotic perspective to what he calls the 'determinate moments' of first 'encoding' and then 'decoding'.

> In the moment when the historical event passes under the sign of language, it is subject to all the complex 'rules' by which language signifies. To put it paradoxically, the event must become a 'story' before it can become a *communicative event*. In that moment, the formal sub-rules of language are 'in dominance', without, of course, subordinating out of existence the historical event so signified, or the historical consequences of the event having been signified in this way. (Hall, 1974: 2)

Questions about the role of language and signification are a can of worms in social sciences. Keeping the can firmly closed leads to a mechanistic and simplistic understanding of social phenomena, but once you open it there is the danger that the worms will eat the whole theoretical structure and notion of society. Hall's solution to just peek into the can is clever: he is able to take the role of rhetoric into account to some extent, but otherwise – for instance as far as his notion of social structures is concerned – he sticks to a realistic conception of language.

However, this solution led to an obsession with 'determinate moments', especially the moment of 'decoding', in reception research. From the perspective of the encoding/decoding model it appears that the ideological effects of programming are dependent on the particular strategic moment when the encoded media message enters the brain of an individual viewer.

Hall (1974) suggests that there are four 'ideal-type' positions from which decodings of mass communication by the audience can be made: within the *dominant or hegemonic code* the connotative level of the messages is decoded in terms of the dominant of preferred meanings; the *professional code* is what the professional broadcasters employ when transmitting a message which has already been signified in a hegemonic manner; the *negotiated code* contains a mixture of adaptive and oppositional elements; and finally the *oppositional code* is the position where a viewer perfectly understands both the literal and connotative inflection given to an event, but determines to decode the message 'in a globally contrary way'.

The encoding/decoding model suggested by Hall created a series of empirical studies about the reception of television programmes by different audiences, the first one of which was David Morley's *The Nationwide Audience* (1980).[2] By selecting different groups of people and showing them the *Nationwide* public affairs television programme, Morley could more or less confirm and develop Hall's idea about the four codes discussed above. For instance, the art students whose reception of the programme Morley studied more or less represented the 'professional code'. An innovative, schematic theory had led to the beginning of an empirical project to be carried on by an enthusiastic group of new researchers.

The second generation: audience ethnography

Morley's seminal study was soon followed by studies about the reception of, especially, romantic serials (Ang, 1985; Hobson, 1982; Katz and Liebes, 1984; Liebes, 1984; Liebes and Katz, 1990). What became known as qualitative audience reception studies meant that one analyses a programme and studies its reception among a particular audience by conducting 'in-depth' interviews of its viewers. However, along with an increasing number of empirical reception studies, there occurred a series of gradual shifts in the whole reception paradigm, so that we could say that a new *audience ethnography* paradigm was created.

First, there was a move away from an interest in conventional politics to identity politics, particularly to questions about gender. This can be seen, for instance, in the fact that a slackening interest in the reception of public affairs programmes was balanced out by a growing interest in fictional programmes, particularly romantic serials. These studies concentrated on the politics of gender, on the discourses within which gender is dealt with in the programmes, and how women viewers interpret and make use of the offered readings against the background of their everyday life and experiences. As Ann Gray points out in Chapter 2, feminist scholarship especially has had an important role here in breaking new ground and addressing new questions in reception research.

Second, at the expense of a diminishing interest in programme contents, much more emphasis was laid on the functions of the medium, as is the case with, for instance, James Lull's (1980a, 1980b) analyses of the social uses of television or David Morley's *Family Television* (1986). The growing interest in the functions of television in the family could be seen partly as a rebirth of the older American uses and gratifications paradigm. However, unlike the old paradigm, in the new audience ethnography one focuses on television as a social resource for conversation or on the way in which television use reflects and reproduces (gendered) relations of power in family life. A large project about the role of information and communication technologies in the home also reflected the increased interest in the social uses of television and other media (Silverstone, 1991; Silverstone et al. 1991).

Third, even when the studies of this second generation dealt with a particular programme or serial, researchers started to look at reception from the audience's end of the chain. One does not try to explain a reception of a programme by probing into an 'interpretive community' (Fish, 1979). Instead, one studies the everyday life of a group, and relates the use of (a reception of) a programme or a medium to it. One studies the role of the media in everyday life, not the impact (or meaning) of everyday life on the reception of a programme (e.g. Gray, 1992; Hermes, 1995).

People representing the second generation of reception studies like to emphasize that they are doing or that one should do proper ethnographic case studies of 'interpretive communities'. One even talks about an 'ethnographic turn' quite comparable to the previous 'linguistic turn'. Like classic anthropologists such as Malinowski (1961 [1922]), it has been argued that a proper ethnographic study in audience ethnography entails at least several months' stay in the 'field' (Drotner, 1992) – a demand which, strangely enough, is presented at a time when anthropologists and qualitative sociologists are increasingly questioning the whole notion of a 'field' (Gupta and Ferguson, 1997). On the other hand, what is called an 'ethnographic study' often simply amounts to qualitative 'in-depth' interviews of a group of people, which is of course quite understandable as one bears in mind that most television or video viewing takes place in very small and private settings. There are restrictions to an ethnographer's possibilities of doing a long-term participant observation study in a home.

The third generation: a constructionist view

The starting point for the new agenda of cultural audience studies could be dated back to the late 1980s, when a number of writers began to question and discuss the premises of audience ethnography (Allor, 1988; Ang, 1989, 1990; Fiske, 1988, 1990; Grossberg, 1988; Lull, 1988; Radway, 1988). For instance Allor (1988), Grossberg (1988) and Radway (1988) emphasized that there isn't really such a thing as the 'audience' out there; one must bear in mind that audience is, most of all, a discursive construct produced by a particular analytic gaze. As Grossberg puts it, 'media audiences are shifting constellations, located within varying multiple discourses which are never entirely outside of the media discourse themselves' (1988: 386). Radway (1988) emphasized that, instead of one particular circuit of producer, text and audience, people's daily lives must be the point of departure and object of research. Traditional ethnography was heavily criticized. On the other hand, other researchers, such as Lull (1988), were concerned with a development where some cultural studies theorists were enthusiastic about the impossibility of doing empirical work, although (or because) they had never even tried it.

We must not, however, conceive of the third generation as a clear-cut paradigm with a definite time of birth, let alone a list of studies or researchers representing it. It is an emergent trend, evident not only in the critical discussion outlined above but also in the 'discussion' parts of many 'second generation' studies, where researchers place their study in a larger framework.

This wave of critique and self-reflection meant a thorough rethinking of the place of the media in everyday life, the concept of 'audience' and, along with that, the place of media research itself in the whole picture. As a consequence, a new agenda or third generation of cultural audience studies emerged, although many of its implications are still to be spelled out.

The third generation entails a broadened frame within which one conceives of the media and media use. One does not necessarily abandon ethnographic case studies of audiences or analyses of individual programmes, but the main focus is not restricted to finding out about the reception or 'reading' of a programme by a particular audience. Rather, the objective is to get a grasp of our contemporary 'media culture', particularly as it can be seen in the role of the media in everyday life, both as a topic and as an activity structured by and structuring the discourses within which it is discussed. One is interested in the discourses within which we conceive of our roles as the public and the audience, and how notions of programmes-with-an-audience or messages-with-an-audience are inscribed in both media messages and assessments about news events and about what is going on in the 'world'. The third generation resumes an interest in programmes and programming, but not as texts studied in isolation from their usage as a element of everyday life. Furthermore, it adds a neglected layer of reflexivity to the research on the 'reception' of media messages by addressing the audience's notions of themselves as the 'audience'.

The second generation of reception studies involved a move away from the media to 'interpretive communities' of the everyday, even to the extent that, for instance, Jensen argued that 'the central object of analysis of mass communication research lies outside the media, in the cultures and communities of which media and audiences are constituents' (1990: 14). As Schrøder puts it, 'this development towards ethnography and the everyday is now threatening to write the media, as the focus of research, out of existence' (1994: 338). The third generation brings the media back to media studies, but conceives of the media and media messages in a broader sense than just as an encoded text to be then decoded by a particular 'interpretive community'. A study may start out from such a research design, but the big picture one wants to shed light on, or the big question to pursue, is the cultural place of the media in the contemporary world. It may entail questions about the meaning and use of particular programmes to particular groups of people, but it also includes questions about the frames within which we conceive of the media and their contents as reality and as representations – or distortions – of reality. And how are these frames or discourses about the programmes and about viewing and audiences inscribed in the programmes themselves? What are the cultural concerns that surround media use and media messages? This big research programme also includes questioning the role of media research itself. How are these concerns inscribed in the theoretical models of mass communication research? What is the place of expert knowledge produced by media researchers in enhancing or quieting down public concerns, and in reproducing or transforming the frames within which the media and 'audiencing' (that is, being in the position of the audience, see Fiske 1993) are perceived?

This does not mean that everything should be attempted in any single study. Neither does it imply that we should return to a macro-level investigation of the function of the media, and forget about 'audience ethnographies'. Rather, in a way the new agenda of audience research reclaims the meaning of ethnography. Among anthropologists ethnography means something like 'social and cultural analysis in a particular setting, based on extensive first-hand research'. Ethnography and 'fieldwork' vary considerably from researcher to researcher, and they also depend on the society being studied, but they often include the gamut from surveys and interviews to naturalistic observations. During recent years anthropologists themselves have begun to question the meaning of 'field' and fieldwork in what is now often called our 'postmodern' world.

Traditionally even anthropologists studying highly developed and urbanized societies have selected a remote rural community, typically a village, to do their fieldwork, but urban and multiple-method ethnography is becoming much more common. And even if anthropologists have selected a particular community as an empirical starting point, they have made use of all the data and statistics available about a country and cultural area they are trying to get a grasp of. Anthropologists are increasingly aware of the difficulties in defining the Other, the object of research. How does an anthropologist, for instance, relate to 'native' social researchers: should the anthropologist assume that he or she can outwit the native informant simply because of an outsider's view, weighed against the native's years and years of 'participant observation' and a lifelong 'field experience'? Or how should an emigrant who has returned to study his country of origin conceive of the 'native' or 'Other' in himself, as John Stewart (1989) questions in his study. Or does an American show on local television represent the 'Other' or a 'foreign' element in the everyday life of a people?

As social researchers studying our own culture and society we are quite comparable to anthropologists studying 'other' cultures. Compared with anthropologists, who often have a cultural distance that enables them to see the forest for the trees, we have the disadvantage of being insiders. That is why we have to work hard, develop theoretical perspectives and methods that will better enable us to take distance, to see the bigger picture and ourselves in it too. On the other hand, we have the advantage of a very long personal field experience. We know a lot about the culture, and we possess what Clifford Geertz (1983) calls 'local knowledge': we master in practice many of the rules and discourses we are trying to make our objects of reflection and questioning. In light of our abundant field experience, it is ridiculous to think of a media ethnography in terms of so-and-so many months of participant observation: 'fieldwork' has actually started years before we knew anything about a particular site we are going to study. Similarly, the duration of participant observation or any active part of data gathering depends on the particular study in mind.

Outlining aspects of the new agenda

Above, the retrospective story of the development of cultural media research has been told in terms of three generations of studies. The development was characterized first as a turn from the encoding/decoding model to audience ethnography and then to a discursive or constructionist view of the media and audiences. The different dimensions and implications of the new agenda are still to be explored by future research, but I suggest that we can already identify certain emergent trends in media research as implications of the discursive or constructionist turn. An increasing reflexivity, a move from audience psychology to sociology, and a development towards addressing a whole 'media culture' instead of only mass communication are such trends, which can be identified by taking a retrospective look at the development of mass communication research. Let me now discuss these trends in the light of previous research and the chapters of this book.

Increased reflexivity

One of the gradual developments in cultural and media studies has been to reflect upon and to take distance from the cultural concerns embedded in the way we conceive of contemporary society and its characteristic new phenomena, such as mass communication and mass culture. The relation to these phenomena has been difficult in cultural studies and in critical social theory more generally, because a central objective of cultural studies has been to be critical of 'modern' or 'postmodern' society, and in that sense it itself includes a moral stance. However, to be 'critical' in the analytic sense requires that in one's perspective to the phenomena under scrutiny one is not led or blindfolded by culturally given concerns.

The Marxist background and influence of cultural studies writing and research has been evident in an interest in ideology, and in the processes through which the working class has been kept content with its social position and conditions. In particular, the Frankfurt School, and especially Max Horkheimer and Theodor Adorno, has emphasized that commercially produced mass culture and the 'culture industry' possess a central role in this respect. Although cultural studies is particularly known for its less elitist and more complex relation to mass culture, Richard Hoggart, as an early figure, still shared many of the Frankfurt School's concerns in this respect:

> The Derby Survey suggests that fiction of one sort or another accounts for between 75 and 80 per cent of public library issues; and most librarians would say, I think, that much of this fiction is of a very poor kind. [. . .] In the public libraries the issues of the class 'history, biography, travel' form the biggest single non-fiction group, probably accounting now for a quarter to one–third of all non-fiction issues. Again, many librarians would say, I believe, that the books included in that general heading are often of little value. (Hoggart, 1958: 332–3)

In Hoggart's view, as a consequence of the consumption of 'poor fiction', the intellectual minority of the working class moves over to the middle class and the class as a whole becomes passive. Previously, Hoggart thinks, the working class read – or was offered – better popular culture, but the new mass culture is demoralizing:

> They can be accused (as can all else for which they stand as examples: the thin *bonhomie* of many television programmes, the popular film, much in commercial radio), not of failing to be highbrow, but of not being truly concrete and personal.

> The quality of life, the kind of response, the rootedness in a wisdom and maturity which a popular and non-highbrow art can possess may be as valuable in their own ways as those of a highbrow art. These productions do not contribute to a sounder popular art but discourage it. (Hoggart, 1958: 339)

As said, Hoggart shares many of the Frankfurt School's views, with the exception that he does not dismiss mass culture offhand. His view does reproduce the cultural distinction between art and mass culture, but it allows the study of highbrow – as well as popular culture – products from the viewpoint of their radicalism or conservatism: whether they produce and reproduce or challenge the prevalent ideology, for instance the relations between the sexes.

It has been a central theme in cultural studies to search for possibilities of resistance in mass culture and everyday life. For instance, Janice Radway finds elements of resistance and compensation in women's reading of the Harlequin series romances:

> It is combative in the sense that it enables them to refuse the other-directed social role prescribed for them by their position within the institution of marriage. In picking up a book, as they have so eloquently told us, they refuse temporarily their family's otherwise constant demand that they attend to the wants of others even as they act deliberately to do something for their own private pleasure. Their activity is compensatory, then, in that it permits them to focus on themselves and to carve out a solitary space within an arena where their self-interest is usually identified with the interests of others and where they are defined as a public resource to be mined at will by the family. For them, romance reading addresses needs created in them but not met by patriarchal institutions and engendering practices. (Radway, 1984: 211)

After the publication of some key texts, such as the book *Resistance through Rituals* (Hall and Jefferson, 1976), it became extremely popular in cultural studies-influenced research to find elements of resistance in the consumption of mass cultural products or for instance in youth subcultures. Whatever researchers studied, they seemed to find symbolic resistance.

Another, related theme in cultural and media studies theorizing was the emphasis on the active role of the receiver; a theme which got one of its most influential formulations in Hall's encoding/decoding article discussed above. The point that messages have to be decoded before they could have any meaning or effect was sound, but detached from a broader theoretical context and reinterpreted in a political framework it ceased to form a basis for innovative research. John Fiske's optimism in the face of television viewer's possibilities to actively produce their readings and interpretations is often considered as an extreme example. Fiske (1987: 236) even talks about television's 'semiotic democracy', by which he refers to its delegation of production of meaning to its viewers. After such a celebration of the role of the viewer or consumer, many people in the field felt that they had had enough of it. That kind of cultural studies theorizing had come to an end.

It is important to notice that the celebration of the active viewer or of possibilities of resistance through mass culture is still fixed to the idea that the consumption of (mass) culture has to be legitimated. Reading romances or watching a television serial is granted a legitimation by showing that it is somehow valuable or useful, or at least not totally harmful. While the older highbrow/lowbrow distinction was totally based on criteria set by the cultural product, the new conception sets criteria according to the way a product is consumed. It is a move away from the sphere of aesthetics to the political, or one could say that it politicizes the aesthetics of everyday life, but it is nevertheless a reproduction of the hierarchical notion of culture.

Ien Ang has been one of the first to question this perspective on mass culture. Although she has preserved the feminist interest in looking for emancipatory potential in media reception, she also notes that the consumption of mass culture always has to do with pleasure, and that it is in no way necessary to think that pleasure has to be instrumentalized.

> It seems therefore impossible to ascertain whether the pleasure of *Dallas* that is based on a recognition of and identification with the tragic structure of feeling is intrinsically progressive or conservative, and therefore politically good or bad – such a question would moreover contain an instrumentalist conception of pleasure, as though pleasure itself doesn't much matter – because that pleasure is first and foremost connected with the *fictional* nature of the position and solutions which the tragic structure of feeling constructs, not with their ideological content. (Ang, 1985: 135)

It is obvious that the instrumentalist perspective of mass communication research on its object is not of its own making; it is only echoing culturally embedded concerns about mass media. In fact, the whole of media research has been formed to address these concerns; for instance, how powerful or harmful are the effects of mass communication and its contents? There is of course really nothing wrong about addressing people's concerns with the help of systematic research, but it is also useful to ask where such concerns stem from in the culture and society. What are the main reasons for the concerns surrounding media use? What do they tell us about the way in which we conceive of the role of mass communication as part of contemporary complex societies? Whose concerns are they particularly?

Recent research shows that media use is in many ways a moral question. For instance, when talking about their TV viewing, people tend to explain, justify and excuse themselves for watching fictional programmes and particularly soap operas, whereas they may talk about watching the news and current affairs programmes as if it were a civic duty (Alasuutari, 1992; Hagen, 1992, 1994a, 1994b).

These observations at once speak to several interesting social and cultural phenomena. For one thing, the 'moral hierarchy' of television programmes shows how hierarchies are reproduced in modern societies: we all contribute to naturalizing the 'legitimate taste' (Bourdieu, 1984), especially represented by the habits and attitudes of upper-middle-class males, by the discourses within which we talk about different genres of fact and fiction. Moreover, in so doing we reproduce a utilitarian attitude to fiction and to the media, and by preferring fact over fiction we naturalize a conventional notion of politics.

Finally, an analysis of these discourses leads us to inquire into their history and present uses in society. As the studies referred to above point out, the moral tensions surrounding our media use are not just private concerns, but instead reflect the discourses within which media policies are organized and legitimated. Public service institutions, especially in their previously common state monopoly position, utilized the notion of 'mass culture' or 'lowbrow' to legitimate the programme policy of showing what citizens *need*, instead of what they *want*. As Ien Ang puts it:

> A history of European public service broadcasting in general could be written from this perspective: a narrative in which the resistance of the audience against its objectification in the name of highminded, national cultural ideals drives the story forward. (1991: 101)

Continuing Ang's line of thought, in Chapter 6 Heikki Hellman discusses how different configurations of viewers also provide the paradigms of programming policy and the discourses by which to legitimate different programme policies. Hellman's analysis leads us to ask whether the recent problematization of the distinction between 'high' and 'low' in media research reflects, perhaps also contributes to, the international and especially European deregulation of media policy. From this perspective, the celebration of the active audience and the emancipatory potential of different programmes and genres can be seen as just another discourse useful in justifying or opposing media policies and politics.

Media researchers' increased reflexivity in relation to the discourses within which we conceive of and talk about, say, the role of the audience has meant that reception studies and qualitative audience research cannot totally ignore a media policy perspective. This also entails that the researchers have to reflect on their own position and the role of research: as researchers we cannot naively assume to hold a detached, divine position outside the society we are studying. No matter how unbiased, neutral and objective researchers want to remain, we have to acknowledge and take into account that, as soon as social science discourses about the media and audiences leave the desk of their author, they become part of public discourse used for different purposes.

We can also talk about increased reflexivity on the side of ordinary people as audiences. Or, to be more precise, it is probably a researchers' delusion to assume that people have become more reflective in their relationship to the media. It is rather that constructionist qualitative audience research, more than previous paradigms, is able to pay attention to the fact that ordinary people do not just watch TV without any reflection on that activity as a whole. As Birgitta Höijer discusses in Chapter 9, there are also common-knowledge discourses within which to talk about, assess or criticize one's own or someone else's media use. As ordinary citizens we also share different cultural images of the media (see Chapter 5), and as Joke Hermes shows in Chapter 4, there are different discourses within which to deal with media figures and celebrities. The shared frames and discourses used in articulating issues related to the media necessarily affect our own relationship to them because, after all, reality only exists to us through meanings, discourses and discursive practices.

The discourses surrounding audiences, media and media use both form and circle around an intersection between everyday life, politics and media research. For instance, as Ingunn Hagen shows in Chapter 7 and John Tulloch in Chapter 8, television professionals – journalists, producers and drama directors – all have their images and constructs of audiences, often partly formed with the help of constructs, such as ratings figures, that media research provides them. Moreover, as John Tulloch vividly shows, national and global politics are fed in, for instance, through soap opera writers, producers or viewers suggesting social problems and political issues that could be dealt with in the series. All these different discourses and audience and media constructs become part of common knowledge, and thus affect our notions about the media and media use.

From audience psychology to sociology

The development toward a discursive or constructionist approach in media reception and qualitative audience research has also meant that researchers have taken more distance from the 'determinate moment' of decoding. A psychological interest in viewers' mental processing and interpretation of media messages has given way to a more sociological perspective, within which one studies the range of frames and discourses on the media and their contents as a topic in its own right, not as a lens through which to peek into individual acts of reception.

This increased distance taken from a psychological research interest can also be seen as a long, gradual process. With his encoding/decoding model Hall took distance from a behaviouralist theory, wherein one conceives of the process of mass communication in terms of 'effects', 'uses' or 'gratifications'. Hall points out that these concepts 'are themselves framed by structures of understanding, as well as social and economic structures which shape its "realization" at the reception end of the chain, and which permit the meanings signified in language to be transposed into conduct or consciousness' (1974: 4). Although Hall, by introducing the semiotic perspective to media reception, did break away from behaviourism, his model retained a fairly psychological aspect by suggesting that there is a determinate moment of *reception* which one should concentrate on. This turned researchers' attention to the mental processes whereby viewers perceive and interpret messages. The underlying idea here is that, since the culture-bound concepts by which one makes sense of reality provide the horizon for interpreting new messages, the same message is not exactly the same for different individuals. As Schrøder (1987: 19), for instance, formulates the big question in a review article assessing the state of the art of audience research as it was at that time: 'Do people who watch the same programme actually see the same programme?'

The first attempts to address that question were simply based on the idea that, instead of a social survey, one needs a more qualitative approach such as 'in-depth' interviews to be able to probe into the cultural reality of a community or an individual. However, it was soon pointed out that meanings are produced in a community. It was emphasized that the individual audience member is a social being with a specific cultural identity created by the interpersonal relations of the communities to which he or she belongs. That is why it was thought that one needs to study groups, preferably natural audiences, which 'negotiate social meanings from their encounter with screen events' (Schrøder, 1987: 19).

Let us take Liebes and Katz's study of cross-cultural readings of *Dallas* (Liebes and Katz, 1990), a typical 'decoding study', as an illustrative example of the methodological problems for which 'third generation' thinking provides a new angle. From this angle, even the same empirical findings can be seen in a new light.

Liebes and Katz wanted to study how 'viewers selectively perceive, interpret and evaluate the programme in terms of local cultures and personal experiences' by studying four different groups within Israeli society (Israeli Russians, Arab citizens of Israel, Moroccan Jews, and kibbutz members who are mostly Israeli-born), second-generation Americans in Los Angeles, and Japanese in Japan (1990: 20–4). Although the research design was ambitious in trying to compare several cultures, actually there was no fieldwork, and the idea about a national and ethnic 'interpretive community' as the explanation for possible differences in 'decoding' was 'operationalized' so that the researchers asked their subject families to invite two other couples to their homes to watch a sample episode together, and to be interviewed. That was their solution to the problem that, as Katz and Liebes put it: 'We do not know how to sample thoughts without provoking them, or how to sample conversations without constructing them' (1985: 10).

The way in which Liebes and Katz present the results of their analysis shows how they conceive of the actual object of analysis. By applying Roman Jakobson's theory, they distinguish 'referential reading' and 'critical reading'. According to them, referential reading connects the programme and real life. Viewers relate to characters as real people and in turn relate these real people to their own real worlds. Meanwhile, critical reading frames discussions of the programme as a fictional construction with aesthetic rules. Referential readings are more emotionally involving, whereas critical readings are more cognitive, since they deal with genres, dynamics of plot and thematics of the story (Liebes and Katz, 1990: 100).

To compare the different groups' 'readings', the researchers counted the ratio of referential to critical *utterances* in the group discussions. The idea was to classify 'every statement that connects an observation about the programme with an observation about real life or about the programme as text or artistic construction' (Liebes and Katz, 1990: 101). Comparisons between the groups then show that they differ significantly in the ratio of referential to critical utterances. The most critical utterances were made by the Russians, followed by Americans and kibbutzniks, followed by Moroccan Jews and Arabs. 'Higher education also increases the proportion of critical statements, but even when education is held constant, the rank order of ethnic differences remains unchanged' (Liebes and Katz, 1990: 101).

Although codes such as 'referential' and 'critical' can quite reliably be identified in interview texts, a major problem in Liebes and Katz's study is that they equate the two types of discourse with two kinds of perceiving or 'reading' *Dallas* as a programme. It is simply assumed that individuals who predominantly speak about the episode by referential utterances take the programme as real.

This hasty equation of interview talk with a decoding of a programme or with cognitive structures inherent in a culture or 'interpretive community' is challenged in present-day media research, influenced by different trends of discourse analysis. From a discourse-analytic perspective, the idea is not to treat the interviewees' talk as a screen through which to look inside their head. Instead, the idea is to start by studying the interview text – or any texts or transcriptions of conversations for that matter – in its own right. What is going on in the interview text and in the interaction situation? How do the participants (the interviewer and the interviewee) co-construct and negotiate their roles, definitions of the situation, or different objects of talk? What frames, discourses or 'interpretive repertoires' (Hermes, 1995; Potter and Wetherell, 1987) are invoked, and what functions do they serve?

This change of perspective from treating interviews as a picture of 'decoding' to treating them as discourses on the media and everyday life, a turn whose implications media researchers have only begun to chart through empirical research, was due to the ethnographic turn discussed above. Since studies such as David Morley's *Family Television* (1986) began to perceive the media from the viewpoint of the everyday, as household appliances used in different ways amidst domestic life, it was natural to start conceiving of individuals' talk on the media and their contents as just topics among other topics. The different discourses within which the media were talked about could then be seen as different uses of the media as a topic, each explainable by the context in which it is used and by the function it serves.

From this perspective, the different 'decodings' or typologies of 'reading' can be assessed in a new context. Let us take Liebes and Katz's (1990) study as an example. Continuing the central problematics of the first generation of reception studies – that is, the question about the media's ideological effects and people's oppositional potential – Liebes and Katz (1990) distinguished *referential* and *critical* readings.[3] Underlying these typologies is the researchers' interest in seeing whether viewers are critical of what they are shown, and what factors have an impact on individuals' ability to be critical. For instance, Liebes and Katz (1990: 101) explain the American *Dallas* viewers' high ratio of critical statements by them being well acquainted both with the real Dallas and with real Hollywood. However, from a discourse-analytic perspective one would ask, what are the contexts, the points people want to make in a discussion, in which people discuss the series as a performance? Or more generally, what are the themes and topics that watching and asking about *Dallas* invoke? For instance, it can be suggested that the American respondents shared the same concern with the respondents in my study (Alasuutari, 1992); when accounting for watching serials they wanted to assure the interviewer that they are not naive in their attitudes towards fictional programmes. Through their explanations and justifications people wanted to dissociate themselves from the specific kind of attitude toward television which is regarded as injurious or shameful.

From this perspective, the 'reception' of a programme or genre can be given a more sociological meaning. We are interested in it as a topic in a given society. What are the embedded problems and concerns that evoke it as a topic? What are the viewpoints and subject positions taken in the discourse? How, and by whom, is it discussed in public, and how do people in everyday-life conversations refer to or comment on the public discussions about it?

A 'reception' study devised along these lines does not necessarily analyse the programme or genre 'itself' at all. For instance, Hermes' (1995) study of women's magazine readers concentrates on the repertoires people evoke in discussing their magazine use, and in that sense defines the cultural position of that media genre. In a similar vein Gripsrud's *The Dynasty Years* (1995) treats *Dynasty* as a historical phenomenon, part of a particular period, tied to certain conjunctures in American, and more generally, Western society. Although he concentrates on a particular series, the object is not the product *Dynasty* 'as such'; rather, it is the totality of '*Dynasty* texts', the public debate and discussion developed around it in the 1980s.

Addressing media culture

All in all, the new agenda of cultural studies entails a shift to addressing media use and reception in an even broader perspective. Instead of only treating media messages from the viewpoint of their truthfulness or effects, the media and programmes and messages are also seen as part of social reality.

Life in contemporary societies increasingly revolves around the media and modern communication technologies. In fact, they are constitutive of the whole world system, where individuals and nation states are complexly dependent upon – and in a real-time connection with – each other. We more or less share the same topics world-wide, be they current events, pop stars, movies or television programmes. As a topic, there is no epistemological difference between fact and fiction, although they are framed differently in everyday conversations.

Because of the relative novelty of the contemporary 'media cultures', and the rapid development in communication technology, world cultures have to continuously renew the frames within which to conceive of the new 'mediascape' within which people lead their daily lives. Old and new epistemologies often live side by side, and rapid social change often causes confusion and fears.

As an essential aspect of contemporary cultures, the media and the frames within which they are conceived deserve critical, reflective, empirical research, and in the face of the social changes, media research also has to renew itself. For instance, the old question of whether mass communication affects its audience or whether the audiences have an active role is – within the broader societal frame – roughly the same as to ask whether society has an impact on the individual. Such questions are framed much too narrowly. As I see it, the task of the emerging new agenda of cultural audience studies is to study different phenomena related to contemporary media cultures empirically, and in such a way that researchers are not blinded by their own fears and concerns.

Organization of the book

The book at hand makes an overview of the present shape and the evolving new agenda of reception research and qualitative media studies. It is divided into two parts.

Part I discusses the development and present shape of the field at a more general level. In Chapter 2 Ann Gray discusses especially the role of feminist scholarship in the development of ethnographic research and reception research as a whole. She also discusses how the increased interest in identity politics in media studies created a partly gendered division between 'public knowledge' and 'popular culture' projects, and how the proponents of the public knowledge project, from the viewpoint of their traditional conception of politics, criticize the popular culture project for redirecting attention away from the 'real' world, without realizing how biased that perspective is. In Chapter 3 Kim Schrøder discusses the methodological development and divisions within mass communication research. He shows how both 'camps', qualitative and quantitative research, have their weaknesses, and by giving a concrete example shows that the two approaches are not mutually exclusive. They can be complementarily combined in a single study.

The chapters in Part II map out different dimensions of the new agenda. These chapters discuss how there are shared images and notions about practically all elements of mediated communication, and how these notions play a crucial role in affecting not only the media but society at large.

In Chapter 4 Joke Hermes discusses the various ways in which media figures, fictive or real-life constructions play a role in mediated communication and everyday life. In Chapter 5 I discuss different cultural images of the media. In Chapter 6 Heikki Hellman discusses how public service and commercial broadcasting policies are legitimized, and how these discourses have changed along with the recent development of the multichannel television universe.

Chapters 7–9 concentrate on the notions and constructions of the audience by different parties. In Chapter 7 Ingunn Hagen concentrates on the images various media employees, especially those of broadcasting institutions, have of audiences and the general public. In Chapter 8 John Tulloch discusses how television fiction professionals' knowledge and conceptions of a targeted audience and its taste are taken into account already in programme production. In Chapter 9 Birgitta Höijer discusses the viewers' notions, or 'meta-cognitions', of the audience.

The last word is given to David Morley. As an active and prominent figure in reception and audience studies through all its phases, Morley gives his assessment of the 'third generation' of reception research in the light of the chapters in this book.

Notes

1. More precisely, that paradigm can be dated back to 1969, when Hans Robert Jauss published his essay Paradigmawechsel in der Literaturwissenschaft'. In that essay, Jauss himself characterizes the ideas he presents as a paradigm shift in literary criticism, and he was not mistaken in that. Instead of studying authors' biographies, German literary critics began to study the social conditions accounting for the reception of a work (Holub, 1984).

2. It was the second part of a research project which started with Brunsdon and Morley's (1978) analysis of the Nationwide programme itself.

3. In that their classification is close to Hall's typology distinguishing between dominant and oppositional codes. Similarly Richardson and Corner (1986) made a distinction between transparent and mediated descriptions.

References

Alasuutari, P. (1992) "I'm Ashamed to Admit it but I Have Watched *Dallas*": The Moral Hierarchy of TV Programmes', *Media, Culture & Society*, 14 (4): 561–82.

Allor, M. (1988) 'Relocating the Site of the Audience', *Critical Studies in Mass Communication*, 5: 217–33.

Ang, I. (1985) *Watching Dallas: Soap Opera and the Melodramatic Imagination*, London: Methuen.

Ang, I. (1989) 'Beyond Self-Reflexivity', *Journal of Communication Inquiry*, 13 (2): 27–9.

Ang, I. (1990) 'Culture and Communication: Towards an Ethnographic Critique of Media Consumption in the Transnational Media System'. *European Journal of Communication*, 5: 239–60.

Ang, I. (1991) *Desperately Seeking the Audience*, London: Routledge.

Bourdieu, P. (1984) *Distinction: A Social Critique of the Judgement of Taste*. Cambridge, MA: Harvard University Press.

Brunsdon, C. and Morley, D. (1978) *Everyday Television: 'Nationwide'*. London: British Film Institute.

Drotner, K. (1992) 'What is "the Everyday" in Media Ethnography?' Paper presented to the Mass Media and the Ethnography of Everyday Life seminar, Holbaek, Denmark, November.

Fish, S. (1979) *Is There a Text in This Class? The Authority of Interpretive Communities*. Cambridge, MA: Harvard University Press.

Fiske, J. (1987) *Television Culture*. London: Methuen.

Fiske, J. (1988) 'Meaningful Moments', *Critical Studies in Mass Communication*, 5: 246–51.

Fiske, J. (1990) 'Ethnosemiotics: Some Personal and Theoretical Reflections', *Cultural Studies*, 4 (1): 85–99.

Fiske, J. (1993) 'Audiencing: Cultural Practice and Cultural Studies', in Norman Denzin (ed.) *Handbook of Qualitative Research*, Thousand Oaks, CA: Sage: 189–98.

Geertz, C. (1983) *Local Knowledge: Further Essays in Interpretive Anthropology*. New York: Basic Books.

Gerbner, G. (1956) 'Towards a General Model of Communication', *Audio Visual Communication Review*, IV (3): 171–99.

Gray, A. (1992) *Video Playtime: The Gendering of a Leisure Technology*. London: Routledge.

Gripsrud, J. (1995) *The Dynasty Years: Hollywood Television and Critical Media Studies*. London: Routledge.

Grossberg, L. (1988) 'Wandering Audiences, Nomadic Critics', *Cultural Studies*, 2 (3): 377–92.

Gupta, A. and Ferguson, J. (eds) (1997) *Anthropological Locations: Boundaries and Grounds of a Field Science*. Berkeley: University of California Press.

Hagen, I. (1992) *News Viewing Ideals and Everyday Practices: The Ambivalences of Watching Dagsrevyen*. University of Bergen, Department of Mass Communication, Report No. 15.

Hagen, I. (1994a) 'The Ambivalences of TV News Viewing: Between Ideals and Everyday Practices', *European Journal of Communication*, 9: 193–220.

Hagen, I. (1994b) 'Expectations and Consumptions Patterns in TV News Viewing', *Media, Culture & Society*, 16: 415–28.

Hall, S. (1974) *Encoding and Decoding in the Television Discourse*. Centre for Contemporary Cultural Studies, Stencilled Occasional Paper No. 7. Birmingham: University of Birmingham.

Hall, S. and Jefferson, T. (eds) (1976) *Resistance through Rituals: Youth Subcultures in Post-War Britain*. London: Hutchinson.

Hermes, J. (1995) *Reading Women's Magazines: An Analysis of Everyday Media Use*. Cambridge: Polity Press.

Hobson, D. (1982) *Crossroads: The Drama of a Soap Opera*. London: Methuen.

Hoggart, R. (1958) *The Uses of Literacy*. Harmondsworth: Penguin Books.

Holub, R. (1984) *Reception Theory – A Critical Introduction*. London: Methuen.

Jauss, H. (1969) *Paradigmawechsel in der Literaturwissenschaft*. Linguistische Berichte, No. 3, 44–56.

Jensen, K. B. (1990) 'Television Futures: A Social Action Methodology for Studying Interpretive Communities', *Critical Studies in Mass Communication*, 7 (2): 1–18.

Katz, E. and Liebes, T. (1984) 'Once upon a Time, in Dallas', *Intermedia*, 12: 28–32.

Katz, E. and Liebes, T. (1985) *The Export of Meaning: Cross Cultural Readings of American TV*. Paper presented to the Manchester Symposium on Broadcasting, March.

Lasswell, H.D. (1948) 'The Structure and Function of Communication in Society', in L. Bryson (ed.), *The Communication of Ideas*. New York: Institute for Religious and Social Studies.

Liebes, T. (1984) 'Ethnocriticism: Israelis of Moroccan Ethnicity Negotiate the Meaning of Dallas', *Studies in Visual Communication*, 10 (3): 46–72.

Liebes, T. and Katz, E. (1990) *The Export of Meaning: Cross-Cultural Readings of Dallas*. New York: Oxford University Press.

Lull, J. (1980a) 'The Social Uses of Television', *Human Communication Research*, 6: 197–209.

Lull, J. (1980b) 'Family Communication Patterns and the Social Uses of Television', *Communication Research*, 7 (3): 319–34.

Lull, J. (1988) 'The Audience as Nuisance', *Critical Studies in Mass Communication*, 5: 239–42.

Malinowski, B. (1961 [1922]) *Argonauts of the Western Pacific*. New York: E.P. Dutton.

Morley, D. (1980) *The Nationwide Audience*. London: British Film Institute.

Morley, D. (1986) *Family Television: Cultural Power and Domestic Leisure*. London: Comedia.

Potter, J. and Wetherell, M. (1987) *Discourse and Social Psychology: Beyond Attitudes and Behaviour*. London: Sage.

Radway, J.A. (1984) *Reading the Romance: Women, Patriarchy, and Popular Literature*. Chapel Hill: University of North Carolina Press.

Radway, J.A. (1988) 'Reception Study: Ethnography and the Problems of Dispersed Audiences and Nomadic Subjects', *Cultural Studies*, 2 (3): 359–76.

Richardson, K. and Corner, J. (1986) 'Reading Reception: Mediation and Transparency in Viewers' Accounts of a TV Programme', *Media, Culture & Society*, 8: 485–508.

Schrøder, K.C. (1987) 'Convergence of Antagonistic Traditions? The Case of Audience Research'. *European Journal of Communication*, 2: 7–31.

Schrøder, K.C. (1994) 'Audience Semiotics, Interpretive Communities and the "Ethnographic Turn" in Media Research', *Media, Culture & Society*, 16: 337–47.

Shannon, C.E. and Weaver, W. (1963) *The Mathematical Theory of Communication*. Urbana: University of Illinois Press.

Silverstone, R. (1991) 'From Audiences to Consumers: The Household and the Consumption of Communication and Information Technologies', *European Journal of Communication*, 6: 135–54.

Silverstone, R., Hirsch, E. and Morley, D. (1991) 'Listening to a Long Conversation: An Ethnographic Approach to the Study on Information and Communication Technologies in the Home', *Cultural Studies*, 5 (2): 204–27.

Stewart, J.O. (1989) *Drinkers, Drummers, and Decent Folk: Ethnographic Narratives of Village Trinidad*, New York: State University of New York Press.

2

AUDIENCE AND RECEPTION RESEARCH IN RETROSPECT
The Trouble with Audiences

Ann Gray

My brief for this chapter is clear from the main heading, but during my research and background reading I became very critical of the ways in which audiences and audience research have been accounted for. What follows is, therefore, a retrospective piece, but not of the 'overview' review type implicit in its title. This would involve me in covering ground which is effectively covered elsewhere and the reader can be directed to excellent existing work which would provide considerations of the above issues and questions.[1] My reading of different accounts of audience and reception research and some of the recent critical accounts of media and cultural studies fuelled a desire to address explicitly the contribution which a feminist politics, scholarship and intellectual endeavour has made and continues to make to the study of audiences within the associated, but different, fields of media and cultural studies. This contribution has produced a significant body of work which has been developed over the past couple of decades, but in the accounts and 'histories' of reception studies it is often included under the category 'new audience studies', which are then used as examples of the de-politicization of media studies or simply overlooked. In particular, very little close attention has been given to the specificity of these studies and their aims. Thus, there is a double meaning in the 'trouble' in my subtitle. It indicates my dissatisfaction with the accounts and suggests that feminist-inspired work causes trouble to certain established ways of approaching audiences.

To begin, let me consider the damage done to audience studies by the 'overview', that familiar academic genre, which attempts to cover or map out the field in question. I suggest that the nature of this damage is threefold: first, there is a tendency to simplify theoretical models, frameworks and concepts which have been developed through these complex studies; second, there is scant consideration of the politics of research practice, and here I would include questions of method, of disciplinarity and institutional context; and third, the process of simplification effectively evacuates a politics and a history of which these studies were and are a part. This is paradoxical, given that the most consistent accusation by critics has been that the 'new audience studies' lack a political and critical edge (e.g. Corner, 1991; Curran, 1996; Garnham, 1997). Clearly, what constitutes 'the political' is at stake here, but this must be understood within a context where these overviews and critical 'position' papers are effectively producing and maintaining a *gendered division* of the field. A paradox is always intriguing, and I will return to this in my concluding remarks by suggesting why the new audience studies paradigm is so deeply troubling to these and other authors.

My aim in this chapter is twofold. First I will suggest a different way of reading audience work, and in doing so will construct a more complex version of the trajectory of 'new audience studies'. Second, by exploring questions of method, I argue that there *are* quite fundamental differences in approaches to audiences, which need to be fully acknowledged before we can develop further this already mature and complex field of study.

The critics are coming at reception studies, and cultural studies more generally, from a range of positions, but I want to begin by looking at a very influential text which identifies two main strands of audience studies: 'the public knowledge project' and the 'popular culture project' (Corner, 1991). For Corner, the public knowledge project is concerned with the investigation of mainly factual media, broadcasting and press, and the ways in which they inform or produce 'knowledge' in the reader. The popular culture project, conversely, focuses on fictional or 'entertainment' texts, and is concerned with the 'imaginative pleasure' offered readers by such texts. Corner identifies those reception studies which fall in the latter category as the 'new audience studies'. I have very high regard for Corner's work and the piece in question is more open than most, particularly in his desire to overcome the divisions. However, his 'distinctions' have become a convenient short-hand for thinking about reception analysis and have been identified as examples of the gendered nature of not only reception research, but media studies in general. Nevertheless, these categories are by no means 'equal but different' in many of the retrospectives and overviews. The 'public knowledge' project is taken to be the *existing* paradigm and those studies reflecting the popular culture project are found lacking. Indeed some of the authors seem to suggest that there is, in the sheer existence of these studies, a general weakening of the public knowledge project, a kind of emasculation of the concerns and vigour of the earlier work (Curran, 1996). The critics incorporate in these images of 'bad' projects the figure of the 'active audience', which notion indicates an abandonment of politics and a concern with individual taste and pleasures and a speculative, loose and non-critical methodology. Corner thus questions 'the general *political* relations at work [. . .] in the sudden burgeoning of "demand-side" research from the mid 1980s onwards' (1991: 269); this is particularly problematic and prevalent, according to Corner, in work within his defined 'popular culture' project.

There is a dangerous tendency for these divisions and distinctions to become set in stone, but this effectively ignores feminist scholarship and sexual politics, which were the impulse behind much of the so-called 'demand-side' research. The sphere of consumption has in general been seen as feminine (compared to production) and in much mass communication theory the audience is characterized as passive. This applies as much to dominant ideology theses as it does to marketing and advertising research. However, when researchers turned their attention to the ways in which meaning is produced at the moment of reading, to the actual viewing, reading, listening contexts, and to the eruptions of daily life into an understanding of media reception, they were also interrupting existing models and approaches. These operated within neat, confinable and measurable models of reception and the 'certainties' of analyses of institution, ownership and control of the media as well as media content and message.

Corner is concerned with issues and questions of power in relation to media and society. However, he and others seem unaware of the implicit hierarchy and reproduction of power relations therein which this representation of the field demonstrates. The importance of current affairs programming, and of the public knowledge project, is simply taken as a given. It has never had to be justified or fought over, and Corner's paradigm categories effectively 'naturalize' these hierarchical and, I would argue, gendered divisions. Feminist media scholarship, on the other hand, has had to argue its corner and justify its theoretical and methodological focus. As such it can be understood, within the academy, as a history of struggle, over appropriate research objects, methods and theories (Brunsdon, 1997). Rarely do overview and 'state of the field' papers pay any attention to the institutional contexts within which academic work takes place, whereas feminists, working in a range of disciplines where their concerns are often marginalized, have emphasized the importance of this dimension in an understanding of the politics of knowledge and the development and financing of research (Bar On, 1993; Bobo and Seiter, 1991; Stanley, 1990).

Corner refers, rather anxiously it seems, to the 'burgeoning' of the 'new audience' research, but there are remarkably *few* empirical audience studies within the interdisciplinary fields of media, communication and cultural studies. This is made obvious by the constant referencing of a handful of studies in every discussion of audience work. These would include Ang (1985) on *Dallas*, Hobson (1982) on *Crossroads*, Morley's *Nationwide* study (1980a) and *Family Television* (1986), Buckingham's (1987) work on children's viewing, Lull's (1990) study of family television viewing, Seiter et al. (1989) on soap opera audiences, Sut Jhalley and Justin Lewis (1992) on *The Cosby Show*, and Katz and Liebes' (1985) studies of cross-cultural readings of *Dallas*. Other studies regularly cited which do not deal with broadcast media are Janice Radway's *Reading the Romance*

(1984), Joke Hermes' *Reading Women's Magazines* (1995) and my own study of the use of video recorders in the home, *Video Playtime* (1992). It is surely significant that most of these studies investigate questions which are broadly within the 'popular culture' project. The increased interest in audience work has been generated by those scholars who have brought different agendas to the field, for example questions of power in relation to gender and 'race' and of media use within domestic contexts.

It is still the case, despite Corner's fears, that there are very few actual studies of audiences/readerships, but the volume of critical work and 'overviews' of audience work are legion. Because the audience and its study is so obviously a key element in thinking about media in contemporary societies, scholars have felt obliged to address the topic. However, they have tended to do this either by producing overviews of 'the field' or by taking theoretical positions on the conceptualization of the audience – some notably managing to theoretically evacuate any study of actual audiences from our agenda (Allor, 1988; Hartley, 1987). The result is that the few existing studies have borne the weight of these critiques and overviews and what we have are over-simplified versions of the studies themselves within which certain tropes emerge which are repeated again and again in the literature. The most familiar trope is that of 'the active audience', a term which is used often in the relevant literature. This character is posited all too readily, simply to be dismissed as evidence of work which is declared to be apolitical, naive, celebratory and banal.[2] There is, therefore, a tendency both in the 'new audience' critical writing and in the simplifying strategies of the overview to elide feminist reception studies with the much denigrated 'active audience' research. The result is that feminist-inspired work is constantly kept on the margins of media studies. This is noticeable if one is trying to recommend texts to students on a general media course where feminist work is not sufficiently or thoroughly addressed, Van Zoonen's study being the exception (Van Zoonen, 1994; and see also readers Baehr and Gray, 1996 and Brunsdon et al.,1997).

I want to propose that the most extreme version of the 'active audience' is a myth, emerging rarely in its 'pure' form, and that most of the studies referred to above provide examples of what Bennett has called the '*determined* active reader' (1996: 152, my emphasis). In many of these studies the researchers are at pains to explore not just reader activity in and for itself, but also under what circumstances and in what conditions those readings take place. This involves exploration of anterior circumstances of readers, social positioning being just one, and how they shape not only readings, but access to particular genres and, more generally, the use and consumption of different media in their daily lives. More importantly, however, they were all undertaken within specific intellectual, political and institutional contexts, some continuous, some discontinuous, but each responding to particular gaps, blind-spots and problematics in the understanding of the interpretation, consumption and use of popular media forms. They developed over time, and when these studies are wrenched from their historical contexts, as they so often are, and used in critical overviews to make academic capital, then readers are given an impoverished version of the development of the field. These various contexts should be made available to students as informed introductions into audience work. Students with access to the complex contexts of these studies are then in a position to ask some key questions about audience/reception studies. These would include: What is the research question? What aspect of 'audience' and media is being investigated? How is the audience being conceptualized? What is the nature of the relationship between the audience and various kinds of media forms? What aspect of audience activity is the central focus of the research? What are the methods employed, and how does the researcher account for them and him- or herself? These elements are by no means uniform or stable, and require more detailed attention and understanding than they have thus far been afforded.

The encoding/decoding model

What better place to start than the 'encoding/decoding' model proposed by Stuart Hall?[3] It is often, after all, where reviews of 'active audience' studies begin. Here, I want to use it as an example in the practice of examining the actual context of its development, compared with the (over-)simplification in its recent manifestations. This is particularly the case in student textbooks, which reduce the model to a simple, almost common-sense model of communication which seems, to students I have encountered at any rate, to be stating the obvious.

In a very interesting and helpful interview, Stuart Hall is encouraged to reflect on the encoding/decoding model which forms the start point for many accounts of the move into the 'active audience' (Cruz and Lewis, 1994). He insists on beginning his responses to various questions by reminding us of the context within which the model itself was developed. It was written and delivered as a 'position paper' and has, in Hall's words a 'polemical thrust' (Cruz and Lewis, 1994: 253). It positioned itself in relation to the state of existing research, and Hall suggests that we must pay attention to at least three aspects of the work.

First, its methodological and theoretical problematic. It was addressed to the Centre for Mass Communications Research at the University of Leicester, which at the time, the mid-1970s, was associated with the then mainstream approaches to communication and media analysis. Hall's paper 'The Television Discourse – Encoding and Decoding' was a challenge to the dominant communication model and to positivistic notions of content analysis and audience understanding. In short, it was complicating the dominant communication model at the time and it 'interrupt[ed] that transparent notion of communication' (Cruz and Lewis, 1994: 254). The second factor is, as Hall describes, political. The paper challenges the idea that it is possible to determine the nature of communication and meaning by the application of measurement techniques. It insists that meaning is multi-layered/multi-referential and as such imports the then new fields of semiotics and structuralism into the study of mass communication. And finally, for Hall, the model was part of a wider debate within Marxism itself and signals the move from the over-determination of the dominant ideology thesis to the more complex notion suggested by Gramsci's hegemony model. However, the encoding/decoding model was concerned with power, specifically with the idea of the encoding of 'preferred meanings' into media products. These are the product of institutional processes, working within the broader cultural and ideological world and, Hall suggests, working within the dominant ideology.

If Leicester were operating within one research paradigm, the other major development in audience work at the time was known as the 'uses and gratifications' model (Blumler and Katz, 1974). Hall's model offered a way beyond the current uses and gratifications approach by insisting that audiences share certain frameworks of understanding and interpretation. Reading is not simply the lonely uses and gratifications individual; it is shared. Hall reminds us of the major purpose of the paper – 'I had in my sights the Centre for Mass Communications Research – that was who I was trying to blow out of the water' – and insists that if the model has *any* purchase, now and later, it's a model because of what it suggests. It suggests an approach; it opens up new questions. It maps the terrain. But it's a model which has to be worked with and developed and changed' (Cruz and Lewis, 1994: 255). Hall locates the encoding/decoding paper at a conjuncture, or paradigm shift. He characterizes it as the one which Barthes made 'from the interpretation of the codes into the notion of textuality, and then later into the notion of desire and the pleasure of the text'. He sees this as a key development which 'took cultural studies from communication studies to literary theory, to the cinematic text, to psychoanalysis, to feminism, and to the beginnings of poststructuralism' (Cruz and Lewis, 1994: 271). Hall's version of the encoding/decoding model is a far cry from the way in which it has become in media and cultural studies textbooks, almost reified as a *description* of media communication process. What he also signals is the shift in cultural studies – a shift which is perhaps at the core of the differences between the conflicting views of audience research.

Hall's suggestive model provided the theoretical framework for the groundbreaking *Nationwide* study (Morley, 1980a), which brought together the constructed text (Brunsdon and Morley, 1978), with its perceived preferred reading, and the interpreting groups of readers with their determinations. Brunsdon, Hall and Morley worked together on the *Nationwide* study as, in Hall's words, a 'small research team', unable to get comprehensive funding, but working on a shoestring to give some empirical substance to the encoding/decoding model. The *Nationwide* study sought to combine textual construction and interpretation, it granted viewers interpretive status (but always within shaping structural determinations) and developed ways of conceiving of the audience as socially structured, suggesting that decoding is not homogeneous. Thus, the text and audience are conceptualized within and as part of the social structure organized in and across power relations of dominant and subordinate groups, of which the media were seen to be occupying a crucial position and role. Although the viewer was considered to be interpreting specific programmes in different ways, these were not entirely and absolutely open to the viewer; she or he was limited, shaped by her or his own social positioning as well as the limitations and closures of the text itself.

Whilst this study significantly attempted a 'double move' into the notion of the socially constructed audience and ideologically constructed text, it also shifted from 'straight' news and current affairs to an understanding of the encoding of the more popular 'entertainment' magazine format of *Nationwide*. It thus challenged the 'hard news' focus of existing work, it placed textuality clearly in the communication dynamic, and it was suggestive of different reader positions.

The suggestive text

Hall notes the important contribution made to the development of the *Nationwide* study by Charlotte Brunsdon, who was beginning to work on the analysis of popular television genres from a feminist perspective (Cruz and Lewis, 1994: 272). The encoding/decoding model gestured towards the influences of structuralism and semiotics, and at the same time textual analyses of popular entertainment genres which were identifying reader/subject positions offered by the text were also coming from literary and film theory, especially from a feminist perspective. Tania Modleski (1983), for example, provided a textual analysis of US daytime television which assumed an ideal reader, distracted, rendered incapable of concentrated and focused viewing. Her more detailed analysis of the structure of the soap opera, such as its multiple storylines and the possibility of multiple character identifications inscribes, according to Modleski (1982), the 'ideal' viewer/reader as an 'ideal' mother. In the UK, scholars were also looking closely at the soap opera in terms of their strong female characters (Dyer et al., 1981, 1997 [1977]), but a more complex formulation of text and reader pleasures came from Brunsdon's (1981) suggestion that pleasures offered by soap required particular 'feminine' skills and competencies, for example 'reading' emotional turmoil, understanding the complexities of familial relationships, which were, in turn, validated within the text, for example a foregrounding of the domestic and the everyday. In these textual analyses the reader/viewer stepped into and out of the text and as such they can be seen as significant interdisciplinary 'moments' within the development of cultural studies. Thus, whilst the text was understood to offer 'preferred' reading viewer/interpretive positions, the questions begged were then about how and in what ways actual readers were taking up those positions. A number of studies mobilized these questions in relation to popular genres; Hobson (1982) on the then popular British soap opera *Crossroads*, Ang (1985) and Katz and Liebes (1985) on *Dallas*, Buckingham (1987) on *EastEnders*.

The 'negotiated space'

To return briefly to Hall's reconsideration of the encoding/decoding model, he acknowledges the importance of 'the negotiated code' in saying, 'So the truth is, negotiated readings are probably what most of us do most of the time' (Cruz and Lewis, 1994: 265). He refers to the introduction to *Resistance through Rituals* (Hall and Jefferson, 1976) and what is described as 'the negotiated space' in which subcultures occupy different positions. With this insight and the kinds of questions which arose from the suggestive textual readings, especially in relation to the gendered audience, we can see studies undertaken in the last ten years, defined within the popular culture project, as exploring the nature and dimensions of that 'negotiated space' via the embodied 'determined active reader'. I will now look briefly at some of those studies. My aim here is not to produce them in any depth, and certainly, given my earlier remarks, I am wary of oversimplification. Rather, I wish to highlight the sheer diversity of the studies and their problematics. Whilst many will be familiar, some will not, and I warmly recommend them to the reader.

One of the most important studies regularly cited in audience works is Radway's *Reading the Romance*. In her introduction to the British edition (1987) she tells of her ignorance of British cultural studies before embarking on her study of female romance readers in the United States, and yet her work is often included as an example of 'demand-side' studies which celebrate the ways in which 'ordinary' people demonstrate 'resistance' through their consumption of popular genres. Hers is an infinitely more complex study than this would suggest. Within the context of publishing and production, she analyses the romance genre, but also explores how these novels are used by a group of identified romance 'fans', to work with their own sense of identity and positioning within marriage and family. Her study remains an exemplar in understanding the complexity of the consumption of this popular genre. Just as Janice Radway's work on romance readers has been an important reference point for work on broadcast media consumption, Joke Hermes' (1995) recent study of reading practices of women's magazines offers another way of approaching the everyday consumption of such popular texts. Her work with a relatively large number of readers is suggestive of the 'embeddedness' of such reading practices in the routines of daily life. Her analysis uses the notion of 'interpretive repertoires' in understanding reading positions and draws significantly on socio-linguistics and discourse analysis. Hermes' study was undertaken from a postmodern feminist perspective and seeks to address the meanings of a specific popular genre within the context of everyday life.

Audience research has been slow to raise questions of 'race' and ethnicity, and Jacqueline Bobo and Ellen Seiter (1991) are critical of the 'whiteness' of much feminist media and cultural criticism. In 1988 Jacqueline Bobo published her important essay on black women's readings of the film of *The Color Purple* and has since published her *Black Women as Cultural Readers* (1994), which builds on this study working with a small group of African-American women and analysing and discussing their responses to other mainstream texts as an 'interpretive community'. Bobo and Seiter suggest that '[i]t can be predicted with certainty that other work by women of color will not only alter the pool of empirical findings in cultural studies, but also challenge, redefine, and renovate the theoretical agenda in ways white academics cannot at present imagine' (1991: 291). Whilst Radway and Bobo's works pay important attention to the texts, for other researchers a crucial aspect of the 'negotiated space' is the 'actual' context of reading or viewing, which Hermes includes in her study. This was an absence identified by Morley in his retrospective on the *Nationwide* study, which had constructed viewing conditions within occupational locations. He anticipated that viewers in the context of domestic viewing might well make very different readings of the same text, or choose not to engage with particular texts at all (Morley, 1986). However, his study of families in East London revealed the domestic as a complex set of social relations within which viewing took place, with gender being a significant organizing category (Morley, 1986). An important historical dimension to domestic media use is provided by the work of Moores and O'Sullivan, who, through oral history methods, investigate early uses of radio (Moores, 1988) and memories of the arrival of television into UK homes (O'Sullivan, 1991).

Attention has been paid to the dynamics of television and video viewing within the contemporary domestic sphere, and there are a diverse range of studies which set out to look at very different aspects of this as a research site. James Lull's (1990, 1991) studies of family viewing activities in the US and China registered different viewing types and practices. Power relations in the domestic contexts of reception and the ways in which media technologies and their products are used and intervene in the construction of gendered, classed identities was the focus of my own study (Gray, 1987, 1992), and Sean Moores' (1996) recent work on satellite television examines gender and generational conflicts around this new technology. Minu Lee and Chong Heup Cho (1990) looked at how Korean women living in the United States shared a pleasure in viewing Korean soaps, which gave them a sense of 'home'. Marie Gillespie's (1995) ethnography of 'young Punjabi Londoners' explores in great detail the ways in which television is central to the formation and transformation of identity within this group. Her aims are to mobilize broader questions of the 'transnationalization' of culture(s) by examining them from the local and domestic point of view. Purnima Mankekar (1993, forthcoming) analyses how the popular entertainment forms of the Indian state broadcasting organization, Doordarshan, are attempting to construct a 'new' national identity around tropes of 'development' and 'consumption'. Her thesis suggests that the Indian woman is central to this construct, and her ethnographic study of viewing families looks at how these representations are negotiated within the formation of class and gender identities.

In different ways these studies are concerned to place media readings and use within complex webs of determinations, not only of the texts, but also those deeper structural determinants, such as class, gender and, still, to a lesser extent, race and ethnicity. These studies have also shed light on the ways in which public and private discourses intersect and are lived out within the intimate and routine practices of daily life. In addition, most reflect on research methods, and especially the location of the researcher in her/his study, and Mankekar (forthcoming) and Bobo and Seiter (1991) respectively raise critical questions about the dominance of the West in the definitions of 'knowledge sites' and the exclusionary practices of academic institutions. Thus, in spite of their small scale, each, in different ways, poses broader questions of structure and agency within the socially structured world of practices and subjectivity, and many reflect on the institutional context of research itself. I cannot comprehend of the questions and issues which these studies raise, and the ways in which they have gone about exploring them, as being of no importance. Nor do I recognize them as representative of the 'loss of critical energy' to which Corner refers, or as trivial aspects of social and cultural communication. I also suggest that these studies cannot be reduced to a set of enterprises which simply reproduce notions of the active audience who demonstrate their 'resistance' in their use of popular forms. Rather, what these studies suggest is that people negotiate – rarely are their readings and positioning oppositional. Where resistance has been noted, this is not particularly in relation to the readings of the text and its preferred meanings, but in the *practice* of reading and consumption.

Although many of the critics take the new audience research to task for attending only to the 'micro' dimension, I would argue that what underpins the questions and problematics of the studies are those of agency and structure. Studies show how public and private are absorbed into the everyday, the mundane, the ordinary. Such studies recognize the false distinctions between micro and macro, and demonstrate how discourses flow in and out of constructions of identity, self, private and public, national, local and global. Boundaries, thus, are permeable, unstable and uneasy, demanding a new way of thinking and looking at the 'audience', the user, the text, and the complexity of relations and discourses which surround and are part of it.

Ethnography and the processes of the everyday

Much of the debate and critique surrounding reception and audience practice could not have taken place without these small-scale studies, which
have mostly employed qualitative or interpretive ethnographic research
methods. Their aim was to see the world as experienced by the participants
themselves, revealing the presence of the researcher in the process of
research. Researchers actively invite those who read and watch to present
their own point of view usually in lengthy open interviews, or in the
course of participant observation. Studies have clearly demonstrated, as
Morley suggests, that 'the value of ethnographic methods lies precisely in
their ability to help us "make things out" in the context of their occurrence – in helping us to understand television viewing and other media
consumption practices as they are embedded in the context of everyday
life' (Morley, 1996: 321–2). We learn a great deal from these audience/
reception studies, which are not necessarily very much to do with the
audiences themselves, but rather the *processes*, by which media forms and
technologies take their place in everyday settings. Furthermore, critical
and analytical empirical work can enter into a productive dialogue with
our theorization of audience and consumption practices.

There is, however, a critical and political commitment which is worth
noting here. The aim of gathering data from the subject's viewpoint was often
motivated by a desire to allow participants to have some say in the research
agenda in this kind of exploratory work, rather than using qualitative methods to reveal 'truths' of the settings. It is possible to reformulate the notion of
'new audience studies' into 'new audience' studies. This is to suggest that
what is actually new about these studies are the new audiences which they
bring to the field. Hall notes (Cruz and Lewis, 1994) that it was impossible to
get research funding for the *Nationwide* study, and this has certainly been the
experience of many researchers wishing to carry out exploratory studies.
Thus, ethnographic methods are particularly well suited to the needs of post-
graduate research students, groups or individuals who have only just gained
positions within the academy and who cannot command large research
funds. Kirsten Drotner (1994: 342) suggests that ethnography was useful for
understanding the new and complex developments instigated by the
women's movement and the emergence of the multicultural society. Thus,
new groups in the academy, such as ethnic studies and women's studies
scholars, chose to explore the (cheap) ethnographic method.

Wild thinking : from 'things' to 'processes'

In conclusion, I will return to John Corner, who, in his discussion about the
'context' dimension of audience research, asks 'what do you include in

context and where does context stop?' (1991: 278). This reveals a central difference in the 'old' and 'new' approaches to audience studies and can be characterized as that between 'object' and 'process' as research focus. This is a question which could be the beginning of a productive debate. Let me start this, at least, by turning to Bausinger's (1984) key article about media technologies and everyday life. He uses an 'example' of the Meiers' Saturday evening tele-viewing practice. This, as it happens, is a 'hypothetical' account which Bausinger used to demonstrate exactly what is at stake in trying to understand the complex processes of media and daily life. However, I believe that this account will get nods of recognition as it indicates the frustrations and general *un*predictability of domestic daily life. Thus investigation and our understandings of media use and consumption will be hampered if we *begin* by deciding what is relevant and what irrelevant. For Bausinger these are issues of ontology and epistemology, which he summarizes as follows: 'others are on the look out for *things*, instead of investigating *processes* which are not easily encloseable, and hence not easily measurable. A bit of wild thinking is needed to catch and describe this complex world in all its rational irrationality'(1984: 347, my emphasis). What reflexive ethnographic studies have suggested is the very boundlessness of media processes, the impossibility of constructing a frame around media text and audience, of the need to take account of and pay attention to the messiness of the everyday, the dull thud of the commonplace, the routine and routinized nature of daily life in all its complexity, and into which media forms are enmeshed.

What might the future be for audience work? Liesbet van Zoonen (1994) and Charlotte Brunsdon (1997) have examined the gendered state of media research and both make relevant points. Van Zoonen notes the gender politics of 'reception analysis', where 'the public knowledge project tends to become a new male preserve, concerned with ostensibly gender-neutral issues such as citizenship, but actually neglecting the problematic relation of non-white, non-male citizens to the public sphere' (1994: 125).[4] This is a clear example of the existence of what Charlotte Brunsdon has referred to as the 'academic parallel universe' and the apparent impermeability of the 'male' work to feminist scholarship. Christine Geraghty's (1996) answer to this sorry state of affairs is for feminist scholars to stop restricting their studies to the sphere of consumption. They should 'overcome their feminine technophobia' (Geraghty, 1996: 320) and begin work on media ownership, control and regulation, and, we might add, the public knowledge project in reception analysis. In my attempt to (re)write a retrospective of reception analysis which tells a story in which feminist work is central, I am suggesting that feminist work and that inspired by feminism has shifted the ground of exploration and inquiry in forcing gender and sexual politics onto the agenda. Rather than, as Geraghty suggests, feminists taking on 'political economy' work, shouldn't we be asking the political economists of media and communication studies some questions? For example, why do their agendas remain closed to the insights of feminist scholarship? These insights would insist that they question their views of the relationship between macro-structures of media and micro-processes of viewing (Corner, 1991: 269) and critically examine their assumptions about what consistitutes 'politics' and where 'power' might reside. Above all, we might suggest that they overcome *their* phobias and fear of the feminine which are barely disguised in their work. Dennis McQuail, writing recently, in an otherwise typically measured piece, accuses cultural studies of being too 'flighty and opinionated' (1997: 55). What more revealingly gendered and patronising a put-down could there be to describe work that has been a serious and consistent attempt over the last two decades to explore and understand the complexities of the processes of social and cultural communication in contemporary societies?

Notes

I would like to thank Charlotte Brunsdon and Joke Hermes for helpful discussions and Pertti Alasuutari for his comments on an earlier draft.

1. For excellent critical retrospectives see Morley (1992) and Moores (1993). Ien Ang (1991) examines the institutional construction of audiences and her later collection (Ang, 1996) addresses issues of media audiences in postmodernity.
2. David Morley (1997) makes a similar point in a recent response to critiques of cultural studies.
3. Here we are presented with an immediate problem: there are three versions of the encoding/decoding paper. The earliest version appears in *Education and Culture*, No. 25 (UNESCO, 1974) as 'The Television Discourse – Encoding and Decoding' (Hall, 1974a) and is reprinted in Gray and McGuigan (1997); then *Encoding and Decoding in the Television Discourse* is CCCS Stencilled Occasional Paper No. 7 (Hall 1974b), an edited extract of which forms the 1980 version 'Encoding/Decoding' in the 1980 collection *Culture, Media, Language* (Hall, 1980), which is the version most usually cited. Thus, Hall was working on this model much earlier than the 1980 reference suggests.
4. Joke Hermes (1997) has taken up the issue of media and 'citizenship' from a feminist perspective.

References

Allor, M. (1988) 'Relocating the Site of the Audience', *Critical Studies in Mass Communication*, 5: 217–33.

Ang, I. (1985) *Watching Dallas: Soap Opera and the Melodramatic Imagination*. London: Methuen.

Ang, I. (1991) *Desperately Seeking the Audience*. London: Routledge.

Ang, I. (1996) *Living Room Wars : Rethinking Media Audiences for a Postmodern World*. London: Routledge.

Baehr, H. and Gray, A. (1996) *Turning it On: a Reader in Women and Media* London: Arnold. New York: Routledge.

Bar On, B.-A. (1993) 'Marginality and Epistemic Privilege' in L. Alcoff and E. Potter (eds), *Feminist Epistemologies*. New York: Routledge.

Bausinger, H. (1984) 'Media, Technology and Everyday Life', *Media, Culture & Society*, 6 (4): 343–51.

Bennett, T. (1996) 'Figuring Audiences and Readers', in J. Hay, L. Grossberg and E. Wartella (eds), *The Audience and Its Landscape*. Boulder, CO: Westview Press.

Blumler, J. and Katz, E. (1974) *The Uses of Mass Communications : Current Perspectives on Gratifications Research*. Beverly Hills: Sage.

Bobo, J. (1988) '*The Color Purple*: Black Women as Cultural Readers', in E.D. Pibram (ed.), *Female Spectators: Looking at Film and Television*. London: Verso.

Bobo, J. (1994) *Black Women as Cultural Readers*. New York: Columbia University Press.

Bobo J. and Seiter, E. (1991) 'Black Feminism and Media Criticism: "The Women of Brewster Place"' *Screen*, 32 (3): 186–302.

Brunsdon, C. (1981) '*Crossroads*: Notes on Soap Opera', *Screen*, 22 (4): 52–7.

Brunsdon, C. (1997) *Screen Tastes: Soap Opera to Satellite Dishes*. London: Routledge.

Brunsdson, C. and Morley, D. (1978) *Everyday Television : 'Nationwide'*. London: British Film Institute.

Brunsdon, C., D'Acci, J. and Spigel, L. (eds) (1997) *Feminist Television Criticism : A Reader*. Oxford: Oxford University Press.

Buckingham, D. (1987) *Public Secrets: EastEnders and its Audience*. London: British Film Institute.

Corner, J. (1991) 'Meaning, Genre and Context: The Problematics of "Public Knowledge" in the New Audience Studies', in J. Curran and M. Gurevitch (eds), *Mass Media and Society*. London: Edward Arnold.

Cruz, J. and Lewis, J. (1994) 'Reflections on the Encoding/Decoding Model: An Interview with Stuart Hall' in J. Cruz and J. Lewis (eds), *Viewing, Reading, Listening: Audiences and Cultural Reception*. Boulder, CO: Westview Press.

Curran, J. (1996) 'The New Revisionism in Mass Communication Research : A Reappraisal', in J. Curran, D. Morley and V. Walkerdine (eds), *Cultural Studies and Communications*. London: Edward Arnold.

Drotner, K. (1994) 'Ethnographic Enigmas: "The Everyday" in Recent Media Studies', *Cultural Studies*, 8 (2): 341–57.

Dyer, R., Lovell, T. and McCrindle, J. (1997 [1977]) 'Soap Opera and Women', in A. Gray and J. McGuigan (eds), *Studying Culture*. London: Edward Arnold.

Dyer, R., Geraghty, C., Jordan, J. Lovell, T. Paterson, R. and Stewart, J. (eds) (1981) *Coronation Street*. London: British Film Institute.

Garnham, N. (1997) 'Political Economy and the Practice of Cultural Studies', in M. Ferguson and P. Golding, (eds) *Cultural Studies in Question*. London: Sage.

Geraghty, C. (1996) 'Feminism and Media Consumption', in J. Curran, D. Morley and V. Walkerdine (eds), *Cultural Studies and Communications*. London: Edward Arnold.

Gillespie, M. (1995) *Television, Ethnicity and Cultural Change*. London: Routledge.

Gray, A. (1987) 'Behind Closed Doors: Video Recorders in the Home', in H. Baehr and G. Dyer (eds), *Boxed-In: Women and Television*. London: Pandora Press.

Gray, A. (1992) *Video Playtime: The Gendering of a Leisure Technology*. London: Routledge.

Gray, A. (1995) 'I Want to Tell You a Story: The Narratives of Video Playtime' in B.

Skeggs (ed), *Feminist Cultural Theory: Process and Production*. Manchester: Manchester University Press.

Gray, A. (1998) 'Learning from Experience: Cultural Studies and Feminism', in J. McGuigan (ed.), *Cultural Methodologies*. London: Sage.

Gray, A. (forthcoming) *Lived Cultures: Ethnographic Methods in Cultural Studies*. London: Sage.

Gray, A. and McGuigan, J. (eds) (1997) *Studying Culture*. London: Edward Arnold.

Hall, S. (1974a) 'The Television Discourse – Encoding and Decoding', *Education and Culture*. No. 25 (UNESCO) and reprinted in A. Gray and J. McGuigan (eds) (1997) *Studying Culture*. London: Edward Arnold.

Hall, S. (1974b) *Encoding and Decoding in the Television Discourse*. Centre for Contemporary Cultural Studies, Stencilled Occasional Paper No. 7. Birmingham: University of Birmingham.

Hall, S. (1980) 'Encoding/Decoding', in S. Hall, D. Hobson, A. Lowe and P. Willis (eds), *Culture, Media, Language*. London: Hutchinson.

Hall, S. and Jefferson, T. (1976) *Resistance through Rituals*. London: Hutchinson.

Hartley, J. (1987) 'Invisible Fictions: Television Audiences, Paedocracy and Pleasure', *Textual Practice*. 1 (2): 121–38.

Hermes, J. (1995) *Reading Women's Magazines: An Analysis of Everyday Media Use*. Cambridge: Polity Press.

Hermes, J. (1997) 'Gender and Media Studies: No Woman, No Cry', in J. Corner, P. Schlesinger and R. Silverstone (eds), *International Handbook of Media Research*. London: Routledge.

Hobson, D. (1978) 'Housewives: Isolation as Oppression', in Women's Studies Group, Birmingham Centre for Contemporary Cultural Studies, *Women Take Issue*. London: Hutchinson.

Hobson, D. (1980) 'Housewives and the Mass Media', in S. Hall, D. Hobson, A. Lowe and P. Willis (eds), *Culture, Media, Language*. London: Hutchinson.

Hobson, D. (1982) *Crossroads: The Drama of a Soap Opera*. London: Methuen.

Jhalley, S. and Lewis, J. (1992) *Enlightened Racism: Audiences, The Cosby Show and the Myth of the American Dream*. Boulder, CO: Westview Press.

Katz, E. and Liebes, T.(1985) 'Mutual Aid in the Decoding of *Dallas*: Preliminary Notes from a Cross-Cultural Study', in P. Drummond and R. Paterson (eds), *Television in Transition*. London: British Film Institute.

Lee, M. and Cho, C.H. (1990) 'Women Watching Together: an Ethnographic Study of Korean Soap Opera Fans in the U.S.' *Cultural Studies*, 4 (1): 30–44.

Lull, J. (1990) *Inside Family Viewing: Ethnographic Research on Television's Audiences*. London: Routledge.

Lull, J. (1991) *China Turned On: Television, Reform, and Resistance*. London: Routledge.

McQuail, D. (1997) 'Policy Help Wanted: Willing and Able Media Culturalists Please Apply', in M. Ferguson and P. Golding, (eds),

Mankekar, P. (1993) 'Television Tales and a Woman's Rage: A Nationalist Recasting of Draupadi's "Disrobing"', *Public Culture*, 5 (3): 469–92.

Mankekar, P. (forthcoming) *Screening Culture, Viewing Politics: An Ethnography of Television, Womanhood, and Nation in Postcolonial India*.

Modleski, T. (1982) *Loving with a Vengeance: Mass-Produced Fantasies for Women*. Hamden, CT: Shoestring Press.

Modleski, T. (1983) 'The Rhythm of Reception: Daytime Television and Women's Work', in E.A. Kaplan (ed.), *Regarding Television: Critical Approaches – An Anthology*. Los Angeles: American Film Institute.

Moores, S. (1988) '"The Box on the Dresser": Memories of Early Radio and Everyday Life', *Media, Culture & Society*, 10 (1): 23–40.

Moores, S. (1993) *Interpreting Audiences: The Ethnography of Media Consumption*. London: Sage.

Moores, S. (1996) *Satellite Television and Everyday Life*. Luton: John Libbey.

Morley, D. (1980a) *The Nationwide Audience*. London: British Film Institute.

Morley, D. (1980b) 'Texts, Readers, Subjects', in S. Hall, D. Hobson, A. Lowe and P. Willis (eds), *Culture, Media, Language*. London: Hutchinson.

Morley, D. (1986) *Family Television: Cultural Power and Domestic Leisure*. London: Comedia.

Morley, D. (1992) *Television, Audiences and Cultural Studies*. London: Routledge.

Morley, D. (1996) 'The Geography of Television: Ethnography, Communications and Community', in J. Hay, L. Grossberg and E. Wartella (eds), *The Audience and its Landscape*. Boulder, CO: Westview Press.

Morley, D. (1997) 'Theoretical Orthodoxies: Textualism, Constructivism and the "New Ethnography" in Cultural Studies', in M. Ferguson and P. Golding, 1997.

Morley, D. and Silverstone, R. (1980) 'Domestic Communication: Technologies and Meanings', *Media, Culture & Society*, 12 (1): 31–55.

O'Sullivan, T. (1991) 'Television Memories and Cultures of Viewing, 1950–65', in J. Corner (ed.), *Popular Television in Britain: Studies in Cultural History*. London: British Film Institute.

Radway, J.A. (1984) *Reading the Romance: Women, Patriarchy, and Popular Literature*. Chapel Hill: University of North Carolina Press.

Radway, J.A. (1987) 'Reading the Romance', in J. Radway, *Reading the Romance: Women, Patriarchy, and Popular Literature*. London: Verso.

Seiter, E., Borchers, H., Kreutzner, G. and Warth, E.-M. (1989) '"Don't Treat Us Like We're So Stupid and Naive": Towards an Ethnography of Soap Opera Viewers', in E. Seiter (ed.), *Remote Control*. London: Routledge.

Stanley, L. (ed.) (1990) *Feminist Praxis: Research, Theory and Epistemology in Feminist Sociology*. London: Routledge.

Van Zoonen, L. (1994) *Feminist Media Studies*. London: Sage.

3

THE BEST OF BOTH WORLDS?
Media Audience Research between
Rival Paradigms

Kim Christian Schrøder

Irrespective of their academic upbringing, media audience researchers share a common goal: to increase our knowledge of how the media are used – in the widest sense of the word – by diverse groups in contemporary culture and society, and how in turn the media may be seen as vehicles of social stability and change.

However, as soon as it comes to selecting the lenses with which to observe the issues and the tools with which to analyse the data, different academic traditions set out in different directions and return with sometimes quite divergent or even contradictory insights. That this is so is evident from even a superficial comparison of the studies presented by researchers from what will here be seen as the two major traditions in media audience research: the qualitatively based ethnographic approach (including reception research) and the quantitative uses and gratifications approach.

This chapter argues that, as traditionally practised, these two approaches have complementary deficiencies and merits. Moreover, it argues that for many tasks in audience research it is by synthesizing these approaches into one research design that we may be able to develop a method to overcome the deficiencies and preserve the merits. This will not be achieved by merely agglutinating the two approaches, as often suggested by adherents of methodological triangulation, since, in a manner of speaking, to combine two wrongs does not produce one right.[1]

At a first glance it may seem over-ambitious to suggest the feasibility of a research design which unites the 'thick description' of the contextualized data of ethnographic inquiry with the reliability and generalizability of social science measurement. No full-scale study has yet demonstrated this kind of synthesis in practice. But the case study reported at the end of this chapter may provide at least an outline of how it may be achieved.

There has been no dearth over recent decades of calls for convergence or cross-fertilization between humanistic and social-science paradigms. In a succinct statement from 1990 Jensen and Rosengren declare that

> humanistic researchers need to establish a terminology which will enable them to deal with issues of reliability, validity and generalizability. [. . .] Social science research, equally, needs to recognize that non-quantitative procedures of analysis, as developed within linguistics and semiotics in the course of this century, may well have an explanatory value in their own right. (1990: 231)

However, when it comes down to implementing such a grandiloquent research platform in practical research, protagonists on both sides of the paradigmatic gulf have seemed unwilling, or unable, to take on its full implications (see, e.g., the recent skirmish between former partners Jensen and Rosengren: Jensen, 1996; Rosengren, 1996).

This chapter presents an attempt to define in terms of concrete methodological measures what the implications are for an audience research that takes the platform of cross-fertilization seriously.

Naturally, the talk about 'cross-fertilization' cannot ultimately be reduced to a question of collaboration between 'qualitative' and 'quantitative' methodologies, but also concerns their epistemological foundations.

When we are talking about these methods we are also talking about the epistemological differences between a positivist, functionalist approach and a phenomenological, hermeneutic approach, traditionally associated with 'administrative' and 'critical' research, respectively (see, e.g., Gitlin, 1978). The 'dialogue' between paradigms is therefore ultimately between such entities.

However, the methodological issue is often a useful short-hand for these differences, because it is in the field of methodology that the epistemological positions must ultimately be evaluated: we have to ask whether we, and the wider society, consider the findings produced with this or that methodology interesting, relevant, useful to our concerns, or not. For many new scholars, methodology precedes epistemology, because the methodological lenses given to new members of research communities simply have built into them epistemological biases which render many issues a priori 'unresearchable'.

What happened to validity? A critical perspective on uses and gratifications research

As has often been pointed out, uses and gratifications (U+G) research, in defining media audiences as 'active', broke decisively with the dominant paradigm of media effects in the late 1950s, asking not what the media do to people, but what people do with the media. As I see it, its well-known seven-point research platform as formulated by Katz et al. (1974: 20) could have served, in a general sense, as a common platform for all subsequent audience research irrespective of the different emphases of different schools and approaches.[2]

However, the gut response to this platform from scholars who study audiences from cultural studies or ethnographic perspectives has been negative. Morley thus vehemently distanced himself from the uses and gratifications tradition, arguing that since 'uses and gratifications is essentially a psychological field, relying as it does on mental states, needs and processes abstracted from the social situation of the individuals concerned [. . .] we need to break fundamentally with the "uses and gratifications" approach' (1980: 14).

This view, which echoes Elliott's (1974) authoritative critique, is one of the factors which has led to the development of the other, ethnographic, paradigm in media audience research, not because the platform's wording necessarily requires it, but because of the theoretical and methodological emphases established through the practice of agenda-setting researchers within the U+G tradition.

The cardinal sins of U+G research, as seen from the other side, have consisted, on the one hand, in ignoring the everyday *social* context of media use, which the platform hides away as a parenthetical 'engagement in other activities' and a ragbag category of 'other consequences'; and, on the other hand, in U+G researchers' complete separation of 'need gratification' from the cultural meanings derived by audiences from media content. Equally serious has been the alleged methodological myopia which in practice has turned the survey questionnaire and other statistical methods into the only permissible research tools.

What is remarkable about such criticism of the U+G approach is that it has recently been rekindled by respected scholars *within* the paradigm, as a kind of revival and radicalization of Elliott's previous critique, which was always respected but has never really left its mark on U+G research practice. On the one hand, these recent intra-paradigm critics celebrate the indubitable achievements of researchers in the tradition, 'the number and breadth of studies which it has stimulated' and 'the depth of the insights which these studies have produced' (Roe, 1996: 81). On the other hand, they expose the methodological shortcomings and criticize the explanatory poverty of many studies within the tradition.

As his title indicates, Gantz (1996) undertakes 'an examination of the range and salience of gratifications research associated with entertainment programming', critically reviewing some of the prominent published research in gratifications research over the last 20 years. His fundamental question is what insights this work has provided into the TV viewing experience.

To this end he compares some studies of the gratifications which people report from 'watching TV'. All the studies reviewed presented respondents with lists of possible gratifications derived from qualitative pilot studies. One study (Greenberg, 1974) found that the watching of TV is gratifying mainly because it is a 'habit', because it is a good way to 'pass the time', and because it provides 'companionship' when there is no-one else to talk to, that is, his respondents watch TV for non-programme-specific reasons.

Another study, by Rubin (1981), found that people's main reasons were to do with programme content – they watch TV primarily for specific programmes – while 'entertainment', 'relaxation' and 'habit' range considerably lower. In other words, this study shows that TV viewing is related to the active choice of favourite programmes.

The different findings from these two studies may reveal complementary insights about why people watch TV, or they may stem from the fact that different age groups were studied, but according to Gantz's analysis the crucial difference is that between the gratifications lists presented to respondents, one with, the other without the option of programme-specific gratifications from watching TV. In other words, the gratifications lists used determine the results. In general terms this demonstrates an unavoidable feature of questionnaire-based studies, namely that their findings are necessarily limited by the researchers' imagination or judgement of relevance when compiling the questionnaire. No matter how exhaustive the list there are always going to be potential gratifications that are not included. This poses a serious threat to the validity of gratification studies, as we cannot be sure that the research results adequately reflect the real-life phenomena we wish to explore.

Summing up his review of these and a host of other gratifications studies of various types of entertainment programming (religious programming, sports programmes, soap operas and music), Gantz concludes that 'the primary gratification associated with exposure to entertainment television is the entertainment such programming provides', continuing that

> above all else entertainment programming is entertaining. It makes people feel good, happy, sad, excited, nervous, thrilled [. . .]. It gets or keeps people in the mood they seek. For viewers, it also helps structure the day, pass the time, reduce boredom, relieve stress, and provide an opportunity for socializing. And, it may be doing all this every day (1996: 24–5).

One may wonder whether this collection of platitudes is really what the concerted efforts of gratifications researchers have been able to produce after years of work, spending millions of dollars and other currencies. It is hardly surprising that Gantz proposes that 'even within the domain of delineating gratifications, there is room for more research' (1996: 25). More bluntly, Lewis, as an outside observer finds that U+G 'quantitative surveys have creaked and cranked their way to unconvincing conclusions' (1997: 88).

Commendably, however, Gantz uses the low explanatory power of

these results to direct a critical eye towards the methodological foundations of gratifications research, pointing to 'the bias in research methods
employed up until now':

> The research agenda is likely to require alternative, if not innovative, methods
> of data collection. Interviews will need to be interactive, a mix of open- and
> close-ended questions. Probes will be critical; interviewers will need to ask
> respondents what they (the respondents) mean when they say, for example,
> that they turn to television to be entertained or they watch out of habit. [. . .]
> gratifications scholars will need to be creative and, as needed, supplement
> survey research [. . .] with depth interviews, where respondents are given ample
> opportunity to reflect and describe the nature of their relationship with media
> content. (1996: 26–7)

In other words, Gantz proposes a remedy for the low validity of survey
research, which has always been its Achilles' heel.

The creation of validity, defined as 'the extent to which an account accu-
rately represents the social phenomena to which it refers' (Hammersley,
1990, quoted by Silverman, 1993: 149), depends on a number of factors,
including adequate theoretical foundations for the field of investigation
and conceptual clarity, but most of all it depends on methodological reflection about the data collection stage. Many threats exist, both in qualitative
and quantitative designs, to the researcher's purpose of obtaining as
authentic data as possible. What Gantz is in effect saying is that 'interactive', more conversational encounters with respondents are superior to
surveys in eliciting respondents' authentic, contextualized opinions, attitudes and meanings.

Roe agrees, claiming that U+G researchers 'have been too concerned
with the (very important) task of assessing reliability, at the expense of the
still more important issue of validity' (1996: 90). He also cites other work
on method to the effect that a study of questions commonly used in television survey research 'found that, even after proper piloting, systematic
major misunderstanding of questions occurs without interviewers being
aware of it' (1996: 91).

He further points to the widespread occurrence of measurement error in
survey research, in a devastating critique that many faithful followers of
U+G doctrine will no doubt see as treacherous fifth column activity:

> [A] typical survey item, even when well administered to a proper population
> sample, can yield up to 50% non-valid variance [. . .]. We all know all of this and,
> as with all deeply disturbing thoughts, we usually do our best to forget it when-
> ever we can. We dismiss the qualitative critiques as 'unscientific' and if someone
> breaks ranks from within, the usual response is to offer platitudes, dismiss the
> heretic as a methodological purist (if not troublemaker), and promptly go back
> to business as usual. This strategy, while ultimately making research possible,
> has prevented any real methodological development, and has given extra
> ammunition to critics. (Roe, 1996: 87)

This, however, does not lead Roe to wholeheartedly embrace qualitative approaches, which he finds just as deficient. Nevertheless, like Gantz, he is open to, and invites scholars from qualitative and quantitative traditions to cross-fertilize their work, through a process in which no-one starts out from a position of strength, but rather from a humble acknowledgement that 'in many respects, they are doing an equally poor job' (Roe, 1996: 90).

What happened to reliability and generalizability? A critical perspective on media ethnography

The contemporary ethnographic approach to the media audience, which in this context includes both 'reception' research and more genuinely 'ethnographic' approaches, is based on the premise that meaning is never just transferred from one individual to another, or from the media to their audiences. Meaning, in media as well as research situations, is generated according to the communicative repertoires, or codes, of the encoder(s) and interpreted according to the communicative repertoires of the decoder(s) – and there is no natural fit between encoding and decoding (Hall, 1973). Moreover, these meaning processes are firmly embedded in the social contexts of everyday life in which people use the media (Lull, 1990 [1980]).

Consequently the ethnographic approach has defined itself in dual opposition: to humanistic textual analysis, with its implied position that media meanings and ideologies are imposed on passive minds and may be brought to light by textual analysis alone, on the one hand; and to the social science approach, whose analysis of media gratifications ignores the meanings which create these gratifications, on the other. It is critical of both for neglecting to explore the everyday contexts in which meanings and uses arise in the first place.

Reception research, which historically precedes the more ethnographically inclined approach, may in itself be seen as a 'first generation' cross-fertilization project, borrowing from both these predecessors as it 'draws its theory from the humanities and its methodology from the social sciences' (Jensen, 1991: 135). It focuses on audience meanings as conceptualized within the humanistic traditions of semiotics and linguistic discourse analysis, and it explores these meanings through methods of empirical fieldwork borrowed from the social sciences (Schrøder, 1987).

In spite of the quite vehement dismissal of U+G research by some of the pioneers of reception research, their programmatic statements nevertheless often show a close affinity with the concerns of this tradition. Thus Radway (1984) criticizes humanistic textual analysis because it 'discounts what readers *do* with texts', calling for an approach which 'focuses on the various ways human beings actively *make* sense of their surrounding world', including the ubiquitous mass media (1984: 8).

While retaining the focus on cultural meaning, then, early reception researchers appear to define themselves mainly in opposition to textual analysis: 'The analytic focus must shift from the text itself, taken in isolation, to the complex social event of reading' (Radway, 1984: 8). But when it comes to the empirical exploration of cultural meaning processes they are highly critical of the prescribed method of mainstream social science research: the survey questionnaire.

The main objection has to do with validity. As Lewis puts it, in quantitative surveys 'we have no way of telling if the respondents are comfortable with the way of thinking that has been imposed upon them. [. . .] The ambiguities of language mean that it is difficult to explore the precise meaning of words or sentences without giving the respondent the opportunity to elaborate' (1991: 78; see also Lull, 1985). In other words, the original reasons of reception researchers for choosing qualitative methods of analysis, usually either individual depth interviews or focus group interviews, are strikingly similar to the opinions expressed more recently by the veterans of the U+G tradition quoted above. As a textbook in communication studies puts it: '[I]nternal validity is more important than external validity. This makes sense; after all, if results are not internally valid, generalizing them to other people is a moot point.' (Frey et al., 1991: 325)

However, the laudable insistence of qualitative researchers on (internal) validity as one of the cardinal virtues of empirical research has not been matched by a similar concern for the equally important virtues of reliability and generalizability (or representativeness). The reasons for this are no doubt many, and quite compelling ones too, as lack of resources and limited or no fieldwork experience imposed inevitable constraints on dozens of pioneering research projects in reception studies (Jensen, 1986; Lewis, 1991; Liebes and Katz, 1990; Morley, 1980; Radway, 1984; Schrøder, 1988 – to mention but a few). In short, most reception studies published so far analyse the media meanings of only a handful, or two or three handfuls, of informants, and usually present insufficient evidence of the reliability of the interpretive process. Rosengren's criticism of this situation is harsh and unremitting: reception analysis, he says, 'is dominated by so-called qualitative studies, based on anecdotal data and defined as unformalized, exegetic studies of the meaning of individual experience. [. . .] these studies, as a rule, neglect otherwise generally accepted tests of reliability, validity, and representativeness.' (1993: 13). Even if his criticism is accompanied by somewhat megalomaniacal claims for U+G research as the epitome of modern social science, it is not totally unwarranted, as I shall demonstrate below.

Criticism, like charity, should begin at home, so let me use some of my own research to demonstrate these points. In a reception study of the American soap opera *Dynasty* (Schrøder, 1989) I interviewed 25 American viewers in the Los Angeles area in 1985. The informants, who were recruited by a market research company, were equally distributed with respect to sex and educational status (with/without college); the individual depth-interviews were open-ended and colloquial, lasted one to two hours, including the viewing of an episode of the serial, and took place in the informants' homes.

This empirical set-up with informants on their home turf, talking informally and dialogically about a TV serial they watched regularly to a researcher from Denmark who was curious to learn of their programme experiences, produced data with high validity.

The analytical interpretation of the interview transcripts found a host of culturally interesting themes, most of them arising from programme experiences that contradicted the prevalent notions of audience passivity and ineptness. For instance, it was demonstrated that the data included evidence of audience aesthetic capacities, such as 'a clear awareness of the mechanisms of drama and narrative, distinguishing between character and actant roles' (Schrøder, 1989: 13). Short 'representative' quotations from four interviews were presented as documentation. Another theme was the informants' inclination to read the serial reflexively as a vision of the human condition in America today; statements from three informants were offered in support of this point.

The value of these analytical insights remains clear in the historical academic context in which they were presented: in the face of then still dominant Frankfurt School notions of passive audiences and misled masses, and in the absence of any empirical studies of the cultural meaning of soap opera[3] (other than bland U+G work on general 'gratifications'), it was necessary simply to demonstrate that such readings were possible, even without specifying how widespread they were. Even Rosengren is prepared to grant us that much, finding that reception research has 'produced [. . .] an impressive number of ingenious and insightful case studies' (1993: 13). These case studies showed, for instance, that even if media messages did have 'preferred meanings' (and some would contest this very concept), these meanings were precarious because empirical audience readings were always 'polysemous' and sometimes 'oppositional', to use just a few of the theoretical keywords developed by reception research (Fiske, 1987; Hall, 1974; Morley, 1980).

The community of scholars in mass communication research at the time was largely favourable towards these and similar results then flowing out of qualitative audience studies, probably because these results were, after all, rather commonsensical even though they flouted conventional scholarly wisdom about mass culture. However, it remains true to say that the results had to be taken on trust, as all reception data were only scrutinized by the individual researcher doing the study, picking and choosing a few select quotations to document the interpretations. No procedures were initiated which might demonstrate the reliability of the findings.

Such procedures were of course available in principle: the researcher could have found someone to go over the data and check the interpretations. But in practice this was not feasible, as the projects were too insufficiently funded to get research assistants to replicate the analysis, and pleas to colleagues for assistance in such a laborious task seemed embarrassing.

Another shortcoming of qualitative work lies in its unrepresentative data. Lack of funding, time and fieldwork experience are the reasons why reception projects have used such small samples, usually 12, 16 or 20 informants. The sheer idea of studying a nationally representative sample through qualitative depth interviews or focus groups seemed absurd at the time, as the interview transcripts would run to thousands of pages. Less would have to do.[4]

In his recent critique of Jensen (1995), Rosengren accuses reception research of using only 'convenience samples', emphasizing that 'results from convenience samples – although often extremely valuable as generators of hypotheses – are not generalizable' (1996: 136). Some samples in the reception tradition are indeed convenience samples, that is, informants who were picked for no other reason than their availability. Again lack of funding has been the main reason. Incidentally, however, if criticism begins at home, Rosengren should perhaps direct his fire against his own allies, who seem to condone endless numbers of studies which use readily available college students as respondents: Frey et al. report that by 1985 '65.5 percent of published communication research [. . .] used samples drawn from the college population' (1991: 326).

The samples used in reception research are usually not convenience samples, they are just small. Two types of sample have been quite frequent: 'network samples', in which a 'snowball technique' has been used (Frey et al., 1991: 135), asking subjects to refer researchers to other people who could serve as subjects, sometimes by inviting them to their home for a focus-group-like interview (Lewis, 1991; Liebes and Katz, 1990); and 'purposive samples', sometimes recruited by independent research companies, as for instance in the *Dynasty* study mentioned above, which recruited 25 informants distributed equally in terms of sex and education, with the purpose of obtaining cultural and social variety in the sample. Often, however, the informant distribution over demographic categories has not been explicitly used in the presentation of results, because of a scholarly caution against making too far-reaching claims for the modest sample investigated, or because the number of respondents was too small for clear demographic patterns to emerge.

At the same time, however, probably responding to a deep urge to find numerical significance in the data, the *Dynasty* study does not abstain from using 'pseudo-quantitative formulations' (Rosengren, 1996: 139), noting, for instance, that 'alongside the playful attitude one *often* encounters a complementary serious attitude', or that '*many* female viewers report their perception of female strength being portrayed in the serial' (Schrøder, 1989: 14, 15, emphasis added). Similar pseudo-quantitative formulations are found in many reception studies (see, e.g., the case study of the *Cosby* audience in Lewis, 1991).[5] Faced with such expressions, any curious reader is bound to wonder just how frequently and just how many.

A countervailing tendency, away from the urge of closet quantificationists in the qualitative camp to generalize and to find (pseudo-)numerical
significance, has appeared in recent years through the rise of a more genuine ethnographic approach to the media audience. Beginning with Lull's
(1990 [1980]) study of the social uses of television in American households,
and gaining momentum after Morley's call for a shift of interest 'from the
analysis of the pattern of differential audience "readings" of particular
programme materials, to the analysis of the domestic viewing context
itself – as the framework within the "readings" of programmes are (ordi-
narily) made' (1986: 14), numerous researchers have begun to
conceptualize and explore the media in the context of everyday life.

While some of these researchers see their ethnographic work as a continuation or extension of reception analysis, others argue that media
ethnography should be divorced from reception research. Thus Drotner
argues that 'media ethnography may be defined as an epistemological
alternative to other forms of qualitative media studies and not as their
extension' (1996: 34; see also Drotner, 1994).

This conceptualization wishes to take its analytical point of departure
not in a particular medium, but in a specific group of people, in order to
study 'how various forms of mass media enter their everyday lives and are
appropriated as material and symbolic cultural resources' (Drotner, 1996:
34). Drotner's approach to a genuine media ethnography further requires
that the group studied is regarded as both recipients and producers of
mediated communication; that the researcher does not just carry out one or
a couple of interviews with the informants, but follows the group in different locations as a participant observer; and finally that the researcher
stays with the group for a considerable period of time.

A number of scholars have taken these political and epistemological
interests even further. Thus Ang and Hermes argue from a post-struc-
turalist-feminist perspective that media research should turn in the
direction of an ethnographic approach characterized by a 'spirit of radical
contextualism and methodological situationalism', in which 'media consumption should be conceptualized as an ever-proliferating set of
heterogeneous and dispersed, intersecting and contradicting cultural practices, involving an indefinite number of multiply-positioned subjects'
(1991: 321–2; see also Radway, 1988; Silverstone, 1994).

This perspective, moreover, stresses its 'wariness of generalized
absolutes' and its 'observance of the irreducible complexity and relentless
heterogeneity of social life', and warns that "the dangers of easy categorization and generalization [. . .] are greater than the benefits of a consistent
particularism' (Ang and Hermes, 1991: 323).

As I have pointed out elsewhere (Schrøder, 1994), this kind of radical
ethnography – which is of course perfectly legitimate as a research perspective – tends to focus attention on the endless complexities of the
everyday and to delegitimate research that foregrounds the media. In
what appears to be a new theoretical and methodological orthodoxy of

diffuseness, proponents of radical ethnography appear to be writing the audience as well as the media out of reality, into the pure realm of situational discourses.

Lewis, on the other hand, urges us to recognize the 'inevitable tension' between 'the desire to maintain a qualitative depth in the analysis and the need to establish a systematic framework for organizing the data' (1991: 95). To deny this tension and insist on particularism – because 'generalizations are necessarily violations to the concrete specificity of all unique micro-situations' (Ang, 1991: 164) – delivers a potentially devastating blow to a media audience research that wishes to enter into a dialogue with people (policy makers, other media researchers as well as ordinary citizens) who do not understand, let alone share, the post-structuralist vision of endlessly nomadic subjectivities. As Morley puts it, 'without [. . .] generalizations, we risk floating in an endless realm of contextual specificity, a play of infinite difference, in which we are reluctant to make any generalization for fear of crudity' (1992: 161; see also Alasuutari, 1995: 15ff.).

As I see it, any piece of media audience research should be prepared to answer simple questions about its findings in fairly simple terms, even if such answers are necessarily an 'incomplete' representation of the 'myriad of dispersed practices' (Ang, 1991: 162) explored by the researcher. Usually with a minimum of analytical effort the researcher will be able to discern the contours of patterns in the audience data, broad categories of similarities and differences of perception and practice in people's everyday interaction with the media and their meanings.

In sum, media reception and ethnographic research – for all sorts of good reasons – has been indifferent to questions of analytical reliability, but has nevertheless been quite favourably received in many circles because of its production of obviously valid findings. It moreover acknowledges that its data and results are not representative in a statistical sense, and it has been reluctant to generalize its data by analytically transforming them into systematically defined formal categories that may be probed by other researchers, let alone subjected to some kind of quantification.

Even with these limitations, the ethnographic tradition has produced ground-breaking research with far-reaching academic, cultural and educational implications. Now it is time that we ask ourselves whether there may be ways in which the limitations may be overcome so as to enable us to deliver research with even greater explanatory potential.

Cross-fertilization in practice: the lure of 'triangulation'

In the lessening conflictual scenario of contemporary media audience research, then, it is generally recognized that survey-based social science approaches and qualitative fieldwork approaches have different strengths and weaknesses: 'Quantitative observations provide a high level of measurement precision and statistical power, while qualitative observations provide greater depth of information about how people perceive events in the context of the actual situations in which they occur' (Frey et al., 1991: 99).

In more precise research jargon, qualitative research has greater *validity*, because informants can put items on the agenda, researchers can probe, the data are contextualized, and so on. Quantitative research, conversely, has greater *reliability*, because its more formalized procedures of data collection and analysis increase the likelihood of obtaining consistent data and consistent codings; and its findings have greater *representativeness*, because of the larger samples and the sometimes random techniques used to recruit them.

Many media audience researchers are likely to just accept this state of affairs and to conduct their intra-paradigm business-as-usual. And the research produced in this manner will probably continue to have its uses and gratifications for the respective congregations. Over the years, however, quite a few people have addressed the issue of mutual inter-paradigm openness and cross-fertilization (one of the more recent is Alasuutari, 1995: 116ff.), sometimes against strong resistance from self-appointed paradigm guardians (Holbrook, 1987).

From the social science side, Blumler et al. (1985: 258) raised 'the prospect of a meaningful cross-paradigm dialogue', while Lull, from the qualitative camp, suggested that 'a convergence of quantitative and qualitative research offers the greatest potential for accurate description and explanation of the significance of communication in all contexts' (1985: 220). And a lot of such cross-fertilization has actually taken place, but mostly in a manner which has condoned the inherent limitations of the respective paradigms, because cross-fertilization has not been defined as the creation of an integrated approach. Instead researchers have explored ways in which the approaches may *supplement* each other.

This in itself is no simple matter and has been useful if only for the general process of promoting dialogue across traditional lines of division. In the conceptual landscape of empirical audience research, 'triangulation' has been an endeavour that has received almost unanimous support, within a logic that is aptly expressed by a much-used textbook in the field:

> Both types of observations can be used together profitably to achieve - triangulation, which enhances both the precision of the data gathered (with quantitative observations) and the contextual influences on those data (with qualitative observations). Using both types of observation also provides a way of assessing the accuracy of the findings from one operational procedure by comparing it with a different operational procedure. If the findings support each other, both procedures are corroborated. If the findings are different, however, this does not necessarily mean that the data are questionable. The difference could be a result of the types of data that are acquired through quantitative and qualitative data. (Frey et al., 1991: 99–100)

Although this logic of corroboration has an uncomfortable ring of having your cake and eating it, triangulation has been an exciting challenge for a number of researchers, a kind of mantra that everyone endorses, probably because of its unique potential as a credibility-enhancing mechanism: if both methods yield the same results, your darling method stands vindicated; if they don't, you simply stick to the results produced by your darling method and dump the conflicting results as due to contextual noise.

Triangulation, Silverman observes, is a term borrowed from navigation, 'where different bearings give the correct position of an object' (1993: 156). Although a certain semantic latitude should be permitted in the use of metaphors, we may nevertheless note that the triangulating navigator does not actually observe his or her object with different 'methods', he or she uses the same method but from different locations.

Triangulation as used in media audience research usually implies that the researcher seeks primary data about a research question in two (or more) different ways. This is what Livingstone et al. (1994) did in their study of TV studio audience discussion programmes. First, they carried out a qualitative study that revealed viewers' scepticism of experts, their involvement in such programmes, and their perception of such programmes as a kind of mass-mediated public sphere; second, they did a questionnaire-based survey about the same questions administered to a nationally representative sample. The two studies corroborated each other, and the survey thus enabled them to relate their findings to a number of demographic variables.

In other cases, triangulation covers a research process which uses another method as an auxiliary to the main method employed. Thus the basically qualitative study by Jensen et al. (1994) of Danish viewers' reception of television as flow in a multichannel environment found through qualitative interpretation that the informants could be divided into three viewer types: moralists, pragmatists and hedonists. Curious about how widespread these types might be, the researchers then went on to operationalize the types in the form of questions whose answers could be easily quantified when administered to a representative sample of Danish viewers.

The fundamental problem with triangulation is that we lack a theoretical framework for specifying the precise manner in which the different methods actually observe, or 'measure', the 'same' object. Simply to say that since each method provides a partial view, together they present a more complete picture still begs this important theoretical question (Silverman, 1993: 157).

In other words, if a U+G survey (whose validity is dubious) comes up with similar findings to a qualitative study (whose reliability is dubious), does this then make the U+G study more valid, and the qualitative study more reliable? Many researchers would probably intuitively accept this proposition. But what then if the two methods do not produce the same findings – is neither then valid and/or reliable? Or do we have to choose which to believe, basing our judgement on how well each method appears to be suited to the research question at hand?

As I see it, triangulation – which is in a sense cross-fertilization without anyone having to change – is by no means the obvious or only solution to the challenge of cross-paradigm dialogue. A survey does not suddenly overcome its inherent problems of validity just because it is done by a qualitative researcher as a token of open-mindedness. And vice versa for a quantitative researcher taking over qualitative designs.

Moreover, data elicitation is always situated in a specific research encounter. Consequently, qualitative and quantitative designs – which do create different research environments – should perhaps not be expected to provide commensurable data, nor findings. To use an alternative metaphor, if a method is a 'lens', no one would expect two different lenses to produce the same visual representation of the object.

The best of both worlds?

If triangulation is in some ways a phantom, or at least not a panacea, how can cross-fertilization then be conceptualized? Is it possible to integrate the strengths of the two main approaches into one research platform? In other words, how can we design an approach characterized by high proportions of reliability, validity and representativeness?

As I see it, *validity*, defined as the ideal that the study should adequately capture the real-world phenomena it seeks to explore, is the starting point and *sine qua non* when planning empirical research about cultural meaning processes involving media audiences. If your findings live up to this criterion, you at least know something. What this means is that the processes of data collection and analysis should be thoroughly qualitative, in the manner and for the reasons given by U+G researchers above (Gantz, 1996; Roe, 1996).[6]

The truly cross-fertilized audience research project should then combine its qualitative data collection and analysis with procedures that ensure both reliability and generalizability. The achievement of these is a complex task for any research project, qualitative or quantitative. In simple terms, however, I take them to mean the following:

Reliability is centrally concerned with the question 'Would other eyes observe the same?' This concerns the consistency of the procedures used in gathering and analysing the data, for example 'the degree of consistency with which instances are assigned to the same category by different observers, or by the same observer on different occasions' (Hammersley, 1992: 67, quoted by Silverman, 1993: 145). Another way of putting this is to say that we must strive to eliminate arbitrariness of measurement and interpretation.

Before anything else the avoidance of arbitrariness means that qualitative researchers have to develop what Rosengren (1993) terms 'formal models' that may mediate between the 'substantive theories' and the 'empirical data'. For Rosengren it is precisely the lack of such formal models in the ethnographic approach which is to blame for the fact that 'key results cannot be carefully compared and, consequently, cannot be falsified' (1993: 11).

To this we may add that it is also the lack of rigidly systematic categories for the presentation of findings that has prevented qualitative studies (including my own) from generalizing their results, instead ending up with descriptive verbal characterizations that may be illuminating, but which often also leave an impression of fuzziness.

Unlike quantitative research, the qualitative study cannot deliver a numerical indicator of reliability. It has to find other ways of eliminating the tendency of researchers to fall for 'typical examples' or to let hypotheses influence the interpretations. As Höijer puts it, 'From one or two concrete, vivid instances we assume there are dozens more lurking in the bushes – but we don't verify whether or how many there are, and there are usually fewer than we think' (1990: 19).

Höijer recommends that the first requirement for the avoidance of such pitfalls is to be very systematic: to carefully describe all steps in the analysis: 'Specify precisely what was done and how, and the underlying assumptions in each phase of the research process' (1990: 16). Second, all analytical points must be supported by extensive illustrative quotations from interview transcripts. To follow these suggestions will certainly do no harm, but more is required to persuade the sceptics.

Another strategy is to give readers insights into the process of data analysis, as when Liebes (1984) publishes a two-column analysis of one full *Dallas* interview with the transcript in one column and the analytical discourse in the other. The implication is that this 'reading over her shoulder' during the analysis of a specimen interview enlightens other scholars about her analytical procedure as a whole.

Two other, related strategies are even more unusual in qualitative work; in both cases 'other eyes' are invited to actually scrutinize the complete data with respect to the interpretations and categorizations made by the researcher. Funding permitting, one strategy could be to imitate the analytical process employed in quantitative research where two members of the research team separately analyse the complete data set, then check for and resolve disagreements about specific points before the report is drafted (see the case study presented below).

Another strategy would be to use 'external auditing' to avoid arbitrariness of analysis. For instance, Belk et al. (1988) submitted their analyses for scrutiny by colleagues not involved in the particular study. They provided three peers familiar with the conduct and interpretation of ethnographic research with the draft report plus the complete data sets (field notes, videotapes, memos, etc.) and asked them to 'examine the report for its grounding in the data [. . .] to criticize the project for lack of sufficient data for drawing its conclusions', so as to 'prevent the publication of works that are not based on careful methods and data collection' (1988: 456).

Having myself filled the role of external auditor for a reception study by Mick and Buhl (1992), it is my belief that the intersubjective scholarly forum constituted by such peer auditing may be an answer to some of the reliability problems of qualitative research, as it decisively improves the dependability and confirmability of the findings.

Generalizability normally concerns the representativeness of the findings and basically has to do with the nature of the sample used. However, in the particular context of the recent scholarly disputes about 'generalization' within media ethnography, the concept is interpretive rather than statistical and has to do with the question of whether or not it is desirable to reduce the kaleidocospic data to a handful of categories that may serve as 'generalized findings' (see the discussion of 'radical ethnography' above).

Generalizability defined more conventionally as *representativeness* deals with the extent to which the necessarily small sample studied may be said to represent the larger population for which the researcher wishes the study to have explanatory power. As is well known, a representative sample must be *random* and of a sufficient *size* to encompass the variety of the population.

Sometimes we *are* interested in finding out about whole populations; then we must observe traditional definitions of representativeness. And it is clear that qualitative research will only rarely be able to fully live up to this requirement. But, as Roe observes, in social science circles there has been 'a gross overvaluing of, and investment in, external validity, in the sense of representative samples at the nationwide level [. . .] social scientists have made something of a fetish of representativeness' (1996: 90).

Many researchers who analyse media audiences, for instance in marketing and broadcasting companies, are not at all interested in the total population of a country; instead they may be exploring the perceptions of a social-issues advertising campaign among people who donate to charities, or the reception of a science programme among a highly educated target group. They do not need to abide by the conventional definition of representativeness – two or three focus groups composed of relevant individuals may fully serve their purposes.

As an alternative to 'representativeness', Roe suggests that we abandon any claim to some kind of 'truth' for our findings, however random and statistically potent the sample, for the benefit of a more modest, and pragmatically oriented, concept of 'the map', that is, our findings should be seen as 'abstract representations of features that are only intended to be schematic' (Roe, 1996: 89). Roe argues that this topographical metaphor enables us 'to bypass the sterile controversy which surrounds the issue of "quantitative" versus "qualitative" method' because maps 'can be made on different scales, covering larger or smaller regions, with lesser or greater detail [. . .] the real question becomes whether the level of generality which a researcher employs is appropriate to the problem at hand, and whether the details are sufficiently accurate to solve it' (1996: 89). Qualitative studies may thus be regarded as charts of local areas with high explanatory power, useful for manoeuvring in local regions where they provide a lot of detail. Acknowledging this much is the concession which quantitatively inclined researchers must give if the interparadigm dialogue is to make any sense.

The qualitative side must concede that it is necessary to draw maps at all: against the claim of some that 'generalizations are necessarily violations to the concrete specificity of all unique micro-situations' (Ang, 1991: 162), those interested in cross-fertilization should insist that even with small samples it is no longer sufficient to merely register the existence of a plethora of topographical features in the area being explored. It is mandatory that future travellers be supplied with 'maps' that indicate, in a formalized manner, the relative 'positions' of the most important features, even if this means initially sacrificing a considerable number of details.

In studies of audience readings such 'positions' can sometimes be schematically displayed in concentric circles, as was the case with the classic reading positions ('dominant', 'negotiated', 'oppositional') employed by Morley (1992: 117) in the *Nationwide* study to conclude on his qualitative findings.

A more recent example could be the categorization of readers of non-product, 'ethical' corporate advertisements as 'sympathetic', 'agnostic', and 'cynical' (Schrøder, 1997); by representing these reading positions in a diagrammatic map as three partly overlapping circles it becomes possible to represent the occurrence of 'pure' as well as 'ambivalent' informants in the 16-large sample (see Figure 3.1).

Such generalized formal categories of reading and viewer types obviously do not present the whole picture – a lot of observational and verbal detail is lost *in* the map, and must be provided *with* the map if it is to make any sense. The challenge for qualitative audience studies therefore consists in accompanying the generalizing maps with full verbal analyses that describe individual 'typical' instances of each category as a kind of depth 'case' study (e.g. a typical 'cynical' reading), as well as extensive profiles that distil the shared characteristics of all members of a category (e.g. the shared characteristics of 'cynical' readers).

With such qualitative anchorage of the generalized positions expressed by the 'map of findings', the distance between qualitative and quantitative exploration may turn out to have been reduced to a minimum (see also Alasuutari, 1995: 116ff.). The placing of the readers of ethical advertisements in Figure 3.1 enables anyone to do a simple count of 'how many'

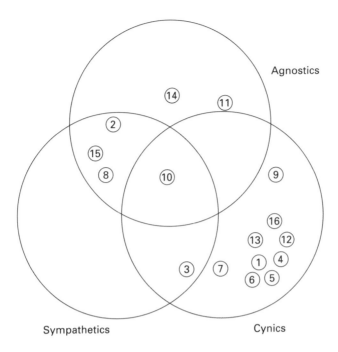

Figure 3.1 *Reading positions of British readers of ethical advertisements*

informants occupy the different reading positions, or types. Such numerical information will no doubt satisfy, if not the demands of real number crunchers, then at least the curiosity of many closet quantificationists in the qualitative camp. Many of them will no doubt fear to tread the path towards full-scale quantification of such qualitative types. Nevertheless, this appears to be an enticing prospect that should be further explored, since, as Alasuutari puts it, 'there is a lot of good in the quantitative approach as long as it is not used in the standard fashion' (1995: 3). It is thus not inconceivable that we may now be able to deal with what once appeared to be a remote ideal:

> One of the tasks ahead will consist in conceptualizing a method which makes it possible to incorporate and preserve qualitative data through a process of quantification, enabling researchers to discuss the demographic patterning of viewing responses, for instance the proportions of 'preferred' or 'aberrant' responses within demographic groups and in the general population. (Schrøder, 1987: 27)

But that is another story.

Towards an integrated approach: a case study of media use in Denmark

The study *The Danes and the Media: Daily Life and Democracy* (Schrøder, 1995) is one in a series of reports about the Danish media landscape commissioned by the Government's Commission on the Media set up by the Prime Minister in 1994. The purpose of the study is to explore through qualitative methods how people are using the media in everyday life in multimedia and multichannel society, and how their use of the media is related to their participation in democratic processes.[7]

The study was conducted with 27 households in a major provincial city that was chosen because it is demographically close to the national average, thus enabling us to come up with results that are 'typical', even though they are not 'representative' of the whole country. The city has a daily newspaper and most households have cable or satellite TV.

By selecting a small geographical area for the study we increase validity because we gain access to informants living in a regional social system: an everyday universe that thinks of itself as such, and which we can familiarize ourselves with through many sources prior to engaging the informants, for example by reading the local newspaper, listening to local radio news and watching regional TV. This enables us to understand and to speak to their concerns, and to better understand the references they make to their everyday world of work and leisure during the conversations.

The 27 families were recruited according to the RISC-system, which divides people into segments according to life values, which have a more direct relation to their behaviour and attitudes than demographic selection criteria. RISC ('Research In Social Change') is a mainly quantitative instrument developed for marketing purposes, and is now used under different names in many European countries. In Denmark it is based on more than 2,500 face-to-face interviews, each supplemented with a self-completion questionnaire. It measures a total of 50 values, each value being based on two to five questions, the response pattern of the respondents determining whether they have the value in question. In this study a reduced version, called MiniRISC, was used, which builds on the same principles. The end product, arrived at through correspondence analysis, is a 'chart of values' (see Figure 3.2).

When individuals and groups are positioned in the chart we may get an indication of the values characterizing these individuals and groups. The south–north axis representing the value continuum from Tradition to Innovation, and the east–west axis representing the continuum from Idealism to Pragmaticism, enable us to distinguish four population segments called respectively BLUE (northwest), GREEN (northeast), PINK (southeast) and PURPLE (southwest). They have the following characteristics (which I here supplement with the Bourdieu-inspired labels given by Dahl, 1995):

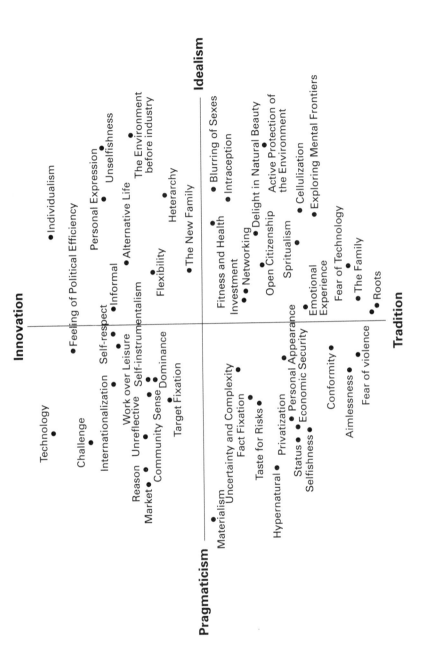

Figure 3.2 RISC chart of values 1994/5

BLUE   Pragmatic–innovative, self-confident, consumption-oriented; rich in economic and cultural capital, but relatively inclined towards the former. Central values: technology, challenge, work over leisure. Five households in the study.

GREEN   Idealistic–innovative, goal-oriented, 'good taste', ecological attitudes; rich in cultural capital, not quite matched by economic potential. Central values: personal expression, the environment before industry, heterarchy. Seven households in the study.

PINK   Idealistic-traditional, family- and health-oriented; more cultural than economic capital, but not too much of either. Central values: fitness and health, exploring mental frontiers, fear of technology. Nine households in the study.

PURPLE Pragmatic–traditional, stability-oriented, low in both cultural and economic capital, tending towards the underprivileged. Central values: conformity, selfishness, economic security. Six households in the study.

I believe that the use of RISC – especially to the extent that the RISC chart, as argued by Dahl (1995), delineates social relationships which are analogous to those of Bourdieu's model of society (Bourdieu, 1984: 128) – enables us to avoid some of the shortcomings of both previous U+G research and qualitative studies of media reception, especially the lack of relationship between individuals and the wider social context.

The RISC approach remedies this macro-level shortcoming, as it conceptualizes media users in social space. By drawing a map for locating people simultaneously in terms of life values and tastes, and to some extent in terms of income, education and status (or economic, cultural and social capital), RISC enables us to identify the cultural relation between a clearly defined social group, its central values and lifestyle, and the media it uses. The RISC chart of values thus allows researchers to position informants in value segments which also indicate relative social position.

Most of the 27 households consisted of two adults, with or without children, but some were singles. The adults covered the ages 25 to 70. Most households had cable or satellite. The interviewer visited each household twice, with three to four weeks in between; each interview lasted between one-and-a-half and two hours and was tape-recorded. The 27 interviews were divided between two experienced qualitative researchers in their mid-twenties, so that the same researcher did both interviews with a household. To ensure high validity, the data collection method used open, relatively symmetrical interviews, where the interviewer navigates through all the relevant topics, in the order which appears natural in the situation.

The first interview dealt with the informants themselves, their everyday life past and present, their obligations, activities and interests, work and leisure, and to a limited extent their use of media, which then became the focus in the second interview. The two interviews thus supplemented each other in covering both everyday life and use of the media.

In order for informants to feel at ease and thus to increase validity, both interviews were held on a concrete level. For instance the talk about TV and radio use took its point of departure in and constantly referred back to TV diaries for the last two days filled out by household members prior to the interview. As regards print media, each informant was asked at the end of the first interview to collect the papers and magazines received and read in the week before the second interview; these publications were dealt with one at a time, and informants were asked to explain why they receive them, how much and when they read them, how they like the content, and so on.

In the data-analytical stage an effort was made to take issues of reliability more seriously than is usually the case in media ethnographic studies. The first interview with each household was summarized topic-wise, with direct quotations of significant passages. The second interview was transcribed verbatim from the tape. In the interpretation of each interview the analyst again listened to the tape and scrutinized the transcripts, then produced a thematically organized 'household profile', which included both components of the household's everyday life and their uses of and attitudes to the different media, and the relationships between daily life and media uses. Each household profile was constructed independently by the project director and by the research assistant responsible for the household in question, so that all profiles were cross-checked back to the tapes/transcripts. Finally the 27 household profiles were synthesized in the project director's report.

Findings

The data available to this study were exclusively of a qualitative kind. And there is a problem of space in connection with the presentation of such data. The following selective and brief summary will therefore not be able to do justice to the many-faceted findings we made in the analysis.

In the original report (Schrøder, 1995), findings about categories of media users, for instance, were reported both in the form of a three- to four-page case profile with lengthy interview quotations of a typical category member, plus a generalized profile of the cases making up each category. Here I shall have to condense the findings even more.

It was one of the main objectives of the study to explore the role of the media in the lives of democratically 'active' and 'passive' citizens. We decided to define these two types of citizen in terms of their involvement in organizations and associations as 'organizers', and to explore the inclination of the two types to seek information through the media: active, democratic citizens are individuals who participate in decision processes at different levels, and who keep informed about the society they live in.

Individuals who do both are good democratic citizens; those who do one or the other need no reprimands either. The problem lies with those individuals who do neither: they pose the challenge for a media policy that wishes to empower those who are, or are in the process of being, disconnected from the democratic process.

'Democratic activity' we defined as participation in public organizations and associations outside of the home; it is not sufficient to be just a member of such associations, it is necessary to be an 'organizer', someone who takes initiatives, gets elected to the board, and so on. It matters less, we decided, whether the association in question is a political party, a grassroots organization, a sports club or cultural association. The essence of 'activity' is to be in a position where one has influence over some aspect of the public or private life of fellow human beings. On this basis we divided the 27 households into democratic 'organizers' and 'non-organizers'.

What really matters for people's ability to function as democratic citizens is their actual knowledge about social affairs from the local to the global. However, our project design did not enable us to test such knowledge. Instead we operationalized the concept of 'information-seeking through the media' as a function of people's use of a range of media which are democratically important:

- substantial TV news programmes (15 minutes and more);
- TV debate programmes and documentaries;
- substantial radio news programmes (10 minutes or more);
- radio debate programmes and documentaries;
- one daily newspaper;
- one weekly or monthly magazine with serious journalism;
- other media with serious social and cultural journalism (e.g. journals, organizational magazines, etc.).

On the basis of the interviews we divided the 27 households between those who do and those who do not use at least three of the above media/genres on a regular basis to keep informed about political, social and cultural affairs.

When the criteria of democratic participation and information-seeking are combined we end up with four categories of citizens (see Figure 3.3). Numbers show how many of the 27 households belong to each category. Below I shall draw a brief profile of each category, concluding with the recommendations we made on the basis of the analysis.

CITIZEN CATEGORY A: WELL-INFORMED ORGANIZERS   The five households in this category consist of individuals who are active information-seekers through the media and who are democratically active, often in broad national or regional associations in the areas of politics, trade unions or culture. They belong to the Blue and Green value segments. They have a

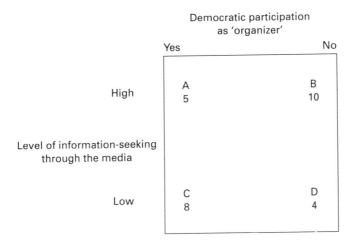

Figure 3.3 *Democratic participation and information-seeking through the media*

selective TV practice that focuses on news, documentaries and films while also including some entertainment. Radio is mostly a background medium, except for news programmes, which are listened to with attention. Newspapers are considered essential, and they read both a national (morning) and a local (afternoon) paper every day. They see these media as a *sine qua non* for their ability to function in democratic contexts.

CITIZEN CATEGORY B: WELL-INFORMED NON-ORGANIZERS   The ten households in this category are frequent users of the informative media, but they have not involved themselves as organizers in democratic contexts. They belong to the Blue, Green and especially Pink value segments. Their appetite for information is due to the fact that they have a generally curious attitude to life, but also because they feel it is a citizen's duty. They are not as selective in their use of TV as category A, and in addition to the informative programmes they enjoy many types of entertainment as well. Radio is a background component of the morning ritual, and may be used attentively for news and informative programmes during the day. They read one daily newspaper, national or regional/local. Under the right circumstances they would be able to become more democratically active.

CITIZEN CATEGORY C: LESS WELL-INFORMED ORGANIZERS   The eight households in this category have involved themselves actively in their surroundings, especially in social and recreational community associations. They do not make a sustained effort to keep informed through the media. They belong to the Green, Pink and Purple value segments. They don't want to go out of their way to watch the TV news, but they often do watch it; otherwise TV is used mainly as an entertainment medium, which accompanies many other activities of family life. Radio, with its mixed music and journalism flows, is a 'sound carpet' at work, and in some home situations, so here they pick up many important bits and pieces about political, social and cultural affairs. They rarely read a daily newspaper, finding the weekly freesheet sufficient. They care enough about their local community to participate in its public activities.

CITIZEN CATEGORY D: LESS WELL-INFORMED NON-ORGANIZERS   The four households in this category are not democratically active, and they do not actively seek diverse sources of information. They belong exclusively to the Purple value segment, that is, a group with few economic and educational resources. Their TV consumption is dominated by entertainment flows that are always there in the background, so they also watch news programmes if such occur in the flow. They do not dislike debate and current affairs programmes when once in a while they bump into them, but they do not actively consult printed or teletext TV listings in order to seek out such genres. Radio is a background medium both at work and at home. The local freesheet is irregularly supplemented with a national tabloid paper. These households focus on their own private affairs and do not feel any need to join in community activities.

Recommendations for media policy

The well-being of a democratic society presupposes that people are well informed and involve themselves in public decision processes, as people in category A and to some extent categories B and C do. However, a democratic society cannot force people to live up to this ideal, only encourage them to do so by creating institutional frameworks that promote the ideal, such as public schools, libraries, electronic media, and so on.

In contemporary Danish society many adults, in categories C and especially D, have organized their daily lives in such a manner that they do not regularly expose themselves to democratically important informative, print or electronic, media. Most people in these groups do tend to follow 'the news', but they do not regularly expose themselves to in-depth coverage of social affairs in newspapers and news magazines.

The qualitative nature of the data-gathering process enabled us to discover that these people do sometimes encounter and get interested in in-depth coverage of such issues, but only when they 'bump into' debate and current affairs programmes on TV. This may happen when such a programme turns up on one of the channels they habitually watch, or when they accidentally zap into one. In the interviews, category C and D informants often speak with great enthusiasm about an engaging documentary about welfare clients, or a debate programme about the educational system, but their having watched it is almost always a result of coincidence.

Media policy in itself can do little to remedy this situation, which is a product of fundamental economic and social forces in Western society. However, one modest thing that an empowering media policy could do, in order to preserve or create media that may connect groups with few social and educational resources to the democratic process, in the community and nationally, would be to ensure through legislation that there remain national TV channels which are required and committed to producing and broadcasting informative programmes and to scheduling them during prime-time when people are actually watching.

Moreover, many statements by informants indicate that it is not sufficient to think only in terms of conventional programme types. It is necessary to develop the aesthetic means of expression of informative programmes so as to not just *inform* audiences, but also to *engage* and to *move* them: the best way to capture audience interest, for current affairs and documentary programmes, seems to be to lean more towards the narrative forms of fiction formats.

As regards debate programmes, many informants spontaneously offered the criticism that discussion programmes were too often 'cut off' by programme hosts anxious to get on with the programme. Broadcasters should therefore aim to develop a range of genuinely dialogic formats in which participants, who should include both ordinary people and experts, can speak their minds and are not all the time 'cut off' in this manner.

Other findings

Other findings of the study enable us to present a *cultural portrait of the role of television in multimedia society*, pointing out the similarities between the uses of television today and the uses of some of television's predecessors in the media landscape, for example the increasing similarity of, on the one hand, TV channel and programme supply and, on the other, print media supply in terms of the diversity which meets the consumer-citizen in front of the screen and at the newsstand, respectively. Other similarities have to do with an increasingly individualized consumption of TV; an increasingly fragmentary 'reading' process (zapping/browsing); and, as a parallel to radio, an increasing use of television as an accompaniment to other activities, or vice versa. The cultural significance of such similarities, the report suggests, might be to remove some of the often expressed public concern about the devastating consequences of television's role in our lives, since what television is 'doing to' modern culture is not that different from what other media have been doing for decades without attracting the same amount of fear and criticism.

The study also produced insights about informants' attitudes on a number of single issues. As already indicated, it turned out that a large number of informants were dissatisfied with the way the participants in

TV discussion programmes are 'cut off' by programme hosts wanting to get on with the programme lest audiences get bored and change channels. It was widely felt that in order to give voice to a society's democratic debate television hosts should not interrupt people so frequently. This issue was not included in the interview guide, but was brought up spontaneously by many informants, thus demonstrating one of the strengths of qualitative research: the researcher's imagination is not the limit of possible insights to be gained from the study.

Another issue that was, often spontaneously, raised by informants was the placement of commercial spots in the TV flow. Danish viewers are in a good position to judge here, as the two commercial channels have different practices: the public service-committed TV2 is only allowed to have commercials between programmes, whereas the fully commercial TV3 places commercials the American way. All informants without exception expressed their great annoyance with commercial interruptions – even if many of them have learned to live with them. If media policy is to reflect the wishes of the population, the study thus shows that new licences to advertising-based TV channels should require them to place commercials between programmes.

Final remarks

The case study presented above is not offered as a flawless model of how to accomplish a paradigmatic integration characterized by perfect levels of reliability, validity and generalizability. The claim that *can* be made for the study is that its conceptualization and execution have taken place in a constant struggle with these methodological ideals in mind. For that reason, whether it is judged to be successful or not, it can hopefully serve for other researchers as a stimulus for methodological reflection and development.

Notes

1. This is not to deny that there are empirical research tasks for which one *or* the other of these approaches is 'right' (cf. Hjarvard, 1995: 25). The argument here is that we should also explore how their application in conjunction should transcend the often-invoked notion of 'triangulation'. Other interesting solutions to overcoming the qualitative/quantitative divide are discussed in Alasuutari (1995: 116ff.).

2. See also McQuail's recent attempt to reformulate the U+G proposition in a less mechanistic manner which, while retaining its implied rationality of media users, puts more emphasis on certain 'key linkages', for instance between social background and experience and expectations from the media (McQuail, 1994: 319).

3. I am here deliberately excluding then forgotten early empirical studies of radio serials (such as Herzog, 1944).

4. To my knowledge the only reception studies to get even close to representativeness are Lewis's (1991) studies of news reception and the *Cosby Show* sitcom, which interviewed 50 individuals and 50 groups, respectively.

5. In contrast, Lewis's news study, which used individual informant interviews, supplies exact numerical descriptions, here about audience perceptions of a politician's speech: 'Of the fifty respondents, forty-one incorporated references to the speech into their readings, thirty-eight incorporated references to his reception, and only twelve incorporated references to the story's history' (Lewis, 1991: 151).

Lewis has recently put forward a strong argument for the rehabilitation of quantitative methods in cultural studies research, where 'the lingering suspicion of numerical data has degenerated into a habit' (Lewis, 1997: 84). For instance, he argues that 'it is important for us to know, roughly, the number of people who construct one reading of a TV programme rather than another' (1997: 87).

6. I would like to stress that I am not arguing that questionnaire-based surveys should be abandoned as a research technique. The research recommendations below are directed specifically towards research into 'cultural meaning processes involving media audiences', that is, the object of study common to the scholars in the two paradigms who call for cross-fertilization. There will still be other, vast fields of study that invite, and indeed require, different types of method: questionnaire surveys, laboratory experiments, introspection, and so on, and various combinations of these, as when a large-scale survey is preceded by a qualitative pilot phase, or a qualitative study is supplemented with a survey.

7. For the benefit of readers not familiar with the media scene in Denmark (population 5 million) here are a few facts. There are three Danish TV channels: TV1 is the old public-service broadcaster ('Danish Broadcasting'), programme-wise much like the BBC in Britain; TV2 is the newcomer, which broke the monopoly in 1988, operating under public service requirements but almost totally financed by commercial revenue, similar to Independent Television in Britain in several respects; the third channel, which has avoided regulation by the Danish Government by operating through satellite out of London, is completely commercial, not too different programme-wise from American network TV. Regional and local TV are still of minor significance as compared with the national channels. A majority of households have access to a range of Scandinavian, European and global channels through satellite or cable.[1]

Radio is dominated by the three differently profiled channels of the Danish Broadcasting Company (which also owns TV1). In addition there is a huge audience for local radio all over the country, mostly commercial stations. There are around ten daily national newspapers, and just over a dozen different regional daily newspapers, with some local editions. Most provincial towns have a weekly or biweekly newspaper that is distributed to all households.

Notes

1. The market share of the three Danish channels is approximately 75 per cent (1999).

References

Alasuutari, P. (1995) *Researching Culture: Qualitative Method and Cultural Studies.* London: Sage.

Ang, I. (1991) *Desperately Seeking the Audience.* London: Routledge.

Ang, I. and Hermes, J. (1991) 'Gender and/in Media Consumption', in J. Curran and M. Gurevitch, (eds), *Mass Media and Society.* London: Edward Arnold.

Belk, R.W., Sherry, J.F. and Wallendorf, M. (1988) 'A Naturalistic Inquiry into Buyer and Seller Behavior at a Swap Meet', *Journal of Consumer Research,* 14: 449–70.

Blumler, J.G., Gurevitch, M. and Katz, E. (1985) 'Reaching Out: A Future for Gratifications Research', in K.E. Rosengren, L.A. Wenner and P. Palmgreen (eds), *Media Gratifications Research.* Beverly Hills: Sage.

Bourdieu, P. (1984) *Distinction.* London: Routledge & Kegan Paul.

Dahl, H. (1995), 'Sociologi og Målgrupper: Om at Operationalisere Bourdieu' [Sociology and Target Groups: Towards an Operationalization of Bourdieu], *MedieKultur,* 24: 5–25, Aalborg, Denmark.

Drotner, K. (1994) 'Ethnographic Enigmas: "The Everyday" in Recent Media Studies', *Cultural Studies,* 8 (2): 341–57.

Drotner, K. (1996) 'Less Is More: Media Ethnography and Its Limits', in P.I. Crawford and S. Hafsteinsson (eds), *The Construction of the Viewer: Media Ethnography and the Anthropology of Audiences.* Højbjerg, Denmark: Intervention Press.

Elliott, P. (1974) 'Uses and Gratifications Research: A Critique and a Sociological Alternative', in J.G. Blumler and E. Katz, (eds), *The Uses of Mass Communications: Current Perspectives on Gratifications Research.* Beverly Hills: Sage.

Fiske, J. (1987) *Television Culture.* London: Methuen.

Frey, L.R., Botan, C.H., Friedman, P.G. and Kreps, G.L. (1991) *Investigating Communication: An Introduction to Research Methods.* Englewood Cliffs, NJ: Prentice Hall.

Gantz, W. (1996) 'An Examination of the Range and Salience of Gratifications Associated with Entertainment Programming', *Journal of Behavioral and Social Sciences,* 1: 11–48.

Gitlin, T. (1978) 'Media Sociology: The Dominant Paradigm', *Theory and Society* 6: 205–53.

Greenberg, B.S. (1974) 'Gratifications of Television Viewing and their Correlates for British Children', in J.G. Blumler and E. Katz, (eds), *The Uses of Mass Communications: Current Perspectives on Gratifications Research.* Beverly Hills: Sage.

Hall, S. (1974) '*Encoding and Decoding in the Television Discourse*'. Centre for Contemporary Cultural Studies, Stencilled Occasional Paper No. 7. Birmingham: University of Birmingham.

Hammersley, M. (1990) *Reading Ethnographic Research: A Critical Guide.* London: Longmans.

Hammersley, M. (1992) *What's Wrong with Ehnography: Methodological Explorations.* London: Routledge.

Herzog, H. (1944) 'What Do We Really Know about Daytime Serial Listeners?', in P.F. Lazarsfeld and F. Stanton (eds), *Radio Research, 1942–43.* New York: Duell, Sloan and Pearce.

Hjarvard, Stig (1995) *Internationale TV-nyheder* [International TV News]. Copenhagen: Akademisk Forlag.

Höijer, B. (1990) 'Reliability, Validity and Generalizability: Three Questions for Qualitative Reception Research', *The Nordicom Review*, 1: 15–20.

Holbrook, M.B. (1987) 'The Study of Signs in Consumer Esthetics: An Egocentric Review', in J. Umiker-Sebeok (ed.), *Marketing and Semiotics*. New York: Mouton de Gruyter.

Jensen, K.B. (1986) *Making Sense of the News: Towards a Theory and an Empircal Model of Reception for the Study of Mass Communication*. Aarhus: Aarhus University Press.

Jensen, K.B. (1991) 'Reception Analysis: Mass Communication as the Social Production of Meaning', in K.B. Jensen and N.W. Jankowski (eds), *A Handbook of Qualitative Methodologies for Mass Communication Research*. London: Routledge.

Jensen, K.B. (1995) *The Social Semiotics of Mass Communication*. London: Sage.

Jensen, K.B. (1996) 'The Empire's Last Stand: Reply to Rosengren', *European Journal of Communication*, 11: 261–7.

Jensen, K.B. and Rosengren, K.E. (1990) 'Five Traditions in Search of the Audience', *European Journal of Communication*, 5: 207–38.

Jensen, K.B., Schrøder, K., Stampe, T., Søndergaard, H. and Topsøe-Jensen, J. (1994) 'Super Flow, Channel Flow, and Audience Flows. A Study of Viewers' Reception of Television as Flow', *The Nordicom Review*, 2: 1–13.

Katz, E., Blumler, J.G. and Gurevitch, M. (1974) 'Utilization of Mass Communication by the Individual', in J.G. Blumler and E. Katz (eds), *The Uses of Mass Communications: Current Perspectives on Gratifications Research*. Beverly Hills: Sage.

Lewis, J. (1991) *The Ideological Octopus: An Exploration of Television and Its Audience*. London: Routledge.

Lewis, J. (1997) 'What Counts in Cultural Studies', *Media, Culture & Society*, 19 (1): 83–97.

Liebes, T. (1984) 'Ethnocriticism: Israelis of Moroccan Ethnicity Negotiate the Meaning of *Dallas*', *Studies in Visual Communication*, 10 (3).

Liebes, T. and Katz, E. (1990) *The Export of Meaning*. New York: Oxford University Press.

Livingstone, S., Wober, M. and Lunt, P. (1994) 'Studio Audience Discussion Programmes: An Analysis of Viewers' Preferences and Involvement', *European Journal of Communication*, 9: 355–79.

Lull, J. (1990 [1980]) 'The Social Uses of Television', in J. Lull, *Inside Family Viewing: Ethnographic Research on Television's Audiences*. London: Comedia.

Lull, J. (1985) 'The Naturalistic Study of Media Use and Youth Culture', in K.E. Rosengren, L.A. Wenner and P. Palmgreen, (eds), *Media Gratifications Research*. Beverly Hills: Sage.

McQuail, D. (1994) *Mass Communication Theory: An Introduction*. London: Sage.

Mick, D.G. and Buhl, C. (1992) 'A Meaning-Based Model of Advertising Experience', *Journal of Consumer Research*, 19: 317–38.

Morley, D. (1980) *The Nationwide Audience*. London: British Film Institute.

Morley, D. (1986) *Family Television: Cultural Power and Domestic Leisure*. London: Comedia.

Morley, D. (1992) *Television, Audiences and Cultural Studies*. London: Routledge.

Radway, J.A. (1984) *Reading the Romance: Women, Patriarchy, and Popular Literature*. Chapel Hill: University of North Carolina Press.

Radway, J.A. (1988) 'Reception Study: Ethnography and the Problem of Dispersed Audiences and Nomadic Subjects', *Cultural Studies*, 2 (3): 359–76.

Roe, K. (1996) 'The Uses and Gratifications Approach: A Review of Some

Methodological Issues', *Journal of Behavioral and Social Sciences*, 1: 81–96.

Rosengren, K.E. (1993) 'From Field to Frog Ponds', *Journal of Communication*, 43 (3): 6–17.

Rosengren, K.E. (1996) Review of K.B. Jensen, *The Social Semiotics of Mass Communication*. *European Journal of Communication*, 11: 129–41.

Rubin, A.M. (1981) 'An Examination of Television Viewing Motivations', *Communication Research*, 8 (2): 141–65.

Schrøder, K.C. (1987) 'Convergence of Antagonistic Traditions? The Case of Audience Research', *European Journal of Communication*, 2: 7–31.

Schrøder, K.C. (1988) 'The Pleasure of *DYNASTY*', in P. Drummond and R. Paterson, (eds), *Television and Its Audience*. London: British Film Institute.

Schrøder, K.C. (1989) 'The Playful Audience', in M. Skovmand (ed.), *Media Fictions*. Aarhus, Denmark: Aarhus University Press.

Schrøder, K.C. (1994) 'Audience Semiotics, Interpretive Communities and the "Ethnographic Turn" in Media Studies', *Media, Culture & Society*, 16: 337–47.

Schrøder, K.C. (1995) *Danskerne og Medierne: Dagligdag og Demokrati* [The Danes and the Media: Daily Life and Democracy], Report for the Commission on the Media, The Prime Minister's Office, Copenhagen.

Schrøder, K.C. (1997) 'Cynicism and Ambiguity: British Corporate Responsibility Advertisements and their Readers in the 1990s", in M. Nava, A Blake, I. MacRury, and B. Richards (eds), *Buy This Book: Studies in Advertising and Consumption since the 1950s*. London: Routledge.

Silverman, D. (1993) *Interpreting Qualitative Data: Methods for Analysing Talk, Text and Interaction*. London: Sage.

Silverstone, R. (1994) *Television and Everyday Life*. London: Routledge.

PART II

THE NEW AGENDA: THE INSCRIPTION OF AUDIENCES

4

MEDIA FIGURES IN IDENTITY CONSTRUCTION

Joke Hermes

When I took my first newspaper subscription (a typical Dutch *rite de passage*), I chose one of our two 'quality newspapers'. I decided against the obvious choice, the left-wing *Volkskrant* and chose instead the far more conservative *NRC*. The *NRC* – a *Times*-like newspaper – I felt could be trusted to give the most reliable information on how the British Royal Family at that time was managing its relational crises. The scandal of all those royal marriages going wrong I savoured all the more by reading about them on *NRC*'s international news page. Of course, the price for my involvement in the discourse of quality news production was that there was relatively little to read, especially preceding the Charles and Diana crisis, the Squidgy tapes and their 1995 television appearances and the subsequent speculation about the future of the British monarchy, a legitimate subject for all of the serious press. Throughout the 12-year period I have been subscribing to *NRC*, though, they published royal gossip, usually while condemning the (British) tabloid press.

In this chapter I will discuss the wide varieties of ways in which we as audience members engage with media figures, ranging from royalty to news readers, to pop stars to the common people brought on the tube by reality television. The relation between audiences and stars has been the object of many disciplines, from theatre and film studies to media studies to mass psychology and social psychiatry. All of these disciplines have their own ways of dealing with this relationship. I will present a media and cultural studies perspective here that uses social discourse as its central term. Psychological theories of catharsis (the cleansing effect of, for example, experiencing mediated violence) or identification (losing one's own identity in favour of taking on the identity of a much-admired other person) from such a perspective are not much help in our media-saturated world today, nor are theories of mass hysteria. Such approaches presume a direct link between individuals and media (persons) that does not give 'culture', or the discursive layer between individuals and their surroundings, its due. Stars are central to our present-day media culture. They will be presented in this chapter as nodes in the discursive meaning-producing machine that culture is. Stars anchor meaning production for us.

Different media genres have different rules for their stars. All, however, need a certain amount of 'personalization', news genres as much as popular fiction genres. After a general discussion of media, meaning and media heroes, I will discuss women newsreaders as a strong example of the importance of media figures and personalization. News production ideology tends to be serious and 'modernist' (as opposed to postmodern and more relativizing) in orientation. It would like to be able to discount the subjective and messy human factor altogether in favour of objectivity and factuality. But the news, like other media genres, functions through its central personalities, its anchor(wo)men. This news and media production-centred discussion of media figures in identity construction will then make way for an examination of the audience.

Towards a new question of audiences, media figures and identity

When I interviewed readers of gossip magazines as part of a wider research project on women's magazines, I discovered that my pleasurable excitement in reading gossip was hardly different from what they felt when reading cheap gossip weeklies. Whereas for me gossip items being printed in the *NRC* made them all the more scandalous and therefore delicious, they had their own strategies for extracting maximum reading pleasure. They tended to take the scandal more for granted than I did and most enjoyed sifting out the 'truth' about so and so's love life, affairs or money mismanagement. My favourite respondent (70-year-old Christine Klein) claimed: 'There is always a kernel of truth. When they write that she [Martine Bijl] is divorcing her husband, she'll leave, but how [. . .] you have to search the other magazines, they write slightly different things' (Hermes, 1995: 125). Practised readers of gossip magazines have learned, in my opinion, how to read them. It is a kind of game: ferreting out a truth that is lodged in the minute details of daily life, which has to be found between the lines or in carefully disguised body language (see also Pursehouse, 1991, on reading the *Sun*). The truth will in the end elude us, both I and my gossip readers know. Still, reading gossip is like coming close to human nature 'in action'. 'You get a buzz from it somehow, I don't know why,' said one of my other respondents (Mona Brooks, 19), 'you feel more alive' (Hermes, 1995: 142).

I found no indications that either my respondents or I myself especially identified with the celebrities we like to read about. There was curiosity, empathy, a feeling of connection, derision and sometimes even anger, but there was no reason to validate the common-sense conviction that people in general would want to model themselves after their media heroes (cf. Fiske, 1987: 170–3). On the contrary, their interest in the details of celebrities' lives would, among other things, seem to be a means of bringing them down to the level of ordinary human beings and to imagine them as part of their extended families. This brings me to my central question: *how, then, are media figures important for identity construction?*

Identity construction here is defined as a sociological rather than a psychological process. More specifically, identity construction needs to be understood as a process of meaning making whereby individual identities are formed as a result of social interaction based on or making use of cultural sources of meaning production. The availability of cultural sources of meaning is structured by societal power relations, as are the rules for using them. There exists as it were a discursive layer between individuals and media culture, referred to as 'cultural capital' (Bourdieu, 1980), vocabularies or 'interpretive repertoires' (Potter and Wetherell, 1987). Vocabularies or repertoires partly overlap with and partly are independent from media discourse. This discursive layer will be central to my discussion of the uses and functions of media heroes in contemporary culture.

It needs to be stressed that media figures, contrary to common-sense conviction, are both more and less than 'role models'. Also neither 'identification' nor fandom (which will be discussed below) is especially emotional or irrational – other standard ingredients of much discussion of media figures – even though they both can be. Both the place of media figures in media production routines and ideologies, whether acknowledged by media producers or not, and readers' strategies to deal with media content are more interesting than the scapegoating accusations we so often hear about. The strict moral rules and codes of our society, and the breaking of those rules, are easily identified with media figures. But although they are convenient scapegoats, it is difficult to hold them responsible. They are as much a product of societal ideologies, of which media ideologies are an integral part, as producers of rules and codes, in the sense that they appear to offer options for dealing with society. What interests me here, rather, are the *underlying* discursive mechanisms of meaning production, and those will be focused on.

Media heroes anchor processes of meaning making

Television is the best example of the importance of what John Fiske calls
'characterization' (1987: 149). He argues that television is centrally concerned with the representation of people (1987: 149). 'About 80 per cent of
prime-time US network television is fiction and this is typically presented
in terms of its leading characters' (1987: 149). However, non-fictional media
genres depend just as much on characterization or personalization. This
holds true as much for the presentation of news – Fiske (1987: 149) claims
that newsreaders get as much fan mail as soap opera stars – as for its
actual content. Galtung and Ruge's (1965) famous 1960s news values
research is another classic example: elite persons are an important characteristic of – printed – news.

The first, very simple point, then, is that mediated communication,
whether fiction or news, apparently needs central characters. This is the
accepted view for fiction content. However, it is also true for the news,
which, in the modernist discourse of quality news, is something akin to a
curse. News and factual content (based on the one-dimensional notion
that a description, a fact or an interpretation is either true or not true, and
that this is all that matters) cannot be understood as next-of-kin to fictional text. There is evidence to this effect, though. For example, Bird and
Dardenne (1988), in an article on the narrative qualities of news, remark
that the kind of news readers are consistently attracted to is 'human interest' news. This is news that is written in 'story' form rather than as a
chronicle or account. Bird and Dardenne suggest that the *form* of human
interest news is at least as important as its content. They go on to remark
that:

> Certain types of news (like unroutine crime) and certain types of audience are
> given the full story treatment, while most 'serious' news is not. And [. . .] while
> undoubtedly many readers have learned the particular narrative code of objec-
> tive reporting, the majority of readers show a marked inability to process
> political news in anything but the broadest of terms'. (Bird and Dardenne, 1988:
> 78)

Stories have characters, heroes and villains, chronicles are far less personalized.

Others too, such as Schudson (1996: 153), have offered examples of the
interwovenness of news and fictional popular culture genres as regards
their 'story' character. Stories need central characters, who in turn are
needed to 'establish identification', as Galtung and Ruge (1965) put it.
What Galtung and Ruge call 'the need to establish identification' becomes
in a discourse perspective 'the need to anchor processes of meaning
making'. Identification in such a perspective becomes less an individual
state of mind seen from a psychological point of view than a process that

motivates meaning making by temporarily attaching the abstract to the living. How this works has been widely documented in popular culture research. Studies of Madonna (Kellner, 1995; Lewis, 1987; Schwichtenberg, 1992), of detectives such as Miss Marple (Shaw and Vanacker, 1991) or V.I. Warshawsky (Pope, 1995), or even of film texts such as *The Sound of Music* (Dyer, 1992) may count as examples.

Dyer's (1992 [1976/7]) case study of the musical *The Sound of Music*, for instance, shows how the film text may set up a number of problems and solutions which are (partly) resolved at the level of the text (dialogue and songs) but also, importantly, in the figure of the actress playing Maria (the protagonist), Julie Andrews. At the heart of the film are the governess Maria's awakened sexual feelings for her employer Colonel von Trapp, a widower, against the background of the German–Austrian Anschluß at the beginning of the Second World War. Von Trapp is from an old aristocrat family and much opposed to Nazism. He shares Maria's love of folk culture. He falls in love with her and, unsuitable though the match may be, marries her. He ends up taking Maria and his children across the border to Switzerland into an unknown future. The exhilaration this film provides those who love it certainly does not stem from its narrative, nor from its rather insecure ending (we leave the von Trapps in the middle of nowhere on a mountain peak), but with the sexual and emotional current running through it, produced by Julie Andrews, according to Dyer. Her clear voice and awkward stance underscore the free sexuality the music suggests but which the narrative cannot handle because there is no model for a positive and free female sexuality. At its most abstract, *The Sound of Music* is about the dialectic between freedom and order. Andrews embodies the two in her singing and her acting: while her singing is unparalleled, her acting is stilted.

Bennett and Woollacott's analysis of James Bond (1987), subtitled 'The Political Career of a Popular Hero', makes much the same point. The figure of Bond anchors a series of processes of meaning making. Bond, for Bennett and Woollacott, is a figure of modernization and the embodiment of ideologies of nation, class, gender and sexuality. In their reconstruction of Bond's popularity (which is, of course, an exercise in how any popular hero comes to have meaning), they recognize how 'Bond' as a figure is made out of a range of texts, including the Ian Fleming novels, the films, gossip about the actors playing Bond (Connery, Moore, Brosnan), the merchandising. They argue that

> Bond's status as a popular hero was clearly illustrated in the programme shown by ITV in May 1983 to celebrate the twenty-first anniversary of Bond's first screen appearance in *Dr No* (1962). The programme consisted of clips from the Bond films interspersed with the views and estimations of Bond held by a series of famous personalities from the worlds of entertainment, sports and politics [among them President Reagan]. Without exception, all of those interviewed spoke of Bond as a real person. Not seriously, of course, to genuinely mistake

Bond for a real person would be a category mistake, a sign of dementia. Rather, the point is that, albeit tongue-in-cheek and knowingly, they all entered into the imaginary game, constructed by the programme, of treating Bond *as if* he were a real person with a real history. (1987: 13)

To have some connection with Bond, so to speak, and for the figure of Bond to have had the cultural significance he had, we make Bond into a 'real person', to be rewarded with the 'Bond' way of looking at the world, undercut by the camp and humour of especially the Connery and Moore interpretations of Bond. We invest popular media figures with reality status.

Seeing media figures as real and as part of our everyday cultural and emotional experience is part and parcel of how media texts come to have meaning. Serious media discourse, such as the discourse of quality news, tends to disallow for this embeddedness of meaning making in everyday fantasy life. When it comes to how we relate to media figures, the choice in serious, modernist media theory would seem to be restricted to mass hysteria (in the case of popular fiction genres) or disavowal (when it concerns news media). In modernism the personal and especially the feminine are part of a chain of signifiers that suggest non-quality, irrationality, emotionality and the loss of control (cf. Huyssen, 1986). A closer look therefore in the next section at a troubling figure in serious news production: the woman newsreader. Since Woman is such an unsettling trope in modernism, it should not come as a surprise that women newsreaders as media figures play a key role in controversies over journalistic performance and quality. Journalism's very identity is seen as being at stake.

News, newsreaders and modernity's fears

In May 1992 then Vice-President of the United States of America Dan Quayle attacked Murphy Brown, protagonist of the sitcom of that name, for encouraging and exemplifying moral poverty. Murphy Brown (played by actress Candice Bergen) is a journalist who at the end of that particular season gives birth to a child, and becomes an unwed mother. Piquant detail: Quayle spoke in California less than two weeks after the Rodney King riots (amateur video footage of a black man being beaten up by the police in the street without any provocation led to mass riots in Los Angeles) and managed to exchange 'poverty in Los Angeles' for a broader poverty of values (Walkowitz, 1993: 40). Rebecca Walkowitz uses this example to show how, in the subsequent society-wide debate, women in journalism are not only the medium of news but integral to news as spectacle. This, in its turn, exposes journalism as other than the 'ungendered, objective mediation of truth' (1993: 43) it sets itself up to be. (See also Hallin, 1996, on high modernism in journalism.) It is intriguing that a fictional character is so 'real' that she set off both the Quayle response and the subsequent debate in and about the press. The show, moreover, did well out of the fracas: it increased its ratings. Quayle fared less well: he disappeared from politics.

Quayle's (unsuccessful) attack on Murphy Brown, fictional journalist, raises questions about how rigidly coded the space for media figures and especially for women is (whether it concerns fictional characters or actually existing persons). Walkowitz uses Murphy Brown to show how 'real' women in journalism are under a heavy obligation to show 'propriety and professionalism', which is less the case for male journalists. Women are implicitly assumed to be a less moral genre of person than men are, easily given to (sexual) abandon. Their authority as journalists is directly related to the extent to which they manage to be 'sexless'. The more they are a spectacle, the more they relinquish authority, is how Walkowitz portrays American (television) journalism, using several other examples as well (1993: 45–6).

The attack on Murphy Brown, the show's retaliation, the uneasiness in addressing Murphy Brown, the fictional journalist (should she be Ms Brown, should her first name be used, should her status as a fictional character be made clear?), in subsequent reporting, give some idea of the issues involved when news media try to come to terms with their closeness to fictional media genres in contemporary media culture. A closer look at those media figures perceived as central to the debate about preserving the qualities of news (the battle between quality news and tabloid news, or between responsibility and commercialism, cf. Hallin, 1996) shows us women carrying the burden of keeping the worlds of fact and fiction apart. They symbolize the threat of the two becoming indistinguishable. Real-life women newsreaders are icons, integral to the discourse of quality news as *sign* of disorder repressed. As media figures they call forth a chain of anxieties about media effects and put them to rest. Women newsreaders are the pegs on which modernist news discourse hangs its queasiness over vulnerability and uncertainty as opposed to factuality, certainty and control.

Media figures do not only function in audience practice. They also function as *link* between the ideologies that inform media production and the everyday repertoires used in media reception. This is important because much is changing in media production and especially in television production. New genres such as reality television, in its many forms, are providing us with a new set of characters in television life, including the talk-show host and the woman or man 'in the street'. These new figures will surely change our relation to the media and to media figures. What the example of women newsreaders makes clear is that they will do so from a severely coded space. What are the confines within which media figures operate and in which, ultimately, audience practice may take place?

Ien Ang's (1985) study of *Dallas* made clear that the audience's interpretive space in that particular case was defined by an elitist ideology of mass culture (*Dallas* as American trash) versus a populist ideology. The debate about television news and documentary production suggests that there, too, two major ideologies stake out the domain in which media professionals, audiences and critics may operate. There is a more old-fashioned, print-based discourse of quality news production, which can be dated to what Daniel Hallin (1996) has called the era of 'high modernism' in journalism. The high modernist view can be characterized by its 'transparent', innocent notion of language. In this view language is still a mirror of reality, which will be damaged irreparably in the so-called 'linguistic turn', although it certainly has not completely disappeared. Language after the linguistic turn is widely recognized to be a construction based on social codes. Language can never directly or fully represent all that is out there. News, like *all* language, involves selection and construction of its raw material: the happenings of life itself.

In television production, modern, pre-'linguistic turn' views of news and language are at war with postmodern, post-'linguistic turn' views. A crude but useful distinction is between the 'modern' production ideology of quality news and the 'postmodern' production ideologies of commercial media production, exemplified in the gossip and tabloid press and in 'tabloid television' (cf. Kilborn, 1994, on reality television; Sholle, 1993). The clash between these two ideologies is partly played out before our very eyes, on the screen, for instance in the strategic choice for more women newsreaders when the Dutch *Journaal* was changed to secure its audience, and in simultaneous allegations of increasing sentimentality and quality loss. The two discourses, this suggests, have strong gender connotations, and women on television, much more than men, are the embodied icons of this genderedness.

A second example then, to show how public service television news could not escape renewal and innovation. It concerns Dutch newsreaders and the decision of the editor-in-chief of the *Journaal* in the mid-1980s (until then the only Dutch television news show) to have more women newsreaders. Liesbet van Zoonen (1991) describes how in the 40 years of its existence the *Journaal* achieved its high point of objectivity (and dullness) in the mid-1970s, a policy that was overthrown in the mid-1980s. Peter Brusse, a new editor-in-chief, who was to stay for only two years, decided that the news should be a popular television programme with natural transitions, more than a dull listing of events. The news should offer opportunities to identify with events and personalities. Human interest stories therefore had to be a major ingredient of the news, and newsreaders were urged to transform their serious mode of address into a more intimate style (Van Zoonen, 1991: 222). Brusse's restyling of the news was accompanied by the hiring of an amazing number of women newsreaders. They, apparently, were felt to be more suited to the new, intimate style of the *Journaal*. Rather than 'decorative performers' (Holland, 1987: 149 in Van Zoonen, 1991), or all-knowing authorities, Dutch women newsreaders, according to Van Zoonen, are like caring mothers, always there to tuck you in after a rousing day (1991: 226).

The Dutch public service news thus found its own way to deal with competition from new non-Dutch channels (available via cable) and commercial news broadcasts. It is intriguing that the changes in style and content needed to be embodied by hiring women. It could be flaunted as an emancipatory move while also signifying a thoroughly reactionary definition of femininity by stressing women as more caring, more personal, more motherly, in short, than men could ever be. The *Journaal* appeared to break with older, rigid modernist definitions of news as objective, abstract and quintessentially dull while it exchanged one type of authority for another. The caring mother can be just as much a figure of power and control, and is perfectly capable of taking up the position of honorary man.

Nothing much changed in the relation between the *Journaal* and its audience. Or did it? Print journalists decried the new *Journaal* for being populist and obvious. From the point of view of quality news discourse, the *Journaal* was about to forsake its political and critical function. From the point of view of the audience, it would seem that the genderedness of news discourse was primarily translated into critical observation of the dress sense of the new women anchors (they lacked it, of course). Women newsreaders are more 'person' than male newsreaders are, and their presence invites different viewing strategies. Having women read the news does not upset its intrinsic values, but it does call them into question, if only just a little (which was upsetting enough for critics).

The case of women newsreaders makes clear among other things how important personalization is for processes of meaning making. Quality news discourse likes to posit an ideal-type news (whether objective or investigative) in which the need to personalize and anchor meaning production is for the most part displaced onto the viewer. He (rather than she) is supposed to be well informed and therefore able to understand the wider implications of everyday news, as well as why the words of political leaders and captains of industry need no further legitimization. But for our knowledgeable news viewer, footage of the French President giving a speech is not so different from an interview with a soap opera star in a gossip weekly: both embody the abstract.

What my anecdotes about fictional and real women newsreaders also make clear is that practices of identification and meaning making are gendered at different levels. Whereas we are used to especially consider gender at the level of the practical and the everyday (e.g. how actual women and men relate to different types of news, cf. Bird, 1992; Jensen, 1986; Morley, 1986), or at a highly abstract theoretical level, for example in feminist philosophy (e.g. Nicholson, 1990), media figures give us access to an intermediate level of meaning production. It links the ideological and the everyday. It is the place where it is suggested more strongly than in mundane-everyday-business-as-usual or than in philosophy that the essence of femininity is lodged in women's bodies rather than in discourse. It is the level of naturalization where the abstract is made concrete, but it is also the level where the embodiment of the abstract may be challenged.

From the perspective of audiences

Audience practice has many ways of dealing with media figures. Since the Beatles conquered the United States in the early 1960s (Douglas, 1994), the most prominent form of the relation between audiences and media figures would seem to have been hysteria. Going by the mass of screaming girls outside the expensive Amsterdam Amstel Hotel sometime in the spring of 1996, where Take That, a now defunct but then popular English boy band, were staying just after they broke up (they were in Amsterdam to give their last concert), girls still claim public space in a most spectacular manner. Fandom gives young women a good reason to assert their right to the street. But it does more. From interviews with Take That fans[1] it becomes clear that fandom provides a focus for fantasy life, as well as for intimate friendships with other fans. The girls used many standard genres (romance, soap opera) to fantasize about themselves married to the band members. Talking about all kinds of possible scenarios (rows that need to be made up; becoming family by marrying different band members) gave them huge pleasure. The breaking up of the group was a true disaster therefore, as well as, it would seem, an opportunity to experience devastation at a more or less safe distance.

Although hysteria may at first glance describe the behaviour of these young women audiences, a closer look reveals that fandom has its rewards: such as belonging to a group of friends, and as a means of writing yourself into highly popular genres, which provides a playground of identity construction. Likewise the Beatlemania of an earlier generation of fans can be seen, in retrospect, to have broken up the rigid gender distinctions of middle-class American life (Ehrenreich et al., 1992: 101). According to Ehrenreich et al. (1992), who also interviewed fans, the Beatles' androgyny was itself sexy. One of their interviewees (13 years old when the Beatles came to Los Angeles) says:

> I think I identified with them, rather than as an object of them. I mean, I liked their independence and sexuality and wanted those things for myself. [. . .] Girls didn't get to be that way when I was a teenager – we got to be the limp, passive object of some guy's fleeting sexual interest. We were so stifled, and they made us meek, giggly creatures think, oh, if only I could act that way, and be strong, sexy and doing what you want (Ehrenreich et al., 1992: 103).

Neither fandom nor hysteria is exclusively a women's domain. Not only did the Beatles have many young male fans as well, as do quite a number of contemporary bands, young male mass hysteria has been documented too. A most interesting example is given in Carol Clover's *Men, Women and Chain Saws* (1992). In it she describes horror film as a typical young males' genre (1992: 6). Astonishing is their taste for so-called 'slashers' and rape-revenge horror films (the genre label may be taken literally), and their identification with the female victim/hero of these genres.

> The only way to account for the spectator's engagement in the revenge drive is to assume his identification with the rape-avenging woman. [. . .] Although earlier cinematic rapes allow for a large measure of spectator identification with the rapist (I am thinking of *Frenzy* and *Straw Dogs* in particular), films from the mid-1970s go to increasing lengths, both cinematic and narrative, to dissociate us from that position. Even when the rapes are shown, they are shown in ways that align us with the victim. (1992: 152)

And her revenge is atrocious indeed. Clover's study is mainly a text analysis in which identification is seen as a necessary step to enjoy the filmic text (1992: 59). However, she also refers to participant observation of the slasher's main audience: 'groups of boys who cheer the killer on as he assaults his victims, then reverse their sympathies to cheer the survivor on as she assaults the killer' (1992: 23).

Clover's analysis is intriguing, as is her assertion that '[i]ronically, it may be the feminist account of rape in the last two decades that has both authorized a film like *I spit on your grave* and shaped its politics' (1992: 152). Feminism has given us woman as a credible and forceful avenger. What is of interest here is that both examples (girls' excessive fan behaviour over pop groups as well as boys' identification with the slasher movie's 'final girl' – all other females, and usually a number of males as well, have been slaughtered by the time she assails the killer) make clear that the image produced by terms such as idolization, hero worship or, indeed, identification obscures the embeddedness of audiences' relations to mass media text in specific social relations as well as the discursive role (as opposed to emotional role) played by the media figures involved.

The popularity of horror as a genre, and the particular form horror subgenres take, only make sense against the broader dynamics of social change. Without feminism there would have been no final girl or avenging woman, nor would young men experience the amount of gender confusion that makes horror an ideal testing laboratory. Beatlemania likewise becomes understandable when seen against the background of a rigid gender role system; a system that was under considerable pressure among other things by the growing economic importance of the teenage market (see Hebdige, 1988: 29–30). The appeal of the male star, according to Ehrenreich et al., was

> that you would never marry him; the romance would never end in the tedium of marriage. Many girls expressed their adulation in conventional, monogamous terms, for example, picking their favourite Beatle and writing him a serious letter of proposal, or carrying placards saying, 'John, Divorce Cynthia.' But it was inconceivable that any fan would actually marry a Beatle or sleep

with him (-) or even hold his hand. Adulation of the male star was a way to express sexual yearning that would normally be pressed into the service of popularity or simply repressed. The star could be loved noninstrumentally, for his own sake, and with complete abandon. Publicly to advertise this hopeless love was to protest the calculated, pragmatic sexual repression of teenage life. (1992: 97)

Both Beatlemania and horror fandom are spectacular examples. It is tempting to understand them as exemplary for our relationship to media figures. That, however, is only to a certain extent the case. More mundane forms of media in their unobtrusiveness perhaps make clear other aspects of the connection between media figures, audiences and identity construction. Some of my gossip readers, to whom I referred earlier, felt deeply involved in the lives of their heroes. They deduced from photos that they had been given medication they had had themselves; they worried over allegations of homosexuality; they admired them for coming to the rescue of those less fortunate in life (see Hermes, 1995: 125–6). Likewise they were indignant at young Dutch soccer players attached to foreign clubs who live abroad and fly to Amsterdam for a night out (Hermes, 1995: 131). There appeared to be two dimensions to their involvement, two ways of talking connected with reading gossip magazines, which I termed the extended family repertoire and the melodrama repertoire.

The extended family repertoire more or less explains itself. On an imaginary level it helps readers to live in a larger world than in real life – a world that is governed by emotional ties, that may be shaken by divorces and so on, but that is never seriously threatened. Sociological realities such as high divorce rates, broken families, children who leave home hardly ever to be seen again, are temporarily softened. The world of gossip is like the world of soap opera: whatever happens, they do not fall apart (cf. Modleski, 1984, on soap opera). Indeed, some of the artists who were mentioned in the interviews had not appeared publicly for a long time as singers or entertainers but they lived on in the world of the gossip magazines and their readers.

The repertoire of melodrama is more complex and gives a stronger sense of the importance of media figures in identity construction. The repertoire of melodrama can be recognized in references to misery, drama and by its sentimentalism and sensationalism, but also by its moral undertone. Life in the repertoire of melodrama becomes grotesquely magnified. In the vale of tears that it is, celebrities play crucial and highly stereotypical roles, reminiscent of oral and folk culture. The moral undertone of the repertoire of melodrama questions what makes life worthwhile, though normally not by rational reasoning, but by emotional appeal or outrage. The repertoire of melodrama appears to provide solace because of the misery of others: readers gave me examples of how the misery of others made them feel better about their own lives, or, at other times, how it allowed to them to have a good cry over frustration and sorrow they chose not to analyse more closely. Gossip magazines' celebrities thus become almost archetypal figures. They embody different aspects of everyday life: frustration, ambition, (the wish for) parenthood, relations breaking up. Using the experiences of celebrities and of the occasional 'ordinary person' in the gossip weeklies, readers build and test scenarios in case the same drama were to occur in their own lives. The repertoire of melodrama appeals to forms of 'connected knowing' (Field Belenky et al., 1986: 113). Knowledge is seen as springing from experience rather than rules or books.

However, at the heart of the repertoire of melodrama, there is also a deep sense that the world is unjust, which points to a more collective sense of social inequality. To enjoy it when things go badly for 'rich and famous people' (as one of my readers put it) is a way of imagining cosmic (rather than political) justice taking its toll. Commiseration and indignation are equal ingredients of the pleasure of reading gossip magazines. The public figures portrayed don't need to come alive to be assigned the classic roles of (oral) folk culture: heroes and villains, and scapegoats for the system and for social inequality. The adulterous priest and the hated tax collector are roles now reserved for incest-committing fathers in the serious press, and for politicians in the gossip press. In gossip magazines and tabloids we also find healers and noble outlaws and the king who did not really die. John F. Kennedy, for example, according to American supermarket tabloids, is still alive. They print stories, photographs and unshakeable testimony of witnesses (Bird, 1992: 175–87). Kennedy, concludes Elizabeth Bird,

> like James Bond (-), Robin Hood (-), or Elvis Presley (-), has become a figure encrusted with narratives that intersect with each other differently, according to the reading of different individuals. (-) [S]pecific stories about Kennedy are often resonant with association that goes beyond him as an individual – conventional narratives of hero, lover, national leader, and so forth (1992: 188).

The two (general) repertoires that govern how gossip weeklies are made meaningful, the extended family repertoire and the repertoire of melodrama, are built on a fantasy of community. The extended family repertoire's friendly manner simply draws a wide circle of media figures into a person's private life by discussing them intimately. On an imaginary level this creates community. The repertoire of melodrama creates community in a different manner. It comes into play when readers are indignant, when they are deeply shocked or moved and wish to evaluate what they have heard. By reading gossip or talking about what they have read with friends, they appeal to and thus construe shared standards of morality, which alternate between disapproval and understanding. Gossip creates an intimate world, a sense of belonging. Moreover, in interpreting the gossip magazine text, readers use and validate their own personal knowledge and experience. When you are faced with understanding motherhood, it doesn't matter that the other is a queen: the moral community of gossip scales down such differences, as well as exploits them when that is more appropriate. As circumstances require, media figures are read as embodying a more formal or a more personal role.

In the case of gossip magazines, media figures are instrumental to the creation of community identity, whether it concerns the prototypical gossip weeklies' audience such as elderly women with lower class backgrounds, or, in the case of my women's magazines research, gay audiences for whom gossip magazines are camp. Reading gossip as camp gives it an extra dimension. Integral to that extra dimension is also a feeling of community, both concretely (flirting with what you have read about the stars) and imaginarily and subversively (bespeaking disdain for mainstream culture as well as for the straight roles gay people are forced into). Gossip as camp contests cultural space and in its contestation undergirds individual and collective identities. Obviously, in the last case, media figures are as much ridiculed as admired and loved.

Conclusions

Media figures are important if we want to know how the media come to have meaning. Two central sites of media meaning production were identified here as media production and audience practice, a conventional view. Of course, actual meaning production goes on continually and can only be grasped by research at specific moments and instances. Media figures provide such instances. The charisma we, as audiences and producers, accord our present-day stars, the link they make for us between the abstract and concrete, offering us a feeling of 'being more alive', also makes them important in a more general quest of media, meaning production and identity construction.

Audiences have many ways of dealing with media figures, that much will be clear. However, despite the multitude of possibilities, culture, the discursive layer between human beings and media texts, channels meaning production into near-tangible forms of discourse. My own women's magazines research suggests that all media or media genres have their own sets of repertoires. Discursive formats such as everyday repertoires are important to audiences because they are built on different kinds of imagined identities, whether communal or individual. Reading feminist women's magazines, for example, for the readers I spoke with, had to do with creating a temporary and imaginary identity of a female *homo universalis*: a woman who is extremely well-read; feminism for her (or him, as the case may be) is something she keeps in touch with rather than what she lives. The ordinary as well as the famous women portrayed were kept at a distance. Reading traditional women's magazines had to do with control, other women's experiences can be learned from, and a woman forewarned stands stronger.

It is a safe bet that watching the news has to do with strengthening one's sense of citizenship. As Ingunn Hagen found out in her television news study, readers experience a deep sense of ambiguity over following the news. On the one hand, they feel it is their duty; on the other hand, they are often bored with it (Hagen, 1994). This accords with what Hagen calls the romantic ideal of the democratic citizen, as opposed to the every-day experience of seeing little of use in the Norwegian public television newscast *Dagsrevyen* she researched (1994: 214–15).

In as far as media figures embody the abstract, and thus anchor processes of meaning making, they are our guides, competing like mad with one another, to the wider world of cultural citizenship. As such they deserve more attention than they have been given. Diana and Charles tell us something about power relations both in class terms and in gender terms; the breakdown of their marriage has spawned many a discussion of infidelity, personal freedom and anorexia. As media figures, these two now have images much bigger than themselves, helped along as much by royal press mismanagement as clever manipulation. As such they break open, in the case of my conservative newspaper at least, the modernist dis-course of quality news. From behind the smokescreen of denouncing the tabloid press (in much detail), Diana and Charles' personal life unbal-anced the careful critical and abstract international news page, inviting close reading of all international news to find the personal in the abstract. Such is the stuff of cultural citizenship: a mix of discourses ties us, each in our own ways, into the larger whole of the cultures we live in.

Notes

1. The interviews were conducted by Ellen Wierda, Amsterdam, as part of a research project on young people and fandom (1996).

References

Ang, I. (1985) *Watching Dallas: Soap Opera and the Melodramatic Imagination*. London: Methuen.

Bennett, T. and Woollacott, J. (1987) *Bond and Beyond: The Political Career of a Popular Hero*. Basingstoke: Macmillan.

Bird, S. E. (1992) *For Enquiring Minds: A Cultural Study of Supermarket Tabloids*. Knoxville: University of Tennessee Press.

Bird, S.E. and Dardenne, R.W. (1988) 'Myth, Chronicle, and Story: Exploring the Narrative Qualities of News', in J.W. Carey (ed.), *Media, Myths and Narratives: Television and the Press*. Newbury Park, CA: Sage.

Bourdieu, P. (1980) 'The Aristocracy of Culture' (translated by R. Nice), *Media, Culture & Society*, 6: 343–51.

Clover, C. (1992) *Men, Women and Chain Saws*. London: British Film Institute.

Douglas, S.J. (1994) *Where the Girls Are: Growing Up Female with the Mass Media*. New York: Times Books.

Dyer, R. (1992 [1976/7]) 'The Sound of Music', in R. Dyer, *Only Entertainment*. London: Routledge.

Ehrenreich, B., Hess, E. and Jacobs, G. (1992) 'Beatlemania. Girls Just Want to Have Fun', in L.A. Lewis (ed.), *The Adoring Audience: Fan Culture and Popular Media*. London: Routledge.

Field Belenky, M., McVicker, B. and Rule Goldberger, N. (1986) *Women's Ways of Knowing: The Development of Self, Voice and Mind*. New York: Basic Books.

Fiske, J. (1987) *Television Culture*. London: Methuen.

Galtung, J. and Ruge, M. (1965) 'The Structure of Foreign News', *Journal of Peace Research*, 1: 64–90

Hagen, I. (1994) 'The Ambivalences of TV News Viewing: Between Ideals and Everyday Practices,' *European Journal of Communication*, 9: 193–220.

Hallin, D. C. (1996) 'Commercialism and Professionalism in the American News Media', in J. Curran and M. Gurevitch (eds), *Mass Media and Society*. 2nd edn. London: Edward Arnold.

Hebdige, D. (1988) *Hiding in the Light: On Images and Things*. London: Comedia.

Hermes, J. (1995) *Reading Women's Magazines: An Analysis of Everyday Media Use*. Cambridge: Polity Press.

Huyssen, A. (1986) 'Mass Culture as Woman: Modernism's Other', in A. Huyssen, *After the Great Divide: Modernism, Mass Culture, Postmodernism*. Bloomington: Indiana University Press.

Jensen, K.B. (1986) *Making Sense of the News. Towards a Theory and an Empirical Model of Reception for the Study of Mass Communication*. Aarhus: Aarhus University Press.

Kellner, D. (1995) 'Madonna, Fashion, and Image' in D. Kellner, *Media Culture: Cultural Studies, Identity and Politics between the Modern and the Postmodern*. London: Routledge.

Kilborn, R. (1994) '"How Real Can You Get?": Recent Developments in "Reality Television"', *European Journal of Communication*, 9: 421–39.

Lewis, L.A. (1987) 'Female Address in Music Video', *Journal of Communication Inquiry*, 11 (1): 73–84.

Modleski, T. (1984) 'The Search for Tomorrow in Today's Soap Operas', in T. Modleski, *Loving with a Vengeance: Mass-Produced Fantasies for Women*. New York: Methuen.

Morley, D. (1986) *Family Television: Cultural Power and Domestic Leisure*. London: Comedia.

Nicholson, L.J. (ed.), (1990) *Feminism/Postmodernism*. New York: Routledge.

Pope, R.A. (1995) '"Friends" is a Weak Word for it": Female Friendship and the Spectre of Lesbianism in Sara Paretsky', in G. Irons (ed.), *Feminism in Women's Detective Fiction*. Toronto: University of Toronto Press.

Potter, J. and Wetherell, M. (1987) *Discourse and Social Psychology*. London: Sage.

Pursehouse (1991) 'Looking at "The Sun": Into the Nineties with a Tabloid and Its Readers' *Cultural Studies from Birmingham*, 1 (1): 88–133.

Schudson, M. (1996) 'The Sociology of News Production Revisited', in J. Curran and M. Gurevitch (eds), *Mass Media and Society*, 2nd edn. London: Edward Arnold.

Schwichtenberg, C. (ed.), (1992) *The Madonna Connection*. Boulder, CO: Westview Press.

Shaw, M. and Vanacker, S. (1991) *Reflecting on Miss Marple*. New York: Routledge.
Sholle, D. (1993) 'Buy Our News: Tabloid Television and Commodification', *Journal of Communication Inquiry*, 17 (1): 56–72.
Walkowitz, R.L. (1993) 'Reproducing Reality: Murphy Brown and Illegitimate Politics', in M. Garber, J. Matlock and R.L. Walkowitz (eds), *Media Spectacles*.
Zoonen, L. Van (1991) 'A Tyranny of Intimacy? Women, Femininity and Television News', in P. Dahlgren and C. Sparks (eds), *Communication and Citizenship: Journalism and the Public Sphere*. London: Routledge.

5

CULTURAL IMAGES OF THE MEDIA

Pertti Alasuutari

The tragic death of Princess Diana in a car crash after being followed by photographers in Paris, on 30 August 1997, invoked questions about the way in which we habitually conceive of the media in everyday life. Throughout the world, people were furious at the photographers, who, by hunting pictures of Diana with her boyfriend Dodi Al Fayed, were commonly thought to be partly responsible for the fatal accident. We read or heard about that anger from the media, often also expressed by representatives of the media themselves. The media were self-reflective of their own role and position. Soon two camps were constructed: self-identified quality papers put the blame on the 'yellow press'. In many commentaries it was noted that the guilt could also be extended to the general international public, whose great interest in the private life of the beloved princess made the pictures of Diana so expensive that the photographers were ready to do whatever it took to get them. All in all, the accident probably made many people throughout the world conscious of the complicated role of the media.

Thus, when we are talking about the media we are in fact dealing with much more than press agencies, journalists, radio, television or newspapers; we are talking about a whole organization of social reality. We could not properly conceive of contemporary society and the world system without the role of the high-technology networks of mass and personal communication that bind people and places together, and are an essential part of business, politics, emotional and public life. In other words, the media are a tough object of knowledge to conceptualize. Yet in everyday life, most of the time the media are taken as massively given, without invoking them as an object of reflection. The media are only brought to discourse in the face of particular problems related to their role or functioning.

We could talk about a basic rule in the 'phenomenology of everyday life' according to which there has to be sufficient controversy over an issue or object of knowledge for it to become 'visible', to be constructed as a known and named object. Second, it follows from that rule that the different ways in which the object is then discussed are relevant to the typical problems or controversies associated with the object in question; that is self-evident, because without those problems and controversies the object would never have been constructed in the first place.

Third, objects of knowledge in social reality – such as 'the media' – are typically constructed by making use of metaphors, that is, by paralleling them to well-known, easily understandable images borrowed from other spheres of life. Consequently, often an object of common knowledge can be understood by identifying the key metaphors invoked in making sense of it, and the discourses related to it.

The images we habitually use in discussing a topic such as the media are in many ways powerful, because the parallel drawn between an image and the present object of attention highlights aspects that could otherwise be missed, but such metaphors also guide perception. The imagery normally used may reflect old sensibilities, and might not speak to present experiences and problematics. Yet, in their clearness and concreteness key metaphors are often so powerful that they tend to lead new discussions in such a direction that they fit the old images.

In this chapter I will discuss the most common images of the media, and how they have been applied to especially radio and television. These images can be grouped into three sets. The first set of images employs the metaphor of a channel or a window, and evokes discussions about how transparent the media are, or how they distort the picture they convey of outer reality. The other set of old images utilizes the metaphor of a square. Within these images, the media can be seen either as a marketplace or as a forum. Finally the third, and most heterogeneous, set of images deals with individuals' personal relationships with the media. Within it, the media may be compared, for instance, to a friend or to addictive drugs or stimulants. After first discussing the role of cultural imagery in general, I will discuss these images of the media. Then, I will discuss how these images have been applied to radio and television. Finally, I will round up the discussion by trying to explain the differences between the cultural images of radio and television.

Cultural images and routinized practices

As said, most of the time we take the media for granted. Daily life and social order are based on routinized, taken-for-granted lines of thought and action, and the media are part of this self-evident, unquestioned environment of modern life. As Paddy Scannell puts it, 'people everywhere listen to radio and watch TV as part of the utterly familiar, normal things that they do on any normal day' (1995: 4). In other words, most of the time we do not waste a single thought on the media as an object of knowledge in its own right. We do not normally interact with, say, TV by first invoking this or that cultural image or frame within which to observe it, in order then to watch it. Instead, we proceed directly to the frames and images needed to make sense of and perhaps to comment on the particular programme – or the events taking place 'out there' that the programme tells us about.

However, although the particular cultural images of the media are only invoked in contexts where there is some kind of 'metadiscussion' about the media or media use, it would be a mistake and a simplification to assume that they do not have any role or importance outside the very instances where they are specifically addressed. The media are an essential part of our everyday life and social reality, and that is why they have a place in the overall 'map' people use in navigating in this more or less shared reality. Individual maps may more or less differ from each other, and when they do, people work out a shared understanding of what is going on, as especially ethnomethodological conversation analysis has pointed out. Working out such a common understanding does not mean that everything we assume about social reality is spelled out; that would be an all too philosophical and complicated (actually impossible) undertaking for all practical purposes of everyday life. We must bear in mind that the key cultural images of the media are also mostly taken for granted, and unproblematically provide us with the common ground on which basis we can talk about 'the media' as an object of knowledge.

Am I saying that people perceive the media through a shared mental map, which is most of the time taken for granted and therefore not made explicit? I suggest that the situation is more complicated than that. There are several repertoires or discourses people invoke when discussing the media at a meta level. Practically only social scientists theorize the media just for the sake of theorizing. Cultural images of the media circle around different problems attached to people's media use, and in that sense we could say that none of them represents a shared map used in dealing with the media. Such maps are nowhere explicated, and the whole image of a complete 'master map' must be rejected. Instead, we could say that there are certain 'landmarks' to which people repeatedly refer when moving about in the terrain of modern life, with the media as an integral part of it.

Several of these landmarks of mediascape entail a moral aspect. For instance, how to 'responsibly' or 'rationally' behave as audience members, or what media contents are appropriate to different audience groups, such as children. In other words, images of the media are constructed in relation to individuals' subject positions as citizens or audience members. Individuals may reject such implicit prescriptions or proscriptions, and when needed justify why they do so, or they may constitute themselves as moral subjects who follow certain normative rules in their media behaviour. To take an extreme example, the American Amish reject mass media altogether, and totally refrain from watching television (Kraybill and Olshan, 1994). To make the picture even more complicated, let me point out that such embedded moralities related to the images of the media may have long ago been taken into account in individuals' media practices and become routinized and therefore not normally invoked, but again this doesn't mean that the cultural frame which accounts for such media routines has no importance.

Transparent and distorting media

During the presidential elections in Finland in 1994 one of the television channels asked people in the street what they thought about the public images of the presidential candidates. 'Have the media influenced your image of the candidates?', the interviewer asked them. Some individuals thought that they had, others said no. None of the interviewees nor the journalists pointed out how absurd the question actually was. Hardly any ordinary citizen would have any means to form an image of the candidates *outside* or irrespective of the media. Still the interviewees were able to regard it as a basically sensible question.

I suggest that the people interviewed could regard it as a sensible question by automatically separating two types of media coverage, or rather two perspectives of the media, from each other. These are two key images of the media.

The first image of the media is a 'weak' one. Within it, the media are equated with 'the world' or 'the news' itself. Over the years we had followed daily political events with the candidates involved: read about them in the newspapers or seen them on TV delivering speeches, negotiating or giving statements as politicians. Seen from this angle, we simply witness what is going on in politics and in the world generally; the media themselves are a self-evident, transparent 'extension of ourselves' (McLuhan, 1964), the technology that enables us to witness events which happen in far-away places. We could call it the link metaphor.

The second image of the media concentrates on the impact of the institution and technology of the media: how they may in various forms distort the picture we get from reality. It may be that not everything is told, or that the image we get is not truthful. To return to our example: during past years we had also seen or heard in the media things that have an image-building aspect. Even the way a candidate puts his or her views into words can be seen from that perspective, but especially personal interviews, knowledge or gossip about the candidate's private life are cases in point. There certainly was more of this kind of media coverage during the candidates' campaigns, although TV advertisements were not (yet) allowed in 1994. The people in the street who were asked about the effects of the media were supposed to make a difference between the 'hard facts' and the media-influenced 'image' of the candidates, although all information about the candidates came from the media. Let us call this the representation metaphor.

In practice these two images of the media blur into each other in many ways, because they both perceive the media as some kind of a channel to the world out there. Especially the image of the media as a representation, as a distorting channel, may at any moment be evoked to overrun the weaker image of the media as a link to the world at large. This is especially true when we consider the different subject positions with which the images provide the audience. Within the image of the media as a link, audience members are typically seen as more or less informed citizens, whose duty should be to keep themselves informed of what is going on, at least as regards politics and other hard news. On the other hand, following 'less important' events, such as sports or popular culture, may be considered as a waste of time, which could have been spent keeping oneself informed. This designation of certain events as 'less important', is often achieved by arguing that they in some ways distort audience members' world view. In other words, argumentation is borrowed from the representation metaphor.

Within the image of the media as a (potentially distorting) representation, typically audience members are assessed or criticized from the viewpoint of their abilities to be critical and doubtful of what they see or hear. As to the news, critical audience members should not rely on a single source, and in any case should assess the way in which an event is represented. As to fiction, critical audience members are supposed to assess how 'realistic' the events and characters are.

Within these two images, the subject position of the audience is more or less equated with that of a nation state's citizens. That is why there is a particular 'media policy' perspective to these images. Within it, citizens assess how appropriately the media function in a given nation state, and such assessments are used as justifications for demanding changes in the ownership, control and legislation of the media. In the case of fact reporting, news and documentary, the media are assessed as to how well they are able to educate the people, keep them informed, and help them form a good and many-sided picture of the world. As to fiction, the media are also seen to have a more or less successful role in not only entertaining people but giving them good models and values.

The media as a forum or a marketplace

The second set of images of the media can be traced back to two metaphoric usages of a square. Within these two images, the media can be seen either as a forum, *agora*, or as a marketplace.

When evoking these metaphors, discussants often appeal to the principle of 'freedom of speech', and to a 'free press' as its guarantee. In the case of newspapers, the image of the media as a forum typically refers to different political parties with their own newspapers or other forms of communication, expressing their views and trying to win citizens as voters on their side. In this instance, newspapers may also be conceived as marketplaces of ideas and other interesting material; it can be thought that citizens buy or subscribe to those papers they find interesting and useful. The principle of freedom of speech is also extended to the realm of art and literature. For instance, Western countries have defended Salman Rushdie's 'artistic' right to write what he wants to in the name of the freedom of speech, whereas Iran seems to have approached it within the channel or window metaphor, arguing that Rushdie conveyed a false and insulting picture of Islam.

Within the electronic media and especially television this set of images has typically been seen in relation to opposing media policy views. Television has been seen either as a public forum or as a marketplace, each metaphor invoking different notions of the audience (cf. Ang, 1991: 26–32).

With the rise of electronic media, the ancient idea of the media as an open forum, as the 'public sphere' where people can express their own views on anything, became problematic. It is of course already true of printed media that not everyone can afford to establish their own newspaper to get their voice heard, but in the case of electronic media it has also been technically impossible. At the dawn of electronic media there were, in a single nation state, a limited number of available wavelength areas for broadcasting. Partly for that reason, partly for other reasons, as soon as radio transmission was invented, in most countries the state controlled radio and television, often in the form of a state monopoly. It has typically been argued that in this way freedom of speech is actually best secured. Thus the metaphor of the media as a forum or *agora* has been used to serve the ideology of public service broadcasting. It was reasoned that a democratically elected organ has to decide about the contents of public broadcasting, the ideal being that the audience-as-public get what they need as citizens: high-quality programming and important information. Public service programming ideology adopted a public educational function. A prime task of state-owned broadcasting was to ensure that news is impartial and the national audience are, or become, educated citizens and informed voters.

The discourse justifying commercial television, on the other hand, sees the media as a marketplace and the audience as market. Within this metaphor, the different channels and programmes are presented as products that the viewers or listeners are free to choose from as 'customers'. In that sense, 'freedom of choice' comes to the fore instead of 'freedom of speech', but it is typically argued that in the system of commercial broadcasting the audience eventually get what they want by 'voting' with their remote controls.

Yet, these two opposing images of the media share certain premises. Whether it is audience-as-public or audience-as-market, whether viewers or listeners are conceived as members in a democratic meeting or as customers choosing between different programmes, in both cases it is considered their business to view or listen to what they like or to draw their own conclusions from it: the voter or the customer is king.

Entertaining and addictive media

There is also a third set of media images, which deals with the media in individuals' lives. They are thought to affect people's lives and personalities by informing, entertaining, and by being a factor in interpersonal relationships within domestic settings. For instance, they can be thought to reflect power relations within the family (Morley, 1986), or be likened to other electric appliances and communication and information technologies in the home (Gray, 1992; Silverstone, 1991, 1994; Silverstone and Hirsch, 1992; Silverstone et al., 1991; Spigel, 1992).

This set of images is quite heterogeneous. As will be seen in the following sections, where I discuss the images of radio and television in the light of qualitative interview studies, people may resort to a plethora of metaphors. The imagery we use to make sense of our experience is very much dependent on a context, and in that sense there is hardly any limit to the images we may employ.

However, many of the images used in this instance address the effects of the media on individuals. It may, for instance, be feared that individuals lose their sense of reality, that is, their ability to see the difference between real life and the imaginary world of TV programmes (Alasuutari, 1992). Thus, the metaphor of the media as a distorting representation is invoked to discuss their psychological effects. In this context, the media may also be likened to addictive drugs to discuss individuals' autonomy as media users (Demers, 1989; Spigel, 1992: 51–3).

The invisible radio

When considering the imagery of the media outlined above, it seems that radio is most often perceived within the image of the media as a link, an extra sense or an extension of ourselves through which we are in immediate contact with the world at large. Of course radio is not nearly the only, hardly even the most important, medium through which we get our daily information about the news of the world, but it is the prime example of our ever-present, self-evident contact with the rest of the world. When listening to or hearing a radio broadcast we seldom conceive of ourselves as doing anything else than 'staying tuned' to events in other places. We do not think that we are being 'exposed' to influences, although we may not like some of the music 'they' play out there.

Because of this image of hearing rather than being addressed 'eye to eye' as an audience member, people do not often notice that they are indeed listening to the radio. This observation of the invisible role of radio, made repeatedly in the history of scarce radio research (Lewis and Booth 1989; McIlwraith and Schallow, 1983; Mendelsohn, 1964), also emerged very strongly in a study of radio listening I made some years ago (Alasuutari, 1997).[1] When people were asked how much they listen to the radio, many of them said that they listen to it reasonably little.

Q: How much do you usually listen to radio?
A: Well every now and then, it depends. When I'm for instance driving my car I listen to it. And, erm, sometimes, when I happen to be at home then I also listen. But not very much anyway.

Q: How much do you usually listen to radio?
A: Well, in the morning [. . .] as I'm coming to school and [. . .] That's about it, and always when I'm driving a car.
Q: How many radios do you have at home?
A: [. . .] Four.
Q: Is there a [. . .] do you have a room of your own?
A: Yeah, yeah.
Q: Is there a radio?
A: Yes.

In many interviews people at first said that they hardly ever listen to the radio, but when the subject was discussed in more detail it turned out that there are several daily occasions in their everyday life when the radio is to be heard. To use Paul Willis's (1978) term, it really seems that radio does not belong to the 'cultural field' of ordinary people; it is not one of the objects or artefacts that have particular symbolic meaning and significance for them. Listening to the radio mostly goes routinely unnoticed.

Why is that so? Why is it that especially radio has that invisible character? Is it because it is perceived within the image of a link, a transparent channel that simply transmits information to us about the world at large, without in any way distorting the picture we get? The study results suggest interesting features about the way radio is typically used as a medium, and the underlying image of radio.

In the study, the particular role of radio was approached by answering why those doing manual work listen to the radio more than others – a finding that has been reported several times in Finnish radio listening statistics (Ruohomaa, 1991; Sarkkinen, 1992). The same finding could be made from my 'mini-sample' of 48 interviewees. In my data, farmers and factory workers held first places. Of the farmers, 85 per cent, and of factory workers, 64 per cent are 'heavy' or 'fairly heavy' radio listeners. As to the proportions of heavy users, the factory workers were the leading occupation.

This finding could be explained by the fact that among these 'heavy radio user' occupations, people typically had a lot of long uninterrupted listening sessions. That, in turn, depends on the listening context. When going to work by car, say, radio listening does not last very long. On the other hand, at work and at home listening may last several hours. The individuals for whom it is possible and who are in the habit of listening to the radio in the morning and at work are the ones whose total listening time will be substantial, because those are often long listening occasions.

To be able to listen to the radio all the time at work requires a particular kind of occupation. It can be said that mechanical tasks enable simultaneous radio listening, whereas tasks that require an individual's full attention prevent it. That is why individuals' total amount of radio listening is correlated with their occupation and, more precisely, with the nature of their work. Manual work is usually more suited to simultaneous radio listening than mental work.

As a side activity we do not pay too much attention to the radio. In that sense it is conceived as a transparent channel: we may pay attention to what we hear on the radio (news), not to the medium itself.

But there are also other explanations as to why the radio is left unnoticed. One is that radio listening as a side activity is socially acceptable, even desirable, because the time spent listening to the radio while doing something else at the same time does not prevent oneself from being active. On the contrary, we could say that it is used to compensate for insufficient mental activity, to provide use for the mental capacities left unemployed by the task at hand. It may support the self-image of an active citizen who, even when being 'held up' by performing a routine task, is also mentally active by keeping up with what is going on out there or by simply listening to what kind of music 'they' are playing.

On a more general level it can be said that by the use of radio we manipulate our mental activity, both the activity level and the content and direction of our attention. We may 'open up' a channel for one of our senses, hearing, in a situation where hearing is not needed to accomplish the task we are engaged in. We may also 'shut down' voices we find uninteresting, disturbing or irritating. By choosing to concentrate on a programme, we may be highly active, while at the same time performing a dull task, such as washing the dishes. The channel and programme may be selected very carefully to adjust one's activity to the preferred level. When performing a task that requires much concentration, we may choose an easy-listening music channel or turn off the radio altogether. In the interviews it turned out that the proportion of music listening is biggest among the descriptions of car listening. On the other hand, less demanding tasks or situations enable and favour speech programmes. At the other end of the continuum we have programmes such as radio drama which require full attention. In the interviews people typically report of listening to such programmes during holidays or weekends.

Adjusting one's activity to the preferred level may also mean that radio is a surrogate friend, a companion during one's lonely moments. By selecting the right kind of channel or record we may also manipulate our emotions (see also Tortzen, 1992a, 1992b). We may tune our radio set to a channel that corresponds to our frame of mind, thus enforcing or stabilizing it, but we may also get attuned to a different emotional state by selecting a suitable channel or record. A woman, age 24, working as an interviewer for a market research company, put it this way:

Q: What are the situations in which you play a record instead of listening to radio?
A: Usually if I have guests or if I get a certain frame of mind – that is, if I'm sad or very happy or something. Or you want to get the feeling more intense, so you know what to do it with when you have records. On the radio you do not necessarily get just what you want.

Another woman, a 28-year-old high school music teacher, uses radio in a similar fashion:

Q: Do you ever listen to the music during the weekends or more than on week-days?
A: Yes, more actually. During Saturday evenings and if I'm going out to have fun I may turn on the radio, you know! [laughter]
Q: When was the last time you went and turned on the radio?
A: It must have been two months ago [laughter].
Q: You said you didn't have the channels in that [preset] [. . .]
A: No [. . .]
Q: How have you found them then?
A: Well I just search for a kind of groovy music that would tune me up to the beat of the city already at home.
Q: So you just keep searching for a suitable channel?
A: Yeah.
Q: How long do you listen to it before going out?
A: Well, let's say I might do my make up for an hour or so and have some white wine [laughter].

Within this discourse of radio use, radio is seen as a sort of product or sub-stance. It is used as a *mind-altering device* that could be compared to drugs as mind-altering substances. However, the way it is spoken of as a device does not suggest that the users would be concerned about becoming addicted to it. It parallels drugs only in that people use it for particular pur-poses; the fear of addiction, the image of the subject being carried away by the drug, is missing. The subject is in full control of its use.

When radio is seen as a product in that way, it fits the image of a prod-uct or products being selected by consumers. In that sense, radio is invisible or unproblematic because radio channels are seen as the market from which consumers may choose the kind of products that fit their frame of mind at any particular time; or they may choose not to listen to it at all.

The morally loaded imagery of television

If we compare the cultural image of television to that of radio, the difference is striking in many respects. Certainly, television – as part of contemporary 'mediascape' – may also be taken for granted in many instances of everyday life, but it is much more of a topic. That is why TV is researched so much more than radio or newspapers. TV can be and is repeatedly articulated within many contradictions characterizing our modern cultures, and in that sense the cultural image of TV is morally loaded.

Let me take an example. When, some years ago, I conducted a study in which people were asked about their TV viewing habits and programme choices (Alasuutari, 1992), it immediately struck me how moral the topic was. There were very few programmes that people freely and plainly said they like to watch. With the exception of the evening news and other current affairs programmes, people seemed to feel a compelling need to explain, defend and justify their viewing habits. Ingunn Hagen (1992, 1994a, 1994b) came across the same phenomenon from the opposite direction. When she studied *Dagsrevyen*, the main TV news programme of the Norwegian public broadcasting corporation, she found that people tended to give an explanation if they for some reason hadn't watched it.

Although the moral aspect of giving an account of one's viewing habits found in those two studies could be made less outstanding by noting that justifications are a routine aspect of ordinary conversations (Heritage, 1984; Nofsinger, 1991), it is still true that television has raised, and continues to raise, strong emotions and heated disputes in many instances and several cultures. For instance, when television came to Finland, the Laestadians, one of the Finnish Protestant revivalist movements, banned it, and maintained the total ban until the 1980s (Melkas, 1985). Similarly, as mentioned above, the American Amish, who are famous for their critical attitude toward modernization, reject mass media, especially television (Kraybill and Olshan, 1994).

Although the Laestadians and Amish are extreme examples, in certain respects they reflect the attitudes of the general public, especially of the upper middle class, who especially in previous decades were critical of mass culture and generally scorned television series. In previous decades critical discussion of television revolved around commercial television and mass entertainment, but now also public television is under fire for its elitist paternalism (Ang, 1991).

In these discussions, there are several images which frame television as a problem. Interestingly, especially in the case of such religious groups as the Laestadians and the Amish, even the 'weak image' of television as a link or as an extra sense that connects us to the rest of the world may be framed as a problem. These groups are not critical of television in the name of truth, by arguing that it would somehow distort the picture we get of the world. They are simply critical of all these 'worldly' things that television brings to our homes, and want to protect themselves from them. As Kraybill (1994) puts it, the Amish community want to restrict their members', especially their children's, consciousness, and the ban on television, as well as on higher education, stems from that attempt.

> Amish children do not study science or critical thinking, nor are they exposed to the relativity and diversity so pervasive in higher education today. The Amish rejection of mass media, especially television, severely limits their exposure to the smorgasbord of modern values. The tight plausibility structure in the Amish community thus helps to hold the forces of plurality at bay. (Kraybill, 1994: 27)

This may again appear as an exceptional case, but in fact a great deal of discussion about television deals with the ways in which and the degrees to which children or other audience groups should be protected from seeing and hearing things that may harm or upset them. It is, for instance, argued that in homes there should be some kind of 'parental mediation' of television viewing, and at the higher level there are laws that censor what can be shown to the general public. The truthfulness of possibly improper programme contents is not the point in this discourse; it is just the contention that showing certain things on TV may shock, offend or harm people.

On the other hand, a great deal of moral concern surrounding television viewing is also articulated with the cultural image of TV as a distorting representation, albeit the underlying image of the 'true truth' is a very fussy one. Often, the (distorting) representation image is invoked when people criticize or justify TV programmes for their (lack of) realism.

For instance, in a study I made (Alasuutari, 1992), when interviewees gave accounts for their viewing habits they often referred to realism. Let me take direct quotations as an example:

Q: Are any of these programmes that you no longer watch?
A: There's plenty, what were they called these [. . .] well, you know, *Dallas* and *Falcon Crest* and what have you [. . .] that sort of thing I just can't watch them any more.
Q: What's wrong with them, why these?
A: Well somehow they're just, they're so far removed from the ordinary world even more than these violence things, I mean really [*laughter*] [. . .] even the wife no longer watches them.

Q: Erm, what would you say are the bad sides about the serial.
A: Er, it's [. . .] what would I say, well I mean it's all so unbelievable everything, isn't it? It can't really be true, can it? I mean if you look out there in the real world.

Analysis of realism was a central form in which especially watching fictitious programmes was discussed, but people depicted realism in many ways. Ang (1985) proposes a distinction between two ways of understanding the realism of the programme: an empiricist and an emotional concept of realism. In the empiricist conception of realism the focus is on whether the representation corresponds to external reality. In the emotional conception the fictional setting of the denotative level of the story is disregarded, and the focus is on whether the characters, models of action, and conflict situations appearing in the story are 'identifiable', that is, whether they are believable within the context of one's own life-experiences.

In my qualitative interview data there were examples of quotations that could fit both of these types. For instance, some of the people who watched action serials explained this by reference to their empirical realism. They pointed out that in spite of all the violence the world that is depicted in action serials or action films is rather realistic: the real world *is* violent. There were also examples of justifying TV viewing on the basis of an emotional conception of realism. In these cases it was pointed out that there is a clear logic of action in TV serials and that the underlying motives of action are recognizable.

In addition to those two ways of talking about realism, there were cases that should perhaps more appropriately be described as references to 'technical realism'. While the content of a programme was not considered to give a truthful representation of reality, the interviewees assessed whether the stunts performed in it could be technically possible.

However, the main reason the interviewees in this study passed a negative judgement on especially soap operas stemmed from still another notion of realism. Within this frame the criticism of 'unrealistic' programmes – and the respondents' willingness to excuse themselves for watching them – is due to their failure to give a true representation of what life is really like for ordinary people. This involves a certain presupposition of what is regarded as the chief function of fictional stories: they should provide ethically sound models of life. This requirement of realism could be described as *ethical realism*.

> Well yes of course I think that very often the value system in these programmes is not necessarily suitable for children, for a growing child, it's not a model you'd like them to follow. No[. . .] I mean I've seen enough of *Dallas*, I've earlier seen the odd episode and these other series, and I think the model they provide is just not good enough.

Within this frame, a programme like *Dallas* is not criticized because the critic would argue that the portrait it gives of the lives of rich people in America is not truthful. From the critic's viewpoint, that may or may not be true, but he or she is concerned about the models of life that are conveyed through TV programmes. By saying that a programme – or a movie or a novel – is 'realistic' in this sense, the speaker in fact says that it portrays a milieu that is familiar to ordinary people (a form of 'everyday life realism'), and tells a story which has an acceptable morale.

On the basis of the Finnish interviewees' attitudes, it seemed that, to be 'ethically realistic', programmes should not give an overly romantic picture of life. Second, fictional stories should not lead us into believing that life is too easy. In real life we must be prepared for unhappy endings. Fictional programmes that are considered realistic are such that describe modest, simple life. In this emphasis on the hardness and harshness of everyday life there are certain traces of Protestant religion and its puritanism. The world that provides an acceptable model for life is often found in films that portray old country life. It is also an ethical principle of the Finnish mode of life to stress that life is hard, because that is the best way to avoid disappointments. Life is hard, and if it's not, it's not good for your character seems to be the guiding line.

In its details my study, of course, reflects Finnish sensibilities and structures of feeling, but I suggest that the various ways in which people invoke the image of television as a channel – a link or representation – are not peculiar only to the Finnish case. When talking about 'realistic' or 'unrealistic' programmes, people imply a 'reality' somewhere else, but often that implied reality is infused with ideals: how reality should be or how people should lead their lives rather than how things are.[2]

In that sense it could be argued that the channel image is mixed with the image of the media as a forum. Fictitious programmes, in particular, are assessed from the viewpoint of their 'message': what opinions the directors or producers express or what lessons they give to the public. Because the 'air time' is limited and because TV is thought to be a politically influential medium and a powerful forum of public education, governments and pressure groups often attempt to influence programme contents. For instance, in American television there are many regulations about the representation of minorities as characters in television serials.

It might even be argued that to refer to realism as a criterion of assessment in fiction is a way of legitimating a moral judgement about a programme. In our contemporary 'emotivist culture' (MacIntyre, 1985; Wilson, 1993) it is commonly agreed that moral arguments are rationally interminable. However, since modern people want to build their views on solid facts, or at least present them in that way, they 'borrow' the distorting channel frame to argue that a programme they dislike is not 'realistic'.

The time people spend (or waste) by watching television is another ground for deeming it problematic and thus treating TV viewing as a topic. This is again intertwined with programme contents and thus with other cultural images of the media, but in this case the main image is TV as a device or substance. When reflecting on TV viewing from this viewpoint, people parallel television to other domestic appliances or utensils. Watching television is simply something that can be done instead of or simultaneously with other activities or chores.

For instance, in my qualitative interview study on TV viewing discussed above, several interviewees accounted for watching 'lowbrow' programmes, in particular, by explaining or self-diagnosing the reason why they watch something they themselves deem silly or a waste of time. Modern culture and cultural citizenship of modern nation states values individuals being active and spending their time usefully, such as doing household chores, keeping up with the news or educating themselves. However, relaxation as a counterbalance to work stress as a way to take care of oneself is a 'respectable' justification for doing something that does not seem to be functional at the outset, and that is how many people explained watching 'silly' series. After a hard week's work, a Friday series, perhaps enjoyed with some wine, is perfect because when watching it 'you don't have to think about anything'.

In these instances, the act of watching television is paralleled with alternative or complementary substances such as alcohol. In that sense, it differs from the way in which radio is paralleled with stimulants. People often talk about radio listening as a way to stay awake and active, or to raise their activity level, but television watching is, at least in these instances, talked about as a relaxant. Of course watching television may be and is used to stay awake, but television is more effective as a relaxant because it prevents oneself from doing much else. Indeed, it is often used to sit back and relax, to cool off and to get one's thoughts away from something they were working on. In that sense, radio could be compared to coffee and television to an alcoholic drink. Modern culture approves of coffee and prizes action, but we have an uneasy relation to alcoholic drinks and idleness or laziness. The discussion and fears of television addiction also stem from using the metaphor of psychoactive drugs to conceive of the media.

Conclusion

In this chapter I have discussed the way in which key cultural images of the media organize and guide public discussions and personal conceptions of the role of electronically mediated communication in contemporary society and the global system. The notion of 'media' itself can be seen as a construction 'put together' from those metaphoric images and the discourses around them.

One of the problems with these cultural images is that the sheer apparent concreteness of the metaphors employed guides reflective consciousness and leads public discussion easily back to old positions. For instance, in the Diana car crash discussion, the guilt hanging on the photographers and partly on the general public was soon levelled at the driver, who turned out to have been drunk. Already by the following week the British yellow press was able to launch a moral crusade against the Queen and the Royal Family for not mourning enough – or in fact not showing their grief publicly in media appearances. Once again, mediated communication was conceived as an object paralleled to objects in the physical world. That is typical of what Pollner (1987) calls 'mundane reason': we always conceive of a world as a 'thing' which is independent of the mode and manner in which it is explicated. For that reason alone the idea of us all being involved in, say, what happens to public figures, and even in the whole construction of them as public figures, does not so easily become part of public discourse.

Yet, cultural images are not eternal. Along with social changes, we come up with new metaphors and images by which to conceive of social reality. In fact social changes are always also, and can be triggered by, changes in key cultural images and discourses. I suggest that the comparison between the cultural images of radio and television illuminates that point.

One of the problems with those who would have been interested in radio research during recent decades has been that – although radio has preserved a role as one of the media in people's lives – academic media research has mainly been interested in television. The reasons for that tell us a lot about mass communication and media research in recent decades, and may give us some hints about future changes.

As in recent years several communication studies journals have published special issues on radio research, the editors have tried to address their public and the main concerns of media research by assuring their readers that – contrary to the common conception about radio as the 'forgotten medium' – radio is important. As the preface to the special 'forgotten medium' issue of *Media Studies Journal* (Summer 1993) puts it, 'a close look at radio demonstrates its vitality, its economic, political and social importance, as well as its staying power in the communication field' (Anonymous, 1993: xi).

As sympathetic and justified as such assurances are, by justifying radio research within the standard media studies political reality, they poorly capture the cultural place of radio in individuals' everyday life.[3] Radio is commonly perceived – or rather taken for granted – within the image of the media as a link to the world. That is why it has rarely been seen as a problem, and worthy of social research that has circled around the images of the forum or marketplace or a potentially distorting representation.

However, I argue that radio shows the future of television, and that all media are becoming radio-like. Just consider breakfast television, MTV or CNN. An ever-greater share of television viewing has become radio-like, a side activity amidst other activities going on in the household, at work or other places. A growing number of television or multimedia sets per household also means that watching television is less often a joint family activity. As a consequence, individual family members less often need to justify their programme choices to others. Using – or rather being linked to – the media will become less often a topic.

Moreover, the future mediascape will be so full of potential channels through which people can find news, information and entertainment that nation states can ever less plan and control programme output. Thus public discourse will be less centred on the discourse of distorting representation or that of audience-as-citizens, and that will also dampen the use of its counterpart configuration of audience-as-market as a critique against commercial broadcasting. More often, as media users, people will be seen simply as consumers, choosing from products and services often also sponsored by advertisers.

The present developments of our mediascape also are reflected in media studies. A turn is evident from media politics to identity politics and to more psychological problem-settings. No matter what the form in which fiction – serials, films or theatre – is consumed or how the programme output is decided, narratives always address morals and personhood (MacIntyre, 1985), and that is one of the reasons why qualitative media studies has turned largely away from fact to fiction. Besides, fiction requires more attention from the audience, and that is why it may be addressed as a time-using problem, for instance, within the addiction framework. Using computers, especially playing computer games, also may be approached from this viewpoint. And who knows, maybe a turn away from 'the media' to 'the audiences' (whose nature as a construction has already been problematized, e.g. Allor, 1988; Ang, 1989; Bird, 1992; Radway, 1988) may lead to new images of mediated communication.

Notes

1. It was based on 48 qualitative interviews, which were then transcribed. The main idea was to 'collect' detailed descriptions of individuals' radio listening situations. The interviewees were asked to describe what time it was; where it was; what else were they doing; whether there were others present; whether anyone commented on anything on the radio; whether their other activities disturbed their concentration on what was on; whether they remembered what the programme was and what was said or what records they were playing; what channel it was, and so on.

2. This infusion of realism with morality has a long history. Aristotle and the Greeks were already concerned with the 'double difficulty' of drama and poetry. On the one hand, it was emphasized that the poet is a moral teacher whose work must fulfil a moral purpose. Others, on the other hand, took the position that art's function is the revelation of reality (Carlson, 1986: 15–16).

3. Scannell puts it this way:

> The only reality that media studies knows is a political reality, set in a field of discourse that – as it would say – mobilizes concepts of power, struggle, conflict, ideology. It has great difficulty with any idea of ordinary *unpolitical* daily life, and its everyday concerns and enjoyments. Since for the politically minded all things are political – and what is not is either marginal or incorrectly understood – it follows that the only *interesting* questions about the media are political. (1996: 4)

References

Alasuutari, P. (1992), "I'm Ashamed to Admit but I Have Watched *Dallas*": The Moral Hierarchy of TV Programmes'. *Media, Culture & Society*, 14 (4): 561–82.

Alasuutari, P. (1997) 'Why Does the Radio Go Unnoticed?', in U. Carlson, *Radio Research in Denmark, Finland, Norway and Sweden. Nordicom Review* No. 1.

Allor, M. (1988) 'Relocating the Site of the Audience', in *Critical Studies in Mass Communication*, 5: 217–33.

Ang, I. (1985) *Watching Dallas: Soap Opera and the Melodramatic Imagination*. London: Methuen.

Ang, I. (1989) 'Beyond Self-Reflexivity', *Journal of Communication Inquiry*, 13 (2), 27–9.

Ang, I. (1991) *Desperately Seeking the Audience*. London: Routledge.

Anonymous (1993) 'Radio – The Forgotten Medium', *Media Studies Journal*, Summer: xi-xix.

Carlson, M. (1986) *Theories of the Theater: A Historical and Critical Survey, from the Greeks to the Present*. Ithaca, NY and London: Cornell University Press.

Bird, S.E. (1992) 'Travels in Nowhere Land: Ethnography and the "Impossible" Audience', *Critical Studies in Mass Communication*, 9: 250–60.

Demers, D.P. (1989) *Breaking Your Child's TV Addiction*. Minneapolis: Marquette Books.

Gray, A. (1992) *Video Playtime: The Gendering of a Leisure Technology*. London: Routledge.

Hagen, I. (1992) *News Viewing Ideals and Everyday Practices: The Ambivalences of Watching Dagsrevyen*. University of Bergen, Department of Mass Communication, Report No. 15.

Hagen, I. (1994a) 'The Ambivalences of TV News Viewing: Between Ideals and Everyday Practices', *European Journal of Mass Communication*, 9: 193–220.

Hagen, I. (1994b) 'Expectations and Consumption Patterns in TV News Viewing', *Media, Culture & Society*, 16: 415–28.

Heritage, J. (1984) *Garfinkel and Ethnomethodology*. Cambridge: Polity Press.

Kraybill, D.B. (1994) 'The Amish Encounter with Modernity', in D.B. Kraybill and M.A. Olshan (eds), *The Amish Struggle with Modernity*. Hanover, PA: University Press of New England.

Kraybill, D.B. and Olshan, M.A. (eds) (1994*) The Amish Struggle with Modernity*. Hanover, PA: University Press of New England.

Lewis, P.M. and Booth, J. (1989) *The Invisible Medium: Public, Commercial, and Community Radio*. Basingstoke: Macmillan.

McIlwraith, R.D. and Schallow, J.R. (1983) 'Adult Fantasy Life and Patterns of Media Use', *Journal of Communication*, 33 (1): 78–91.

MacIntyre, A. (1985) *After Virtue: A Study in Moral Theory*. London: Duckworth.

McLuhan, M. (1964) *Understanding Media: The Extensions of Man*. New York: McGraw-Hill.

Melkas, J. (1985) 'Lestadiolainen televisioideologia elämismaailman puolustuksena' [The Laestadian TV Ideology as a Defence of Life-World], *Sosiologia*, 22 (4): 261–72.

Mendelsohn, H. (1964) 'Listening to Radio' in L.A. Dexter and D.M. White (eds), *People, Society, and Mass Communications*. New York: The Free Press.

Morley, D. (1986) *Family Television: Cultural Power and Domestic Leisure*. London: Comedia.

Nofsinger, R.E. (1991) *Everyday Conversation*. Newbury Park, CA: Sage.

Pollner, M. (1987) *Mundane Reason: Reality in Everyday and Sociological Discourse*. Cambridge: Cambridge University Press.

Radway, J.A. (1988) 'Reception Study: Ethnography and the Problems of Dispersed Audiences and Nomadic Subjects', *Cultural Studies*, 2 (3): 359–76.

Ruohomaa, E. (1991) '1990 radiouudistus ja yleisöt' [The 1990 Radio Reform and Audiences]. *Helsinki: Yle, Tutkimus- ja kehitysosasto, tutkimusraportti* 13.

Sarkkinen, R. (1992) 'Valtakunnallinen radionkuuntelu marraskuussa 1992' [Nationwide Radio Listening in November 1992], Helsinki: *Yle, Tutkimus- ja kehitysosasto, tilastoselvitys* 36.

Scannell, P. (1995) 'For a Phenomenology of Radio and Television', *Journal of Communication*, 45 (3): 4–19.

Scannell, P. (1996) *Radio, Television and Modern Life: A Phenomenological Approach*. Oxford: Blackwell.

Silverstone, R. (1991) 'From Audiences to Consumers: The Household and the Consumption of Communication and Information Technologies', *European Journal of Communication*, 6: 135–54.

Silverstone, R. (1994) *Television and Everyday Life*. London: Routledge.

Silverstone, R. and Hirsch, E. (eds) (1992) *Consuming Technologies: Media and Information in Domestic Spaces*. London: Routledge.

Silverstone, R., Hirsch, E. and Morley, D. (1991) 'Listening to a Long Conversation: An Ethnographic Approach to the Study of Information and Communication Technologies in the Home', *Cultural Studies*, 5 (2): 204–27.

Spigel, L. (1992) *Make Room for TV: Television and the Family Ideal in Postwar America*. Chicago: University of Chicago Press.

Tortzen, A. (1992a) 'Unge, musik og radio' [The Youth, Music and Radio], *Mediekultur*, 18: 22–33.

Tortzen, A. (1992b) 'Youth, Music and Radio'. Paper for the third Nordic Youth Research Symposium, Copenhagen, 23–5 January.

Willis, P. (1978) *Profane Culture*. London: Routledge & Kegan Paul.

Wilson, J.Q. (1993) *The Moral Sense*. New York: Free Press.

6

LEGITIMATIONS OF TELEVISION PROGRAMME POLICIES
Patterns of Argumentation and Discursive Convergencies in a Multichannel Age

Heikki Hellman

There exists an established distinction between two paradigms of television audience. The first approaches viewers as a public, or a group of citizens, while the other is a view of the audience as a market, or a group of consumers.[1] According to Ien Ang, these two alternative configurations are 'each connected with one of the two major institutional arrangements – commercial and public service – of broadcast television' (1991: 29). In this chapter I suggest that these two conceptions of the audience also provide the founding paradigms of programming policy and, logically, of the legitimating discourse on programme policy.

The chapter deals with how programme policy discourse has changed along with the recent development of the multichannel television universe. In Western Europe, broadcasting regulations have traditionally emphasized general values like universality, diversity of opinion and a wide range of offerings. These were the core values that were employed to legitimize the privileged status of national public service broadcasting institutions. Commercial television was based on different values, those of popularity, choice and economic calculation. However, the recent liberalization of the airwaves appears to have contributed to a convergence of programme policy discourses.

With the two discursive ways of understanding the audience as my starting point, I will try, first, to sketch how the recent technological changes in the television landscape have resulted in an 'audience-oriented' turn in broadcasting which highlights the role of programming as the main instrument in broadcasters' constant struggle for an audience. Second, within these two basic approaches I will point to several patterns of argumentation, or subdiscourses, and provide examples of how they are reflected in public debates on programme policy, particularly in the Nordic countries and Britain. Finally, I also wish to discuss a 'discursive convergence' between the two major philosophies of programming: public service and commercial television.

Two paradigms of the audience

According to Ang (1991: 26–32), the two paradigms of the audience stem from two diverse theoretical models of mass communication. The first, the idea of the *audience as a public*, fits the so-called 'transmission' model of communication. Implied in this model is the conception of audiences as 'receivers' of messages sent and meanings transferred. The other, the *audience as a market*, is related to an attention model of communication. Here transfer of meaning is of secondary importance, while communication is considered effective as soon as attention is given to it by audiences (see also McQuail, 1987).

It was the public broadcasters who traditionally approached their audience as a public to be served with social responsibility. National broadcasting institutions constituted a 'paternal system', as it was once called by Williams (1968: 117–18), which aimed at protecting and guiding the majority by transmitting values, habits and tastes deemed desirable by the enlightened minority. The audience of public broadcasters consisted of *citizens* who were to be informed, uplifted and educated. The purpose was to transmit the message to the entire nation – hence the principle of universal service.

In contrast, commercial broadcasters' purpose was primarily to gain the attention of the audience, and here it was the quantity of attentive audience and the duration of its attention that were important. The audience consisted of *consumers* of the messages. The viewers constituted 'a market to be won', as Ang (1991: 29) puts it, which also explains the importance of audience ratings in commercial television. In this view, the link between the TV station and the viewer is a consumer–product relationship, and 'not a moral or social relationship, as in the case of the audience as public' (McQuail, 1987: 221).

These two conceptions of the audience fit also with two distinctly different ways of legitimating programme policies. If the audience is regarded as citizens (audience-as-public), programming tends to be justified within a discourse of 'what the audience needs'. When translating the abstract principles of public service philosophy into concrete guidelines, this discourse 'puts a distinctive emphasis on programmatic comprehensiveness (i.e. varied range of informative, educational, high cultural and entertainment programmes) so as to offer the [. . .] citizen a responsible, meaningful TV diet' (Ang, 1991: 38).

If, then, the audience is considered as consumers (audience-as-market), programme policies are justified within a discourse of 'what the audience wants'. Here programming is characterized by 'a regular and predictable flow of entertainment programmes, so as to secure the prolonged attention of the [. . .] consumer' (Ang, 1991: 38).

I will later discuss selected patterns of argumentation, or subdiscourses, within these two alternative philosophies, but first a question must be raised whether and how these different lines of discourse are applied in public debates on programme policy. Therefore I will start by referring to a recent case which illustrates the present conflict and confusion between market-oriented arguments of 'giving the audience what it wants' and the public service-oriented rationale of 'giving the audience what it needs'.

Conflicting values: a Finnish case study

Finland launched its fourth national television network – the second commercial one – in June 1997. The Government's decision to liberate the broadcasting sector stemmed not from the needs of cultural policy to widen programme supply but, rather, from the interests of technology policy (to pave way for digitalization), competition policy (to stimulate competition) and industrial policy (to promote independent programme production). Nevertheless, in the public debate around the issue, arguments justifying – or judging – the new channel referred constantly to its programme policy.

A preceding strategy report, assigned by the Ministry of Transport and Communication (see Mykkänen, 1995), explicitly advised policy makers *not* to stipulate any strict obligations for commercial broadcasters. Quite the opposite, it suggested that

> detailed standards concerning programming should not be applied in granting the licences. Instead, attention should be paid to the assessment of candidates. Too detailed definitions included in the licences easily become a dead letter impossible to obey for several reasons, the central explanation often being an economic one. (Mykkänen, 1995: 35)

However, the report set forth that in granting new licences candidates offering 'new alternatives' should be favoured, and held that YLE, Finland's public service broadcaster, and commercial stations should operate 'complementarily' (Mykkänen, 1995: 16). Still another central criterion for the assessment of the applicants was the amount of domestic content offered.

When applications for the licence were invited in June 1996, it was required of the candidates that 50 per cent of the European content, as defined by the EU Television Directive, should be in domestic languages (Finnish or Swedish), and that half of the domestic programmes should be made by independent producers. The Minister of Traffic and Communications, Tuula Linnainmaa, also announced that the candidates were expected to give an account of their programming plans.

Implied in this strategy of providing alternatives was an idea of increasing 'consumer choice' by liberalizing the radio spectrum. At the same time, a pragmatist tradition typical of Finnish media policy (see Hellman, 1996; Silvo, 1988) was continued, as only scant attention was paid to programme policy while safeguarding that a sound structure of the media industry and the viability of the business dominated. Instead of strict regulation of programming, the licensee would be obliged to pay an annual 'public service fee' to YLE and to make considerable investments in the build-up of the digital network.

What did the applicants promise to supply in order to complement YLE, on the one hand, and to propose an alternative to the existing commercial broadcaster, MTV3, on the other? How did the applicants argue for their programme offerings and how did the public debate react to them?

One of the two major candidates, A4 Media Oy, which was founded by distinguished ex-YLE journalists but financially backed by the Luxembourg-based media giant CLT, offered a 'quality channel' option targeted to selective viewers. A4 Media explicitly wanted to avoid the 'populism' of MTV3 by investing in news and current affairs, quality drama and arts programmes. Although resembling the public service YLE's fare, particularly that of YLE1, the candidate's justification for its programming profile was that it wished to serve viewers who were otherwise poorly catered for. Hence, A4 Media wanted to provide a genuine alternative that, as it argued, would contribute to the quality of television and was aimed at new audiences. Nevertheless, the company also put forward an economic argument. With the general-audience-oriented MTV3 already being the most popular TV channel in Finland, A4 Media believed that a carefully targeted commercial service would appeal better to advertisers, thus making it worthwhile in business terms too.

The other major candidate, Ruutunelonen Oy, an affiliate of the nationally powerful Helsinki Media Company[2] with the Danish media conglomerate Egmont participating as one of the minor owners, offered a diet typical of a commercial station. A clear majority of its offerings consisted of theatrical films, series and serials, sports, talk shows, and so on. In its application Ruutunelonen also emphasized domestic popular programmes. In line with its rival candidate, Ruutunelonen underlined the need to increase 'programme quality' and to serve small target audiences. This was considered feasible, because 'the audience distribution between a greater number of channels has a decreasing effect on average ratings' anyway.

In the public debate, intellectuals strongly favoured A4 Media due to its quality profile, recognized professionalism and independence – in spite of the CLT connection. A central argument in support for this candidate was that 'we Finns don't need any more of the MTV3 type of nonsense', as a leading TV critic wrote.[3] Also the Minister of Culture, Claes Andersson, a noted poet, referred to the 'needs' of the audience: 'We do not need a "poor man's" commercial television with a flimsy programme policy, interested only in hoovering the advertising money in the market. What we need are quality productions that pay attention to the needs of domestic production, minorities and cultural fare.'[4] In other words, Ruutunelonen was considered to provide a diet very similar to that of MTV3 and not as good quality as A4 Media. Another negative argument for Ruutunelonen was that independent producers who had allied with it were known not for quality programmes but, on the contrary, for their format-based quiz and talk shows. Here, a discourse of 'what-the-audience-needs' was applied by culturally committed actors who insisted that quality principles should have a decisive role in the competition for the new licence.

However, it was Ruutunelonen that was more successful in lobbying the support of the pragmatist policy makers. Also YLE, with its authority, backed Ruutunelonen's plans. This was perhaps because of respect for its major owner, the Erkko family – a superior player in Finland's media industry – and because the consortium was believed to provide a strong institutional structure not in danger of slipping into foreign control. Unlike CLT, the Helsinki Media Company was considered a trustworthy and interested partner in accomplishing the digitalization of the terrestrial network as a 'national project' in cooperation with the state, YLE and MTV. Indeed, the Government's decision explicitly referred to the 'national interests' that tilted the balance in Ruutunelonen's favour.

Thus, while finally granting the licence to Ruutunelonen, the Government only appeared to apply the policy lines agreed upon: the choice was based on the assessment of the candidates, not their programming policy. However, this is not the whole truth. The candidates' programme offerings, too, were considered, and with due economic pragmatism. The policy makers reasoned that if the schedules did not appeal to advertisers, they would be subject to major changes anyway. Although the diet suggested by A4 Media was ambitious and justifiable in cultural terms, the economic viability of its plans aroused scepticism. If the programming was too exclusive, it would not yield sufficient profit to allow investments in digitalization.

Ironically, the first comments after the launch of the channel expressed disappointment. It was not only the critical intellectuals who vented their frustration, but also the very same key politicians who had supported Ruutunelonen's application. One of them was Finland's Prime Minister, Paavo Lipponen, who remarked that the new channel appears to have 'passed under the bar rather than cleared it'.[5]

Ambivalence of legitimation discourse

The Finnish broadcasting licence debate suggests that argumentation still follows the 'paradigmatic' lines of broadcasting organization. On the one hand, there are public service institutions that have particular, commonly agreed obligations in their programme policy. On the other hand, commercial stations are more or less free to apply another rationale, that of audience demand and economic viability.

At the same time, the debate points to an ambivalence of legitimation discourse. In principle, the new entrant was not obliged to supply public service fare. In spite of this, the public debate tended to use public service as a standard against which the candidates' offerings were weighed. On the other hand, the entertainment-centric fare of Ruutunelonen, providing a broader appeal and demonstrating better economic calculation than its rival candidate's offerings, won the support of the policy makers due to pragmatic reasons of economic viability and popular appeal. Indeed, a programme policy legitimized by economic reasoning of 'what the audience wants' outdid a policy seeking cultural justification from 'what the audience needs'.

However, in another sense it was the cultural, or ideological, rationale that was in the winning team. The launch of the new channel was justified by a version of 'cultural nationalism' (cf. Lowe and Alm, 1997) which, instead of having illusions about programme quality, aimed simply at combining the goals of competition, industrial and technology policies with a national interest to promote 'Finnishness' in general. It was the fear of international satellite channels and 'imported digitalization' that motivated policy makers and domestic industry. Whoever the licensee and whatever its production ambitions, according to this logic, domestic programming would be supported simply by ensuring that the main winners from commercialization were domestic forces.

In fact, this cultural nationalism combines discursively 'what the audience needs' with 'what the audience wants' by an intervention of institutional structure. Domestic programmes, it suggests, are best promoted and their popularity is best protected within a media structure which is firmly in domestic hands. Or as an experienced independent producer, an initiator of the Ruutunelonen consortium, said, 'We feel it is vital that we can provide a channel that supplies domestic programmes to the Finns, particularly now when broadcasting is rapidly expanding via satellite dishes and cables.'[6] The same strategy of cultural nationalism, a reconciliation of programme policy and industry structure interests, was applied earlier when Finland, in 1986, launched a semi-commercial Channel Three in order to fight back against the international satellite channels (Hellman, 1996). It can also be claimed that a similar rationale guided Sweden, Norway and Denmark when they liberalized their television sector in the late 1980s or early 1990s (Hellman and Sauri, 1997; Hultén, 1996; Humphreys, 1996).

For example, Meier and Trappel have remarked that it is in small states that 'the contradiction between economic competition and cultural obligations is particularly obvious. Whilst larger states can fulfil both requirements to a certain extent, small states reach their limits considerably earlier for structural reasons' (1992: 141). Indeed, the fact that economic necessities constrain culturally justifiable programme policy explains the ambivalence of the Finnish broadcasting debate. However, this contradiction is not necessarily restricted to small states, such as Finland. Rather, it characterizes broadcasting industry in general.

From a single market to a multiple market

The Finnish case indicates that the legitimating discourse on programme policy offers several arguments that conflict but also merge with each other. Several actors also participate in the debate, and it is as if different justifications were used in different arenas of discussion. Here these arenas are referred to as *markets* (see Lowe and Alm, 1997), by which I mean that they are instances where programme schedules are exchanged for revenue, political support and popular acceptance. Decisions on programme policy are made with reference to and in order to satisfy these markets.

For decades Western European television enjoyed a privileged status with almost no competition within the industry, thus operating in a 'single market' of national economies. National broadcasting institutions were state-owned, public service enterprises, financed by a flat-rate tax, a licence fee, paid by all television set owners. As they were 'creatures ultimately of the state', as Blumler (1992a: 12) puts it, it was the *political market*, consisting of appointed and elected national political elites competing over broadcasting policies, that gave a legitimation to broadcasters and their programme policies. Of course, the *popular market*, that is, viewers with their wishes and interests, was important, too, but as audience attention was taken for granted, the question of legitimation based on popular support never really arose.

Since the early 1980s, European broadcasting has experienced a termination of national public broadcasters' hegemony (de- or re-regulation), unleashing of competition for revenue and viewers (liberalization), introduction of private commercial channels (commercialization), and an invasion of transnational players (internationalization). Spectrum scarcity, which justified monopolistic, or duopolistic, institutional frameworks, was relieved by compressing bandwidth, opening up new frequencies as well as substituting over-the-air distribution by cable, thus providing the public with an unprecedented channel abundance.

This 'paradigmatic change' (Humphreys, 1996) in broadcasting has decreased the importance of the political market in the public legitimation of television services. Instead, broadcasters, public and private stations alike, are thrown into a *multiplicity of markets*, as has been suggested by Lowe and Alm (1997). It is the interdependent but distinctive interests of technological development and substitute technologies (or the 'technological market'), policy makers (the 'political market'), rival broadcasters (the 'business market'), broadcasting professionals (the 'professional market') and the audience (the 'popular market') that the broadcasters are forced to negotiate with. The multiple marketplace creates the battleground where socio-political legitimation and economic viability are sought and gained – and sometimes lost.

Due to this paradigmatic change, programme policies in general are increasingly justified on economic grounds and, in particular, with reference to the audience. It appears that actors within the multiple markets are joined, or separated, by their very conception of the audience, that is, the way they understand the status, needs and demands of the viewers. In other words, even the political and business market, both influential themselves, tend increasingly to justify their interests with respect to the popular market.

The audience is the new king

The changing television landscape has resulted in a growing *audience orientation* of broadcasters' strategies. This is due to at least two reasons. First, it stems from the change in the financial basis of television services. As advertising and subscription are increasingly replacing public measures of funding, such as the licence fee, it is natural that justification for programming is sought directly from audience ratings. No wonder the popular market has outplaced the decisive role of the political market.

Second, as a logical outcome of channel multiplication, audiences tend to fragment. Viewers are no longer stuck with the fixed schedules of established stations as videocassette recorders and specialized cable and satellite channels enable them to multiply the range of their viewing activities. What this means for the television industry is a growing uncertainty about audience preferences and the unpredictability of its choices.

The multiplication of channels and variety of programme offerings is gradually leading to a saturation of the television market. Although further technological leaps towards an interactive 'entertainment/information superhighway' are imminent, already today a 'policy of supply' has given way to a 'policy of demand' (Wolton, 1992). An increase in programme supply has emphasized the strategic role of 'consumer choice', which explains why individual programmes and even channels are carefully focused to reach the desired target group. Audiences 'must be continuously "targeted" and fought for, grabbed, seduced', as Ang (1996: 10) has put it. Yet broadcasters have no ultimate means to ensure that the audience will make the 'right' choice, because ratings figures acquired through people-metering systems only provide indirect evidence of the demand, favour majority tastes and do not measure the intensity of preferences (e.g. Ang, 1991).

These factors of uncertainty, together with the new financial basis of the industry, contribute to the increasing audience orientation of programme output. Each programme, not to mention each programming schedule, is expected to produce its public. The range and choice of its offerings are now of strategic importance for the station's survival in competition. The programming schedule is broadcaster's best attraction for the audience. At the same time, expectations concerning the economic efficiency and viability of programming are pronounced.

While I in the following analyse the various patterns of argumentation used in the programme policy discourse, I will concentrate on the political market, business market and popular market, as it is within these three core arenas that most battles over programme policy are waged. I try to demonstrate the core arguments of the two paradigms of broadcasting, but I will also point to shifts and erosion within these discourses.

Legitimation by the audience-as-citizens

If the ideal-typical audience of public service broadcasting does not constitute a market but a public, consisting of citizens, how do public broadcasters, or those in favour of public service-type television, articulate in order to justify their programme policies? Thematically, at least four patterns of argumentation can be detected.

1. The audience needs diversity

Diversity, pluralism and range have been an established part of the public service legacy from the very beginning. It was already John Reith, the first Director-General of the BBC, who, according to Scannell (1990), decided that a wide range of mixed programming – a triad of information, education and entertainment – would best serve the promotion of national and social unity. Yet his understanding of diversity was biased by educational purposes and an elitist definition of enlightenment. As Curran and Seaton (1991: 178–9) have pointed out, the service was not planned to serve *different* interests; rather, Reith was determined that the audience should encounter the whole range of the company's offerings. Thus, the BBC's programme policy, and, it is suggested here, programming principles of most European public broadcasters, were originally based on an assumption of cultural homogeneity, according to which 'culture was single and undifferentiated' (Curran and Seaton, 1991: 178), and not on a more recent concept of cultural pluralism. This hierarchical juxtaposition of 'what the people need' and 'what they want', as already Reith had expressed the confrontation, resulted in a paternalistic 'better knowledge' of what is good or what people should watch or hear, not necessarily in a genuine multiplicity of programmes and ideas.

Although the public broadcasters had already gone a long way towards popularizing their programme outputs, the fundamental turn towards pluralism did not occur until much later. In Britain the differing broadcasting interests of an increasingly diverse society were recognized by the Annan Report (1977) and materialized, for example, in Channel Four's minority approach, whereas in the Nordic countries paternalist statements based on a homogeneous concept of culture predominated until the mid-1980s, when they were gradually replaced with a commitment towards cultural diversity (e.g. Silvo, 1988; Søndergaard, 1994; Syvertsen, 1992).

Indeed, this new definition of a balanced diet of programming is multi-faceted, referring to diverse programming at several levels: in the multiplicity of audience types served; in terms of programme types supplied; and in respect of responsiveness to society (e.g. Blumler, 1992a, 1992b). The new orthodoxy of audience-oriented pluralism is well manifested by explicit statements of media laws, operating licences, and so on, as well as other principled definitions.

For example, the resolution by the Council of Europe, which in 1994 provided the first officially established mandate at the European level for public service broadcasters, states that these institutions have an obligation to develop 'pluralistic, innovatory and varied programming' and 'services of interest to a wide public while being attentive to the needs of minority groups' (CE, 1994: 9). Similarly, in Britain the Broadcasting Research Unit (BRU), which submitted its exposition of public service principles to the Peacock Committee in 1985, named the goal that 'broadcast programmes should cater for all interests and tastes' as the second of eight central principles, and supplemented it with another principle, claiming that 'disadvantaged minorities should receive particular provision' (BRU, 1985: 3–7).

These examples suggest that the principle of multiplicity of audience is aimed to cover both the general audience and special interest segments, or minorities. Perhaps the most detailed explication of this thinking is included in the BBC's 'statement of promises' (BBC, 1996), which, in addition to supplying 'the widest range' of programmes that 'inform, educate and entertain', also promises to 'work harder to reflect the wide interests and varied cultures of the whole of the United Kingdom' and to 'provide programmes of particular interest to ethnic minority audiences', too (BBC, 1996: 3).

Interestingly, the BBC argues for a division of labour between its two channels, with BBC1 offering 'a wide range of programmes that we hope will have a broad appeal for all ages and lifestyles, reflecting national issues and interests. BBC1 is the channel for a big event [. . .]. ' (1996: 4.) In contrast, BBC2 is presented as 'a clear alternative to BBC1. It is at the heart of the

BBC's reputation as a broadcaster which takes creative risks by trying out new programme ideas and performers. It serves a wide variety of tastes and explores a range of ideas. BBC2 aims to cater for special interests [. . .]. ' (1996: 5.) In this way, by programming two channels so as to complement each other, a public broadcaster can use a 'dual strategy' (Søndergaard, 1994: 217) that balances between the general audience and minority interests.

However, today this programme policy is not applied because of the virtues of diversity in itself. This approach is not merely an effort to reflect better the various needs of information for and education and entertainment of the public, but is justified also on grounds of maintaining channel reach and popularity. Because it is no longer possible to capture all viewers all the time, it has become vital to provide at least something for everyone every once in a while. For example, in the late 1980s Denmark's DR already gave preference to reaching every Dane at least once a week (Søndergaard, 1994: 222). Diversity of programming is the principal method of attaining this goal and, as an evidence of their good performance, public broadcasters have willingly referred to the vast body of research results revealing that they, indeed, provide a broader diversity of offerings than their commercial rivals (see, e.g., De Bens et al., 1992; Ishikawa et al., 1996).

On the other hand, diversity is no longer monopolized by public broadcasters only. Commercial channels can also claim to provide a wide variety of programmes, not lagging far behind public broadcasters. This holds true particularly for stations that apply a generalist strategy and represent a hybrid organization, constrained by certain public service obligations, such as Britain's ITV, Finland's MTV3, Norway's TV2 or Sweden's TV4. Here, diversity can easily be turned into an argument for 'what-the-audience-wants', thus being conflated with the expansion of consumer choice (cf. Ang, 1991: 168). In other words, broadening of programme options can be justified on the basis of the positive utility it produces for those who consume television (see, e.g., Litman, 1992).

In the new competitive environment, diversity, 'the most prominent substantive principle in programming policy', as Ang (1991: 116) characterizes it, has an ambivalent purpose. While, on the one hand, it fits perfectly with the performance goal of public broadcasters to balance between the various aspects of needs the public is considered to have, on the other hand, it also serves as a strategy to meet audience demand. Thus, diversity can be used as an argument in the political and popular market alike, while in the business market it provides a feasible differentiation strategy.

2. The audience needs quality

This pattern of argumentation was clearly present in the Finnish example. Instead of low-budget entertainment and televisual nonsense, as it argues, the public should be supplied with quality programmes with high production values. In informative programmes this suggests an analytical procedure, impartiality and responsibility of reporting, and so on. In drama, 'quality' refers to an innovative and artistic approach, and in entertainment, for instance, to portraying the best of popular performances.

Apart from technical standards, the principle of quality can be divided into two elements: first, it refers to 'good programming' in general and, second, to an 'innovative' approach. This was clearly expressed, for example, in Britain by the BRU's requirement that '[b]roadcasting should be structured so as to encourage competition in good programming rather than competition for numbers' and that '[t]he public guidelines for broadcasting should be designated to liberate rather than restrict the programme makers' (BRU, 1985: 15, 19). The Council of Europe also refers to quality, while it expects public service broadcasting institutions to develop 'innovatory' programming which 'meets high ethical and quality standards' and 'not to sacrifice the pursuit of quality to market forces' (CE, 1994: 9). Similar to the BRU guidelines, quality is here presented as an opposite to the quantity-based philosophy of commercial services.

As a guiding principle, quality is not necessarily included in the official mandates of European public service broadcasting institutions. For example, the recent agreement which defines the duties and responsibilities of the BBC does name 'high general standards in all respects' as one of the two governing principles of the company ('a wide range of subject matter' being the other; Department of National Heritage, 1996: 4), whereas Finland's Act on YLE (1993) makes no reference to this argument in its definition of public service. Although absent in the explicit stipulation, today YLE strongly promotes its quality profile as a distinctive feature of its operations. Similarly, in the 1990s Denmark's DR and Norway's NRK have also applied a similar differentiation strategy (see, e.g., Søndergaard, 1994; Syvertsen, 1997), encouraging 'programmes of the highest possible quality' (NRK, 1987: 2).

Indeed, the importance of quality appears to have increased along with the intensification of competition. It has become, as Ang puts it, 'one of the spearheads of modern-day public service institutions' (1991: 167). In the arguments of broadcasters themselves, quality has become a discursive differentiation strategy that serves to distinguish public service institutions from their commercial rivals. For example, the BBC argues for its uniqueness in the following way: 'The more broadcasters you have to choose from, the more you might expect the BBC – the broadcaster you pay for through the licence fee – to provide something different. We should also have high standards, and a dedication to integrity in all we do' (BBC, 1996: 2). Accordingly, the company promises to 'provide a service which is acknowledged as a world leader' and 'to experiment and take creative risks' (BBC, 1996: 3).

On the other hand, one must remember two things. First, commercial broadcasters also provide quality programmes with high production values. Second, it is the quality as defined by programme makers and broadcasters that has dominated the discourse (Mulgan, 1990). Quality may also be approached from other perspectives, such as individual viewers' personal interests, programme appreciation, consumer demand, and so on (see also, e.g., Ishikawa, 1996), or, even more radically, as a 'contingent criterion of judgement to be made by actual audiences in actual situations', as Ang (1991: 167) puts it.

3. The audience needs information and education

Newscasts, current affairs programmes, features and documentaries, educational programmes and other social or practical information have gained a particular emphasis in public broadcasters' offerings (see, e.g., De Bens et al., 1992; Ishikawa et al., 1996). Their specific mandate to provide information and education stems directly from the audience-as-public approach. The public is regarded as a group of citizens that need to be informed in order to secure an enlightened public discussion on public affairs.

Thus, public service broadcasting is 'obliged to address its audience as rational citizens and to provide them with the information upon which alone rational debate can be based', as the BRU (1985: 8) puts it. Similarly, Finland's Act on YLE (1993) stipulates, as the first duty involving public service, that the company shall 'support democracy by providing a wide variety of information, opinions and debates on social issues'. A conviction that only information can help people to understand political and social processes is well expressed also by the BBC, which justifies its news and information services by claiming them to 'help people understand national and international events' (BBC, 1996: 3). Hence, it is an idea of democracy, best maintained within an informed public sphere, that justifies informative programming.

Perhaps an extreme example of this 'democratist' rationale was provided by Finland's YLE, which in the late 1960s started a radical experiment, known as 'informational broadcasting'. By activating citizens, this project aimed to democratize the whole of society. Programming policy, being considered the central tool of activation, promoted objective, accurate and challenging information as the elemental resource of democratic participation; entertainment was appreciated, but only as far as it had critical and activating potentialities (see, e.g., Hujanen, 1995).

In the discourse of 'what the audience needs', information and education are presented with respect to the political function of public broadcasting, which is intended to provide an arena of debate, characterized by plurality, balance and access. For example, the Council of Europe's resolution requires public service broadcasters to provide 'a forum for public discussion in which as broad a spectrum as possible of views and opinion can be expressed'. In addition, they are obliged 'to broadcast impartial and independent news, information and comment' (CE, 1994: 9). Thus, the traditional values of impartiality and independence – the BBC's 'statement of promises' links 'accuracy' into this context as well (BBC, 1996: 3) – are also justified in relation to democratic goals.

However, information is not only emphasized in the political market, or as a resource of the political realm. Owing to increased competition, informative programming policy also provides a differentiation strategy that helps public broadcasters to legitimize their existence. When commercial channels turn more and more towards international entertainment formulas, information has, paradoxically, become a niche that can be targeted and marketed to selective viewers. This is perhaps best illustrated by the BBC, which promises to 'provide more factual programming during peak time on television than other broadcasters' (BBC, 1996: 3). In the same vein, the Nordic public service broadcasting institutions also wish to perform as the major source of news and information for their citizens, in contrast to their rivals (see, e.g., Syvertsen, 1997).

In addition to the political and business market, information is widely used in programme policy discourse in the popular market too. As Alasuutari (1992) has pointed out in his study of Finnish television viewers, newscasts, current affairs, features and documentaries are ranked high in the 'moral hierarchy' of viewing preferences. According to him, news and documentaries represent 'the most highly valued types of TV programme in the Finnish moral hierarchy' (1992: 563), and although ranking orders do not necessarily reflect actual viewing habits, what is reflected here is the popular acceptance of the educational public service ideology. On the other hand, commercial broadcasters also can utilize the political and popular value of informative genres. For example, Finland's MTV3 is actively marketing itself as being 'the leading supplier of news', referring to the great number and innovative profiling of its daily newscasts.

Hence, 'informing the national debate' (BBC, 1992: 19) is a flexible argument in the legitimation of programme policies, as information and education can be justified in the political, business and popular markets alike. Emphasis on information by public broadcasters – and the popular appreciation of informative genres – provides a practical counterargument to the entertainment-oriented supply of commercial channels, but, at the same time, information involves values that can be shared by all broadcasters.

4. The audience needs cultural integration

National and cultural integration was one of the early legitimations for public broadcasting institutions. In the first place, this was expressed in the goal of providing a universal and comprehensive service, available to the whole nation – a goal which can be justified with reference to both equality and integration. However, integrating purposes can be traced also to the cultural vocation that characterized European public broadcasters from their early days. In other words, broadcasting organizations were taken to be part of the sector of society which is responsible for generating and disseminating its linguistic, spiritual and aesthetic wealth (Blumler, 1992a: 10–11).

In the vision of the BRU (1985: 7), public service broadcasters 'should recognise their special relationship to the sense of national identity and community'. Here, programming duties are connected directly to the idea of the audience as citizens, addressed in a common public sphere. This integrating function of programming may also be justified as a counter-measure to disintegrating tendencies within societies, as is done by the Council of Europe (CE, 1994: 9) when it ranks the duty of providing 'a reference point for all members of the public and a factor of social cohesion and integration of all individuals, groups and communities' as a principal mission of public service broadcasters.

What does this actually mean in terms of programme policy? It appears to refer, first, to a pluralist and sober reflection of the society in the media as discussed above, and, second, to providing integrating experiences and social interaction through programming. The latter function justifies broadcasting as 'a crucial means – perhaps the only means at present – whereby common knowledges and pleasures in a shared public life are maintained as a social good for the whole population' (Scannell, 1989: 164). According to this argument, broadcasting can contribute to a common 'universe of discourse' (Scannell, 1989: 143) that goes beyond the restricted public topics involved in news and current affairs. This integrating function is served by documentaries, drama, entertainment, sports and other broadcast events, such as royal coronations, Olympic games, Eurovision song contests, and so on. From this perspective, what the audience 'needs' is any broadcast which creates a feeling of togetherness and contributes to social cohesion. In programme policy, this has sometimes resulted in public broadcasters' tendency to monopolize major national events in order to be able to provide a 'national common arena' (Syvertsen, 1997: 184).

Integration purposes have also justified public broadcasters' special duties to domestic programming, particularly emphasized during the last few years. In Britain, the BBC's commitment to 'new modern drama and situation comedy' and 'period drama and classic adaptations' (BBC, 1996: 4) demonstrates the corporation's multiple duties to 'support and stimulate the development and expression of British culture and entertainment' (BBC, 1992: 21). In smaller nations, such as Finland and Norway, where original productions are constrained by market size and shortage of resources, public broadcasters' special responsibilities for domestic fare tend to be even more pronounced. Emphasis on domestic programming with 'a significant proportion of original productions', as the Council of Europe requires (CE, 1994: 9), serves also as a comfortable differentiation strategy. On the other hand, the great popularity of domestic programmes, drama in particular (see Biltereyst, 1995), has encouraged commercial channels, too, to promote domestic culture and talent.

Finally, cultural programming and patronage of the arts by public broadcasters also are often justified by their culturally integrating functions. For example, the BBC is expected to 'enrich the cultural heritage of the United Kingdom through support for the arts' (Department of National Heritage, 1994: 6), and the corporation itself promises to 'support and stimulate the development of the best talents so that British culture in all its forms' can be represented in its programmes (BBC, 1996: 3). This argument is used to highlight the public broadcasting institutions' role as cornerstones of their respective national cultures and cultural policies. Hence, arts programmes, broadcast concerts, and so on, which do not necessarily perform so well in ratings, can be legitimized as a common property of the nation.

In conclusion, justification of programme policies based on integrating functions of public broadcasting is used as an argument for cultural nationalism that may take several forms, applicable to the political, popular and business markets alike. Nevertheless, as was demonstrated by the case of Finland's fourth television network, this pattern of argumentation can be extended to promote and protect domestic broadcasting industry in general too (Lowe and Alm, 1997).

Legitimation by the audience-as-consumers

Legitimation by addressing the audience as consumers is not necessarily expressed in written policy documents. Rather, appealing to 'what-the-audience-wants' is manifest in promotional campaigns, media policy debates and broadcasters' day-to-day choices. This discourse can be analysed in terms of two major subdiscourses, complemented with a related economic argument.

1. The audience wants choice

'Consumer choice' is the magic word of this discourse, which suggests that consumers should have the widest possible choice of broadcasting services and that diversity of choice can best be guaranteed by the discovery mechanism of trial and error in a competitive market. What does 'increasing choice' mean as a programme policy goal?

First, it sometimes refers to a widening of the channel choice set, thus providing more simultaneous programme options for the viewer. 'The fundamental aim of broadcasting policy should be to enlarge both the freedom of choice to the consumer and the opportunities available to programme makers to offer alternative wares to the public', as the British Peacock Report (1986: 125), perhaps the most authoritative manifestation of this thinking, put it. This thinking often sees subscription television, with its unlimited range of offerings, as a realization of consumer sovereignty while it 'liberates the consumer by making him or her the best judge of good broadcasting – it gives them choice' (Veljanovski, 1990: 19).

The argument of providing new alternatives to the viewer underlies every recent decision to introduce, at national level, new terrestrial channels. It was one of the justifying rationales behind Finland's Channel Four as well as Britain's Channel Five, both commercial enterprises. However, the argument for increasing choice played a role also in the launch of Norway's NRK2 and Denmark's DR2, both public service channels (see, e.g., Syvertsen, 1997). Hence, increasing choice is not a justification used by commercial channels only.

This justification does not necessarily claim to provide something qualitatively different. Rather, here 'choice' is reduced to quantity of options. As Dowding (1992: 312–14) has provocatively pointed out, the argument for 'increasing choice' does not usually refer to adding to the value of the choice set or necessarily provide the viewers what they really want. Instead, it assumes that adding new alternatives to a choice, first, increases statistically the probability of satisfying their needs; second, may also help viewers to discover their preferences through the very act of choice itself; and, third, may appeal to consumers, as it appears to give them a measure of control over the alternatives.

In this way, programme policy that values choice in itself is well justified in the popular market, but it provides a viable strategy for the business market, too, as it helps TV stations to map out consumer preferences and provide programmes that might meet viewer demand.

Another meaning of 'increasing choice' refers to providing something 'different' as compared to the existing offerings. Here, 'choice' refers to an 'alternative', qualitatively speaking. As the number of channels increases and the audience per channel, logically, falls, new commercial services can lay claim to apply new, alternative programming strategies. The argument of providing a new choice was used, for example, by Finland's Ruutunelonen as it offered a more focused programme diet than its main commercial rival. According to the Channel Controller, Jorma Sairanen, the entrant would not try to compete with MTV3 with similar programming:

> We can manage with some 200,000 to 300,000 viewers [compared to the 800,000 to 1.2 million viewers of MTV3's top programmes], but it must be a targeted audience. Perhaps some two-thirds of our programmes are pretty similar to those of MTV's but, as far as I can see, our opportunities are in the remaining one-third. We can take risks as we are not aiming at big volumes like MTV is.[7]

Here, the alternative is created by means of targeting, which in this case meant focusing on young, urban, female viewers. This strategy also can be justified with reference to both the popular market and the business market. Indeed, specialization as applied by various cable and satellite channels today provides a major programme policy strategy that has

enabled dozens of new outlets to establish their own audience segments
and programme niches. While major TV stations, whether public or private, operate principally as generalists differentiating their products within
a framework of a wide range of broad appeal programming, pay channels,
in particular, introduce a choice by focusing on thematic programming
and narrow appeal.

Currently, increasing choice is enthusiastically promoted in the popular
market by the electronics industry promising by signal digitalization to
multiply the present channel capacity and, hence, provide the consumer
with an almost limitless abundance of programme options. Whether the
business market can bear the forthcoming fragmentation and how much
consumers will be prepared to pay for the improved service are critical
unknowns, however.

2. The audience wants popular programmes

If a broadcaster is determined to 'give the audience what it wants', it tends
to favour programmes that are watched by the greatest possible number of
viewers. Indeed, as micro-economic theory of competition suggests, both
advertiser-supported and pay television are biased against minority-inter-
est tastes – and in favour of programmes that produce large audiences
(e.g. Owen and Wildman, 1992: 148). However, commercial broadcasters
have been able to justify their emphasis on the most popular categories
such as fiction, sports and entertainment by appealing to audience
demand, as expressed by people-meter figures.

Indeed, the argumentation for a popularity-based programme policy is
strongly characterized by what Ang (1991: 50) calls a *ratings discourse*.
Audience ratings, expressed as a percentage of all television households in
the country, and shares, expressed as a percentage of all households that
are watching television during a particular hour, have become a discursive
framework that, on the one hand, enables the industry to know more about
its audience and, on the other hand, has been accepted also by viewers
themselves as an indication of what is popular and what might be worthwhile watching. Even more importantly, ratings provide the advertisers
with vital information of audience size and composition and the rival
channels with strategic knowledge of successes and failures.

As Ang notices, the ratings discourse 'charts the ways in which the
industry defines the audience as a market' (1991: 48). In ratings, popularity is reduced efficiently to a matter of numerical superiority – and
numerical superiority, then, is equated with audience preference. Ratings
appear to provide an unambiguous measure of consumer demand, thus
generating programming decisions that can be easily defended.

But public broadcasters also have discovered the opportunities provided by the ratings discourse. Ratings are now widely employed by
these institutions as a measure of popular support, an issue of increased

importance. For example, Finland's YLE had started its audience research department already in the 1960s, but it was not until the mid-1980s, and the introduction of people meters, that viewing figures grew in importance in the Finnish debate. While lists of top programmes are published weekly by, for example, the major TV guide, *Katso*, and the leading national daily, *Helsingin Sanomat*, ratings are extensively used as an argument for and against individual programmes. Hence the performance of broadcasters has come under a continuing public jurisdiction based on viewing figures and company viewing shares (see, e.g., Soramäki, 1994).

In his analysis of the Danish public service broadcaster, DR, Søndergaard (1994) notices a new responsiveness towards audience demand emerging during the 1980s. What was earlier termed the 'public' becomes 'customers', while the daily schedule in terms of programme placement becomes divided into separate sections for the general audience (prime-time) and special target groups (daytime, late night). Without changing dramatically the composition of offerings, a completely new pro-gramming schedule is created, based on targeting, standardization and regularity.

Hence, popularity serves as an argument not only in the popular and the business markets but also in the political market, where popular legit-imacy can be used as a measure of performance and exchanged for political legitimacy.

3. Viability of programming counts

Relative to justifying programme policy on the basis of popularity, an explicitly economic argumentation claims that programming decisions should obey a strict cost–benefit analysis. Here, programme production and scheduling are guided by economic calculation or, to put it more poignantly, what reaps a profit. This rationale promotes low-cost pro-gramming that appeals to a large viewership, thus favouring imported serial drama instead of domestic original productions and studio-based talk shows instead of genuine features or documentaries, for example.

However, broadcasters whose driving force is the maximization of their long-run profits seldom use this argument publicly as a justification for their programme policies. Instead, while being well understood by rival broadcasters, this argument is valid in the business market, in particular. Interestingly, it is often understood in the political market, too, as was illustrated by the Finnish example, in which the state department in charge of media policy explicitly recommended not constraining commercial broadcasters by any strict stipulations on programming as, for economic reasons, they would easily become a dead letter.

On the other hand, public broadcasters' programme policy is also increasingly guided by an effort to spend the licence-fee income 'as effi-ciently as possible so that you get the maximum benefit through our programmes', as the BBC (1996: 27) puts it. By appealing to cost-effectiveness, the British public broadcaster addresses its audience as a group of *informed consumers*, a hybrid representing properties of both a consumer and a citizen. This shows that economic reasoning serves as an argument in the popular market too.

Conclusion: Signs of discursive convergence

Above I have traced patterns of argumentation in issues of programme policy. I have distinguished between two discourses and several subdiscourses that are common in the multiple policy-making arenas. The two discourses appear broadly to follow the paradigmatic distinction between public service and commercial broadcasting. However, while the distinction between the two paradigms is broad, it also is vague and full of compromises. Whilst traditional arguments based on 'what-the-audience-needs' have partly been replaced by arguments based on 'what-the audience-wants', commercial broadcasters also have compromised their populist programme policies, resulting in a *rapprochement* between the two policy discourses. In conclusion, I shall summarize certain patterns of this convergence.

1. Popularity rules

Owing to increasing fragmentation of the audience, broadcasters will become more dependent than ever on viewers' expressed or anticipated interests, their actual viewing choices and, perhaps more than has happened so far, their programme appreciation. In order to 'keep what are defined as satisfactory audience shares' (Hultén and Brants, 1992: 122), public broadcasters have followed their commercial competitors by opening up new programme slots in the schedule and by standardizing their schedules. By 'popularizing' their fare, public broadcasters wish to appeal directly to audience demand, thus addressing the audience as consumers.

The outcome of the general acceptance of ratings discourse is a convergence of argumentation between public and commercial broadcasters. According to Ang, who has analysed the discursive shift among public broadcasters, '[these] institutions [. . .] have responded [to competition] by adopting the discourse of the marketplace in their approach to the audience: defining "television audience" as a collection of consumers rather than citizens, thinking of it in terms of "what the audience wants" rather than "what it needs"'(1991: 165–6).

This tendency reflects the effort of these institutions to adapt to competition by balancing between normative justifications of range, quality, information and integration and pragmatic requirements of popularity and economic reasoning. This means applying a *mixed strategy* (Syvertsen, 1992), according to which, on the one hand, they confront their commercial competitors by representing the informative, cultural and national ideals they consider to be unique and crucial to their identity as public broadcasters, while, on the other hand, they take compromising steps towards popular genres in order to protect their share of viewing (see also Achille and Miège, 1994; Hultén and Brants, 1992).

2. Money buys

At least two reasons contribute to the fact that public broadcasters are more exposed than before to economic constraints. First, stagnating licence-fee revenue and growing production costs constitute a syndrome which can be faced only with due financial management. Second, criticism of public broadcasters' extravagant spending has resulted in demands for efficiency and accountability as well as promises by them to 'provide value for money', as the BBC (1996: 77) puts it.

As Achille and Miège notice, the tendency to cut costs by externalizing productions also 'favours the convergence of the structures of public and commercial television'(1994: 38). This is supported by industrial policy, too, aiming to consolidate national culture industries. Here public broadcasting institutions are regarded as key players, whose programme purchases and co-productions can encourage the expansion of the independent sector, thus promoting the general interests of cultural nationalism (Lowe and Alm, 1997).

3. Variety is popular

In the new competitive situation, in which the most important arena of legitimation is the popular market, diversity, as an argument for programme policy, is no longer monopolized by public broadcasters only, or by the discourse of 'what-the-audience-needs'. This shift towards a more multifaceted conception of diversity parallels the challenge of the new media and private commercial television and coincides with the development of audience measurement technologies. It also reflects a general cultural change in society as a result of which 'citizens' who formerly were served as equals become 'consumers' who demand various tailored services.

This suggests that the term 'diversity' conceals differences of meaning from one discourse to another. While the private, commercial sector tends to regard diversity narrowly as an economic concept, public broadcasters emphasize the cultural dimension of the concept. While the first approach understands diversity as a pragmatic goal, achieved by means of competition in the marketplace, the second approaches it as a pluralist and principled concept, acquired by public policy measures (e.g. Blumler,

1992a). However, these two meanings appear to be converging and merging with each other.

4. Duties are shared

Another source of discursive convergence is provided by commercial channels which are constrained by various public service-type obligations. The combination of commercial funding and regulation by public policy has resulted in programme policies that resemble more of a public service tradition than a genuine commercial diet (Hellman and Sauri, 1997). The willingness of these hybrid broadcasters to use the 'what-the-audience-needs' argumentation also reflects a 'prestige strategy' (Hellman and Sauri, 1994) which helps them to enhance their legitimacy.

Owing to this discursive convergence between 'what-the-audience-wants' and 'what-the-audience-needs', traditional public service justifications may be partly eroded, but more obvious is that they are transposed to carry new meanings so that both public and commercial broadcasters can use them. The justifications of genuinely commercial programme policy will also be shared, because public broadcasters find it difficult to escape economic necessities and the temptations of popularity. This will result in a legitimation pattern where programme policies are increasingly argued for by a mix of values of citizenship and consumerism, applicable to the popular, political and business market alike.

Hence, the sharp borderline between the public service and commercial way of arguing for programme policy is, if not disappearing, blurring and decreasing in importance. It appears not to be feasible to treat the audience *either* as citizens *or* as consumers. Parallel with a general trend in modern-day society, the two roles overlap and merge with each other.

Notes

1. The distinction is widely used both in theoretical literature of the media (see, e.g., McQuail, 1987) and in empirical analyses of broadcasting and broadcasting policy (see, e.g. Ang, 1991: Søndergaard, 1994; Syvertsen, 1992).

2. The Helsinki Media Company is owned by the Erkko family and its Sanoma Corporation. While the Sanoma Corporation is the biggest newspaper publisher in Finland, the Helsinki Media Company has interests in magazine and book publishing and was the major owner of a national cable network, PTV.

3. *Helsingin Sanomat*, 14 June 1996, p. D11.

4. *Helsingin Sanomat*, 20 May 1996, p. A6.

5. *Ilta-Sanomat*, 4 June 1997, p. A13.

6. *Länsi-Suomi*, 12 December 1996, p. 10.

7. *Helsingin Sanomat*, 31 May 1997, p. C1.

References

Achille, Y. and Miège, B. (1994) 'The Limits to the Adaptation Strategies of European Public Service Television', *Media, Culture & Society*, 16 (1): 31–46.

Act on YLE (1993) *Laki Yleisradio Oy:stä.* No. 1380. Helsinki: Valtion painatuskeskus

Alasuutari, P. (1992) '"I'm Ashamed to Admit it but I Have Watched Dallas": The Moral Hierarchy of Television Programmes', *Media, Culture & Society*, 14 (4): 561–82.

Ang, I. (1991) *Desparately Seeking the Audience.* London: Routledge.

Ang, I. (1996) *Living Room Wars: Rethinking Media Audiences for a Postmodern World.* London: Routledge.

Annan Report (1977) *Committee on the Future of Broadcasting.* Cmnd 6753. London: HMSO.

BBC (1992) *Extending Choice: The BBC's Role in the New Broadcasting Age.* London: British Broadcasting Corporation.

BBC (1996) *Our Commitment to You: BBC Statement of Promises to Viewers and Listeners.* London: British Broadcasting Corporation.

Biltereyst, D. (1995) 'European Audiovisual Policy and the Cross-Border Circulation of Fiction: a Follow-up Study', *Cultural Policy*, 2 (1): 3–24.

Blumler, J.G. (1992a) 'Public Service Broadcasting before the Commercial Deluge', in J.G. Blumler (ed.), *Television and the Public Interest: Vulnerable Values in West European Broadcasting.* London: Sage.

Blumler, J.G. (1992b) 'Vulnerable Values at Stake', in J.G. Blumler (ed.), *Television and the Public Interest: Vulnerable Values in West European Broadcasting.* London: Sage.

Brants, K. and Siune, K. (1992) 'Public Broadcasting in a State of Flux', in K. Siune, and W. Truetzschler, (eds), *Dynamics of Media Politics: Broadcast and Electronic Media in Western Europe.* London: Sage.

BRU (1985) *The Public Service Idea in British Broadcasting.* London: Broadcasting Research Unit.

CE (1994) *The Media in a Democratic Society: Political Declaration, Resolutions and Statement.* 4th European Ministerial Conference on Mass Media Policy, Prague, 7–8 December, MCM (94) 20. Council of Europe.

Curran, J. and Seaton, J. (1991) *Power without Responsibility: The Press and Broadcasting in Britain.* 4th edn. London: Routledge.

De Bens, Els, Kelly, M. and Bakke, M. (1992) 'Television Content: Dallasification of Culture?', in K. Siune and W. Truetzschler (eds), *Dynamics of Media Politics: Broadcast and Electronic Media in Western Europe.* London: Sage.

Department of National Heritage (1994) *The Future of the BBC: Serving the Nation, Competing World Wide.* Cm 2621. London: HMSO.

Department of National Heritage (1996) *Agreement Between Her Majesty's Secretary of State for National Heritage and the British Broadcasting Corporation.* Cm 3152. London: HMSO.

Dowding, K. (1992) 'Choice: Its Increase and Its Value', *British Journal of Political Science*, 22 (3): 301–14.

Hellman, H. (1996) 'The Formation of Television in Finland: A Case in Pragmatist Media Policy', in I. Bondebjerg and F. Bono (eds), *Television in Scandinavia: History, Politics and Aesthetics.* Luton: University of Luton Press.

Hellman, H. and Sauri, T. (1994) 'Public Service Television and the Tendency towards Convergence: Trends in Prime-Time Programme Structure in Finland, 1970–1992', *Media, Culture & Society*, 16 (1): 47–71.

Hellman, H. and Sauri, T. (1997) 'Hybridikanavien nousukausi: Kilpailu ja televi-sion ohjelmarakenteen muutos Pohjoismaissa 1988–1995' [The Rise of Hybrid Channels: Competition and Trends in Programming in the Nordic Countries, 1988–1995], *Tiedotustutkimus*, 20 (2): 20–39.

Hujanen, T. (1995) 'Political versus Cultural in Critical Broadcasting Research and Policy: A Reevaluation of the Finnish Radical Experiment in Broadcasting in the Late 1960s', in J.A. Lent (ed.), *A Different Road Taken: Profiles in Critical Communication*. Oxford: Westview Press.

Hultén, O. (1996) 'Public service och den mediepolitiska utvecklingen i Norden' [Public Service and Developments in Nordic Media Policy], in O. Hultén, H. Søndergaard and U. Carlson (eds), *Nordisk forskning om public service: Radio och TV i allmänhetens tjänst*. Gothenburg: Nordicom.

Hultén, O. and Brants, K. (1992) 'Public Service Broadcasting: Reactions to Competition', in K. Siune and W. Truetzschler (eds), *Dynamics of Media Politics: Broadcast and Electronic Media in Western Europe*. London: Sage.

Humphreys, P.J. (1996) *Mass Media and Media Policy in Western Europe*. Manchester: Manchester University Press.

Ishikawa, S. (ed.) (1996) *Quality Assessment of Television*. Luton: University of Luton Press.

Ishikawa, S., Leggatt, T., Litman, B., Raboy, M., Rosengren, K.E. and Kambara, N. (1996) 'Diversity in Television Programming: Comparative Analysis of Five Countries', in S. Ishikawa (ed,). *Quality Assessment of Television*. Luton: University of Luton Press.

Litman, B. (1992) 'Economic Aspects of Program Quality: The Case for Diversity', *Studies of Broadcasting*, 28: 121–56.

Lowe, G.F. and Alm, A. (1997) 'Public Service Broadcasting as Cultural Industry: Value Transformation in the Finnish Market-Place', *European Journal of Communication*, 12 (2): 169–91.

McQuail, D. (1987) *Mass Communication Theory: An Introduction*. 2nd edn. London: Sage.

Meier, W.A. and Trappel, J. (1992) 'Small States in the Shadow of Giants', in K. Siune and W. Truetzschler (eds), *Dynamics of Media Politics: Broadcast and Electronic Media in Western Europe*. London: Sage.

Mulgan, G. (1990) 'Television's Holy Grail: Seven Types of Quality', in G. Mulgan (ed.) *The Question of Quality*. London: British Film Institute.

Mykkänen, J. (1995) *Yleisradiotoiminnan strategiaselvitys: Radio ja televisio 2010* [A Strategy Report on Broadcasting: Radio and Television in 2010]. Publications of the Ministry of Transport and Communications No 45. Helsinki.

NRK (1987) *NRK mot år 2000* [NRK Towards the Year 2000]. Oslo: Norsk Rikskringkastning.

Owen, B.M. and Wildman, S.S. (1992) *Video Economics*. Cambridge, MA: Harvard University Press.

Peacock Report (1986) *Committee of Financing the BBC*. Cmnd 9824. London: HMSO.

Scannell, P. (1989) 'Public Service Broadcasting and Modern Public Life', *Media, Culture & Society*, 11 (2): 135–66.

Scannell, P. (1990) 'Public Service Broadcasting: The History of the Concept', in A. Goodwin and G. Whannel (eds), *Understanding Television*. London: Routledge.

Silvo, I. (1988) *Valta, kenttä ja kertomus: Televisiopolitiikan tulkinnat* [Power, Field and Narratives: Interpretations in Finnish Television Politics]. Helsinki: Yleisradio.

Soramäki, M. (1994) 'Yleisradio ja kilpailu 1990-luvun alun tv-toiminnassa' [Competition and YLE in the TV Broadcasting of the Early 1990s], *Tiedotustutkimus*, 17 (3): 33–44.

Søndergaard, H. (1994) *DR i tv-konkurrencens tidsalder* [DR in the Age of Competition]. Frederiksberg: Samfundslitteratur.

Syvertsen, T. (1992) *Public Television in Transition: A Comparative and Historical Analysis of the BBC and the NRK*. Oslo and Trondheim: Norwegian Research Council for Science and Humanities.

Syvertsen, T. (1997) *Den store TV-krigen: Norsk allmennfjernsyn 1988–96* [The Great TV War: Norwegian Broadcast Television, 1988–1996]. Bergen: Fagbogforlaget.

Veljanovski, C. (1990) 'Market Driven Broadcasting: Not Myth But Reality', *Intermedia*, 18 (6): 17–21.

Williams, R. (1968) *Communications*. Harmondsworth: Penguin.

Wolton, D. (1992) 'Values and Choices in French Television', in J.G. Blumler (ed.), *Television and the Public Interest: Vulnerable Values in West European Broadcasting*. London: Sage.

7

SLAVES OF THE RATINGS TYRANNY?
Media Images of the Audience

Ingunn Hagen

In this chapter I will discuss what image various media hold of audiences or the general public. I will pay particular attention to the medium of television. Especially in a competitive situation like the multichannel environment, there are more desperate attempts to reach, maintain and measure audiences. Thus, media employees might feel that they are slaves of 'the ratings tyranny'.[1]

I choose to approach media perceptions of the audience on two levels. First, I will deal with notions of the public held by media employees like journalists and producers. In this part, I will concentrate particularly on media professionals involved in news production, an area that was the focus of many of the early, classical works on media images of the audience. Second, I will discuss how media institutions relate to the public. Here I will concentrate on TV institutions, since their interest in audiences has increased in recent years.

It is also possible to extract media conceptions of the audience from the way the media approach audiences in their texts and programmes. Through textual analysis one can discuss the media's implicit readers or viewers, or their particular discursive mode of address. However, I choose to limit my discussion to the images of the audience employed in the media by media professionals and in institutions interested in audience measurements. While discussing more general phenomena, I will draw most examples from the Norwegian context.

Thus, it may be necessary to give some sketchy background information about media availability and use in this country. In Norway, people spend over 5 hours and 9 minutes on mass media on an average day (Vaage, 1999). Most of this time is spent on TV, radio and newspapers. In 1998 the average time spent on TV viewing alone was 1 hour and 59 minutes (or 151 minutes, according to the TV meter report by the Market and

Media Institute [MMI], Rolland, 1999). Norwegians spend on average 1 hour 23 minutes daily on radio listening, while newspaper reading takes 34 minutes (Vaage, 1999). In Norway, there is a high number of newspapers per inhabitant (almost 200 papers for 4 million people) and one of the highest levels of newspaper consumption in the world. Thus, Norway has been characterized as a press nation, rather than a TV nation (cf. NOU, 1992). This is despite the fact that most of people's time is spent on TV viewing.

In Norway, NRK (the state-owned public service broadcasting institution) had a monopoly over radio from 1933 and over TV from 1960. This monopoly situation was broken in 1982, when the then conservative government opened up to allow for independent radio and TV. But even though cable and satellite channels have been available since the early 1980s, it was not until recently that more than half of the population had access to cable or satellite dishes. The second national TV channel, the commercial TV2, was established in 1992. By 1996, 90 per cent of the population could watch TV2, in addition to NRK. In the autumn of 1996, the second NRK channel started, resulting in NRK1 and NRK2. These structural changes and the increased competition are changing the relationship between broadcasting institutions and their audiences (cf. Syvertsen, 1997).

Media images of audiences

What images of audiences are held by media producers and journalists? The answers to this question may be extracted from interview accounts with these media actors, or from examining the work processes and practices of news production, and of other journalistic work or programme making. The essential question is to what degree various audience feedbacks and images are incorporated (or not) into the production process.

If one examines news production, for example, one can find both studies with a focus on the organizational level and studies with emphasis on the actors. Two studies, which often are described as classics within the field of news sociology, can illustrate these two levels of analysis. Both of these studies deal with journalistic work in newsrooms.

Epstein's study of newsrooms in American national TV networks – published in the book *News from Nowhere: Television and the News* (1973) – has an organizational perspective. The results from Epstein's book indicate that an institutional demand is to keep the audience; to have them 'stay tuned', rather than trying to keep them informed.

Another often quoted study is Gans' book *Deciding What's News* (1980 [1979]), in which he studied journalistic work in national news magazines and TV networks. As this analysis is more actor-oriented, news is perceived as a result of journalists' judgements. Journalists make their decisions based on, among other things, what they perceive as appropriate for the public. But as Gans writes about journalists' perceptions of the audience:

> I was surprised to find, however, that they had little knowledge about the actual audience and rejected feedback from it. Although they had a vague image of the audience, they paid little attention to it; instead they filmed and wrote for their superiors and for themselves, assuming [. . .] that what interested them would interest the audience (1980 [1979]: 230).

Thus, while journalists often claim to provide the audiences with what they need or want, their standards are often those of their professional peers. While independence from economic and political interests is important for journalists' autonomy, the lack of regard for the interests of the audience is more problematic. However, the question remains whether a clearer image of the audience would have impact on journalistic work.

It is common, as Gans (1980 [1979]) observed, to equate audiences' taste with the taste of producers. From such a perspective, producer autonomy will serve to guarantee diversity and quality for the audience (cf. Gentikow, 1997). Since programme makers are professionals, they know most about production conventions; technically, aesthetically and ethically. At its best, producer autonomy might result in programmes of high quality that are also popular. Examples of such programmes are some of the productions of the BBC and Channel Four, and also some of NRK's productions (e.g. the historical documentary series of the Norwegian war criminal and torturer Henry Rinnan, broadcast by NRK in 1996). Producer autonomy holds potential for both high quality programmes and innovations. However, producers' cultivation of their own artistic inclinations can also result in arrogance, and in unbridgeable gaps with the audience.

Media images of the audience obviously also play a role in the production of fictional programmes. In his book on the soap opera *Dynasty*, Gripsrud (1995) points to the relationship between the creator's images of the audience and the so-called 'implied' or 'model' readers who can be deduced from the programme itself. In fact, the primacy of the audience in the heads of Hollywood personnel – resulting, for example, in audience previews – is seen as a key to understand the success of many American audio-visual products. Thus, Gripsrud thinks that:

> The constant attention to how this or that element or scene will 'work' for an anticipated audience marks Hollywood's production culture in a variety of ways. Precisely because it is so integral to the culture, it may not even be explicated by writer-producers [. . .] the attention to audience response is a basic part of their knowledge of formal principles: they know from experience what 'works' with a serial's audiences and what doesn't. (1995: 57)

One way to secure heterogeneous audience images sufficient to match the heterogeneity of modern audiences is the collective production team so common in audio-visual productions. Such teams will know (often tacitly) from experience how to engage and entertain an audience, how to take into account their knowledge and expectations, and how to avoid being too provocatory (avoid objectionable programmes). The chief producer often tries to secure that the result of these various audience images, in programme production, will achieve maximum ratings.

When discussing media images of the audience or public one enters into one of the key issues of the social sciences – the relationship between structure (here: media institution) and actor (journalist, media employee). The point is that news and other media texts are produced in a hierarchical organization that limits the work of journalists and producers, while also providing opportunities for them. As Giddens formulates this: 'structure is not to be equated with constraint but is always both constraining and enabling' (1991 [1984]: 25). Giddens labels this 'the duality of structure'; a duality that has implications for the interaction between actor and structure (for a discussion of news journalism between structure and agency, see, e.g., Eide, 1992). The relationship between media professionals and media institutions may be characterized as both complementary and mutually dependent.

The image that media professionals and media institutions hold of the audience will be based on different types of experience and knowledge. One may distinguish between two ways of developing these images, related to two kinds of organizational learning (see Argyris and Schön, 1978).[2] In what can be characterized as single-loop learning, journalists develop their image of the audience within the institution and in cooperation with each other. Single-loop learning often implies that organizational norms and standards remain unchanged. Double-loop learning, on the other hand, means that media professionals and institutions get information from outside – such as from companies that provide audience measurement (the most important of these are now the TV meter panels in various countries). These different kinds of learning horizons could also be characterized as closed and open loops (see Sivertsen, 1987). Double-loop learning implies that new standards are developed. The single loop is clearly insufficient. In my view, the normal double loop also should be expanded in order to gain an adequate image of audiences. But first a look at the relatively closed single loop of media professionals.

Audiences as 'the missing link'[3]

Many researchers and others have pointed to the fact that journalists and other media professionals often lack knowledge about the audience (e.g., Burns, 1969, 1977; McQuail, 1969; Schlesinger, 1987 [1978]; Tuchman, 1978; Tunstall, 1971). In the Norwegian context, anthropological studies of newspaper production (Klausen, 1986; Siverts, 1983) and a study of informational TV broadcasting (Puijk, 1990) point to the same conclusion.

Also in a recent review of literature on media images of the audience, Ettema and Whitney (1994) conclude that professional mass communicators lack a clear or complete image of their audiences. There are also several classical studies which demonstrate that the image journalists and producers have of the audience is decisive for the message they produce (e.g. Bauer, 1964; Darnton, 1975; de Sola Pool and Shulman, 1964). In the struggle for high ratings, many employees in, for example, TV institutions develop a rather negative view of the audience. What Altheide characterizes as a cynical view of the audience is often the result: viewers are perceived as 'stupid, incompetent and unappreciative. From this perspective, viewers threaten the "success" of the news operation [. . .]' (Altheide, 1977 [1974]: 59).

Such negative images of the audience (or lack of interest in the audience?) relate to the increasing professionalization of journalists and other media employees. The fact that many journalists go through formal education is a sign of increasing professionalization, and so is the fact that there are active discussions about professional ethics amongst media employees. Increased professionalization often implies that expectations of greater autonomy also develop (cf. Johnstone et al., 1976). Thus, to meet demands and wishes from audiences is perceived as a threat to professional autonomy (see Schlesinger, 1987 [1978]). It is from colleagues that one can expect the most immediate and most qualified feedback. Darnton describes such a closed single-loop learning for newspaper journalists: 'With specialization and professionalization they have responded increasingly to the influence of their professional peer group, which exceeds that of any image they may have of the general public' (1975: 192). Thus, much research points in the direction that a more defined professional identity makes media professionals more concerned with peer evaluations than with that of audiences.

Regarding journalists' images or perceptions of the audience, several authors have pointed out that these often are subjective and intuitive, rather than based on audience research. Conceptions of the audience held by producers and journalists are often stereotypical, based on accidental meetings, on the bus, train or in their own canteen. Or they try to approach their idea of the 'ordinary man or woman'; perhaps their relatives or their neighbours. 'The milkman in Kansas' is an expression often used in American journalism textbooks in order to illustrate that one should write for a general audience. Appropriate for 'the dog of Mrs Hansen' is the expression the Norwegian author Jon Michelet used, in order to characterize the headlines in *VG*, the most widely circulated Norwegian tabloid newspaper (see Sande, 1989).[4] 'Don't produce for viewers above high school level' was the message to an acquaintance of mine who had internship in an American local TV station. The relationship with the public will also vary according to the actor's place in the hierarchy and function in the media organization. For example, Gans (1980 [1979]) observed that while producers and editors were concerned with the viewpoints of audiences, journalists were often more concerned with the relationship to their sources.

However, in production one indirectly has to take the audience into consideration, especially when facing increased competition. In a report from the newsroom in Danmarks Radio (the Danish public broadcasting institution), Pittelkow describes 'a development towards defining one's role more on the basis of the preconditions and (subjective) needs that one attempts to address in viewers' (1986: 188). This means a greater concern with the 'experiential value' of the news; with the way that news items engage viewers emotionally.

Another example can be drawn from Helland's (1988) interviews with some representatives from NRK.[5] One part of this study was the question of feedback and the role of audience research in the institution. The most important source of the partly imaginary relationship to the audience was from regular internal feedback from professional colleagues within NRK. Those with a background in production claimed that they were very concerned with the audience when producing; and that contact with the target group helped them in this regard. However, internal feedback, especially informal contacts with colleagues, was taken as the most valid. Another source of indirect, external feedback taken quite seriously was reviews in newspapers. The Broadcasting Council and debates in Parliament were also mentioned as sources of external, indirect feedback, supposedly important for the self-censorship practised in NRK. External, indirect feedback, in terms of phone calls and letters, was not taken as seriously as other kinds of feedback. Such responses were not seen as representative. An interesting observation in this limited study was that the interviewees did not mention the audience research carried out by NRK before they were specifically asked about it.

As indicated, a clear image of the audience is often a 'missing link' between media producers and the audience. For example, according to Schlesinger (1987 [1978]), those who produce TV news have little knowledge about the public's background and level of information. Except for audience measurements, which often provide information about ratings for a particular programme, there is little feedback about audiences to the producers. Some are also sceptical of the value of more detailed feedback: 'The pressure on those responsible for programmes is such that fuller or deeper analysis of audience reactions would amount to an intolerable strain' (Burns, 1977: 141). In my view, a clearer image of the audience could also reduce the stress, or at least the uncertainty, related to being a producer. Studies of audience reception, interpretation, experience, comprehensibility, fascination, identification and use can provide useful information. At this point I will continue by discussing the media organization's relationship to audiences from an institutional point of view.

Audience measurement and news

Like in many countries, in Norway broadcasting institutions have shown an increasing interest in the audience in recent years. Obviously, this relates to the liberal media policy that was initiated in the early 1980s, which abolished the TV monopoly of NRK. The 1980s and 1990s have been a period of deregulation, in which Norwegian TV has changed from being a regulated public business to becoming an industry (for a description of this development, see Syvertsen, 1997). The 1990s have been characterized as a period of media revolution (cf. Lundby and Futsæter, 1993), resulting in increased competition between the different television channels.

During the 1980s and 1990s NRK increased the frequency of its audience measurements – often taking the form of telephone interviews. These surveys were performed by the Norwegian Central Bureau of Statistics (SSB). In 1989 the listener and viewer surveys were taken over by the Market and Media Institute (MMI) (see Høst, 1993, 1998). In 1992 the Norwegian version of the much-debated TV meters was initiated, and earlier the same year the second national TV channel, the commercial TV2, was established.[6] The TV meter studies were and are still performed by the MMI, financed especially by NRK, TV2 and TVNorge (a Norwegian commercial channel, broadcast only through cable). The company Norsh Gallup is taking over the Norwegian TV meter panel at the end of 1999.

What is the reason for this great interest in the audience? Naturally, for a commercial channel audiences are the coin of exchange to draw advertising money. But the public service channel is also concerned with audience numbers, as an indirect source of its licence fee. Some critics claim that the broadcasting institutions carry out audience measurements based on their own interests, with little genuine interest to know their audiences. The main reason for the TV institutions to produce this knowledge is in order to control and conquer the audience (e.g. Ang, 1991; Gitlin, 1978). Let us examine the background for such claims.

In Norway, as indicated, the dissolution of the NRK monopoly changed the TV situation radically. Like in many countries with a state-owned public service broadcaster, NRK could take the audience for granted. The deregulation in 1982 changed its conditions radically by introducing competition. Thus, NRK had to be more concerned with the audiences than previously. While NRK does not have to compete for commercial reasons, it still has to maintain legitimacy (for a discussion of this situation facing NRK, see Gripsrud, 1986; Syvertsen, 1992a). The institution is faced with contradictory pressures: on the one hand, it needs a certain viewership, and thus has to compete with the commercial channels; but, on the other hand, NRK cannot become too similar to its competitors, because that would undermine the institution's privileged position as financed by a licence fee.

News broadcasts are often regarded as the flagship of TV stations, because they provide a legitimacy that few other programme genres are able to. Especially for public service channels – like NRK – news programmes have always been important for fulfilling their purpose, and also to build and maintain legitimacy with their audience. While the licence fee makes a public service channel like NRK less dependent on the 'normal' audience, the institution is dependent on the political authorities who decide about the licence fee. Despite the fact that NRK does not have to constantly consider high audience numbers, generally low ratings would clearly be a reason for questioning the licence fee.

Since news has great prestige, news departments often do not have the same economic limitations as other programme departments (cf. Puijk, 1990). Commercial channels – like, for instance, TV2 – also give their news broadcasts high priority. For commercial channels, news becomes an important means to 'have an audience to sell the advertisers', and to contribute to the general image building of the channel. In the public sphere, audience ratings for the newscast in particular become a measure of the success of the channel. But even though both a public service channel and a commercial broadcaster are preoccupied with the audience, there will be important differences in their interests.

Providing citizens with what they 'need'

Public service institutions like NRK often have a normative relationship to the audience; they provide audiences with what they 'need', what is good for them. The public service channel's relationship to the audience can be characterized by the fact that the institution is supposed to be culturally and socially responsible. The image of the audience is then that of a citizen; a citizen who primarily is supposed to be educated and informed (the enlightenment ideal), but also given experiences and entertainment. All of these factors are accounted for in NRK's programme rules, for example (for a further discussion, see Hagen, 1992a). The public service TV institutions see it as their task to enable the audience to perform their democratic rights and duties. Thus, the institution perceives the audience as rational citizens, concerned with collective problems and issues.

There is disagreement regarding a proper definition of the 'public service' concept. However, a common trait in several public service broadcasting definitions is that such institutions should serve societal goals (Søndergaard, 1992; for a problematization, see also Syvertsen, 1990, 1992a). In line with public sphere or democracy ideals, such institutions are supposed to make the audience into well-informed citizens who can participate in political and cultural debates and decisions (for a further discussion of the media's relationship to the public and for the audience's citizen role, see, e.g., Garnham, 1986; Golding, 1990; Murdock, 1990). This could be characterized as a public responsibility view of public TV. An example could be provided from Finland. In his discursive analysis of media policy documents regulating Finnish public TV, Silvo finds that there is an emphasis on 'public responsibility, common national, cultural and political values, unified audiences and democratic media politics' (1988: 275).

These expectations that the institution should inform the audience can be characterized as a fact or news genre contract. This notion of 'fact contract' is used, among others, by Bondebjerg (1989). Others, like Kjørup (1992), have questioned whether the notion of 'contract' is appropriate, since it is not mutually committing. However, there is an indirect contract, at least in the sense that audiences pay a licence fee to NRK for which they expect to get something in return. Moreover, the point is that historically, a relationship has developed between the public service broadcasting institution and the audience that forms the horizon of expectations that the audience brings to news and other programmes broadcast by that institution. From NRK, for example, audiences expect to get the most important news, presented in a balanced manner.

Most public service institutions, such as NRK and the BBC, for example, were established with enlightenment functions, supposed to provide audiences with 'worthwhile experiences'. One might then ask: what is worthwhile experience, and who decides this? The public service institutions' images of the audience vary historically and with national context. Previously NRK, like many public service institutions with a monopoly situation, had more of a paternalistic attitude towards the audience. In his discussion of the paternalistic phase of Danmarks Radio, Bondebjerg (1989) suggests an appropriate name for this phenomenon: 'school teachers' television'. An often quoted definition of a paternalistic system is as 'an authoritarian system with a conscience: that is to say, with values and purposes beyond the maintenance of its own power' (Williams, 1968: 117). Such broadcasting institutions have traditionally seen it as their duty to protect and guide the public; to communicate (often middle-class) values, habits and taste to the majority of the people. This resulted in an ideology of social responsibility with an almost missionary attitude towards the audience.

The legitimation of the state monopoly public service broadcasting policies is, as indicated, in terms of the 'needs' of the audience. These needs are often formulated such that the public are unaware of their 'real' needs. The assumption is that the public lack something that they might not be aware of. Thus, decision-makers can start from what they often regard as objective needs; what the audiences *should* want, if they were educated enough. In the early days of TV and radio in Europe, and particularly in social democratic Scandinavia, the broadcasting institutions were seen to promote indisputable 'quality culture' (see Bondebjerg, 1990). However, audiences did not always approve of what was available; the mocked symbol of dreary high culture in NRK was 'Finnish TV theatre'.

In the early days of Norwegian TV, this kind of emphasis on educational programming revealed itself in both programme selection and scheduling. Serious programmes dominated prime-time. The strategy seemed to be to fill prime-time with what the audience ought to watch. In the new multichannel situation, this strategy has been abandoned. Now the competition from both national and transnational channels forces the public service channels to take the audiences' interests more into account. In a recent 'goals and strategies' document by NRK (1996), these new concerns with the audience are illustrated. The institution still aims to be in the service of the public as a public arena for debate, information, culture, education and entertainment. But NRK also announces that the technological development has created demands for a service which is more oriented towards 'target groups and individual viewers' (1996: 4). The document states that 'NRK will put the interests and needs of the audience at the centre of its programme policy' (1996: 6). However, the strategy is self-contradictory too, as it is also stated that NRK plans a programme policy 'not dictated by economy or audience support' (1996: 6). Thus, while also trying to meet audiences' interests, NRK is still trying to maintain its freedom to define what audiences need. In the strategy document, it is seen as unfortunate if 'NRK develops to be more like the commercial channels [. . .]' (1996: 4).

Satisfying consumer's 'wants'

Prior to the establishment of the second Norwegian national channel, the commercial TV2, there was at least a decade of political controversy and a number of public documents debating the potential channel. Political parties were divided along right–left lines regarding having a TV channel financed by advertisement. The positive arguments for TV2 were nationalist: the new channel was supposed to create a national counter-pressure to the international cultural influence that the increasingly available satellite channels represented (cf. NOU, 1985). TV2 was supposed to strengthen Norwegian culture, identity, language and values. An alternative national news broadcast (to NRK's TV news – *Dagsrevyen*) was seen as important. Very little was said about other kinds of programmes, except that they should represent local and national culture.

A commercial TV institution – like Norwegian TV2 – must to a larger extent take into consideration what the audience 'want' and 'desire'. This notion of want is often promoted as offering the audience something extra, satisfying a desire that stems from the audiences themselves. Much commercial broadcasting, and other commercial media industries, uses a consumer sovereignty argument: if consumers did not like the product, they simply would not buy (watch) it. From such a perspective, the ultimate power is that of consumers or audiences. Thus, commercial institutions are concerned with popularity, expressed by high ratings or high numbers of readers.

A commercial broadcasting institution has as its goal to maximize the audience in order to maximize profit. Consequently, its relationship to the audience is guided by its attempt to reach large audiences. The audience become consumers in two ways: for TV programmes but also for advertised products (cf. McQuail, 1987). Thus, it is not only the maximum size audience that is the most interesting, but also the target groups with the maximum spending power (like the young and affluent).

Commercial broadcasting institutions often perceive the audience as individual consumers who take care of their personal interests (Søndergaard, 1992). In Norway, however, the commercial TV2 also has 'public service obligations' as part of its licence conditions. Still, one could argue that TV2, like other commercial broadcasters, is more responsive to advertisers than it is to its audience. While the arguments for introducing a second, commercial national channel in Norway focused on TV2's potential strengthening of Norwegian culture and identity (see Hagen, 1987), the channel's main programmes are light American entertainment series. However, TV2 also broadcasts news with an alternative to NRK's *Dagsrevyen* (a popular angle, often accused of being tabloid, with heavy emphasis on crime), and popular Norwegian entertainment programmes.[7]

For commercial channels, obviously audience ratings are much more important than for public service channels, since they provide the basis for their income from advertisements. Thus, the audience becomes a product to sell to advertisers. In principle, it is more important for them to get the public's attention and that they watch than that they become informed. But even though the commercial ideology is to 'give the audience what they want', news broadcasts are important for the channel's image building and credibility. Thus, it is quite accurate when the acting chief editor of TV2 characterized the news and actuality broadcast as the 'engine of TV2'.[8]

The main concern of commercial channels is to make people watch and to keep them watching. Thus, programme quality is reduced to popularity expressed by high ratings. When the goal is to avoid viewers zapping to another channel, the result is often to produce programmes that will not offend anyone, so-called 'Least Objectionable Programming' (LOP). According to Meyrowitz 'the key is to design a program that is least likely to be turned *off*, rather than a program viewers will actively seek out'(1985: 73). Public service channels are also concerned with LOP: in the words of the BBC in its 'Promise to Viewers and Listeners': 'We promise to keep in touch with our audiences' views on taste and decency and *not to cause widespread offence*' (BBC, 1997; emphasis added). However, for commercial channels, rather than caring about how people watch and what they get out of it, it is sufficient that they watch – so they are exposed to commercials. Thus, the logic of commercial broadcasting or of what Gentikow

(1997) calls 'consumer quality' is rooted in the needs of advertisers, not in the wants or desires of audiences.

Different logics: still searching for the audience

However, in the competitive situation a public service channel's role also becomes redefined: from serving the public sphere to more of a market situation. Even though a public service channel's role is based on political rationality – as a medium for the political and cultural public sphere – the institution also has to relate to the audience according to an economic logic, because the audience who are 'the public' are 'consumers' in another system.

Consequently, the relationship to the audience may develop the way Søndergaard describes for the Danish public service institution: 'Thus, audiences are defined not primarily through their political and social identity, but rather as individualized, private viewers' (1992: 49). One may interpret this as an indication of conflicting requirements within the organization.

Such conflicting norms motivate interest in sources outside the organization; for broadcasting institutions this is often an increased attention to audience measurement. This is also the case in Norway, where NRK's increasing interest in audience measurement could be interpreted as an indication of conflicting organizational norms. While competing with commercial channels, the public service channels also have to be something else. Such a promise is also given by the BBC, in their 'Promise to Viewers and Listeners': 'The more broadcasters you have to choose from, the more you might expect the BBC – the broadcaster you pay the licence fee – to provide something different' (BBC, 1997).

Audience measurements were originally developed to satisfy the interests of the American TV industry (for a discussion of this, see Gitlin's book *Inside Prime Time*, 1983). In the 1990s this kind of measurement has become very technically sophisticated, and great resources are spent measuring audiences.

The latest development are the earlier mentioned TV meters. Since the broadcasting institutions are dependent on the audience both for economic survival and for legitimacy, it is understandable that they constantly try to conquer and control the audience. The way TV institutions are organized, according to Williams, results in 'deep contradiction, of centralised transmission and privatised reception' (1974: 30). Since the broadcasting institutions get little feedback beyond audience measurements, they have to live with uncertainty about the audience. Several authors (e.g. Elliott, 1979; McQuail, 1969) emphasize this uncertainty. Exceptions in terms of feedback are the letters broadcasting institutions receive from audiences (cf. Bastiansen, 1991), as well as more public or official responses, as discussed earlier. Institutions also initiate studies of audience satisfaction related to the coverage of certain events, such as, for example, the Gulf War (see Bakke and Futsæter, 1991).

Within the broadcasting institution, the scientific status of audience measurements is often emphasized. Such measurements are interpreted as 'seemingly systematic, impersonal, reliable ways to predict success and failure' (Gitlin, 1983: 31). The numbers based on audience measurements are often used to legitimize decisions regarding programme policy (examples of such use of audience measurements are also mentioned in more classic studies, e.g. Burns, 1969). However, the role of audience measurement numbers is also contradictory. The measures often show accurate numbers for programme ratings. In Norway for example, the number watching the public service channel's news (NRK's *Dagsrevyen*) is almost double the number who watch the commercial channel's (TV2) news. But the size of the viewing audience does not necessarily indicate what the viewers are satisfied with. While *Dagsrevyen* has one of the highest ratings among NRK's programmes, only 6 per cent of the viewers thought it was a very good programme (Bakke and Eie, 1992). The audience statistics do not indicate what worked in the programme and what did not. Neither do the numbers normally give any indication of what motivated viewers to watch and what they got out of the programme (cf. Hagen, 1992a). Thus, audience measurement provides an insufficient basis for programme planning and production, unless the aim is only to provide audiences for advertisers.

Beyond ratings

In Norway, like in many other countries with a state-owned public service broadcaster, the public service institution NRK has to relate to a commercial logic, due to the competition with the commercial TV2 (and satellite channels). The other main actor, TV2, is commercial, but also has public service obligations. However, both in order to 'serve the audience' as citizens and to 'give the audience what they want', one must have knowledge of the audience. In Norway, few studies address how TV journalists or producers conceive the audience. But based on Anglo-American research one can assume that they know little about the audiences they approach. Such uncertainty can be an extra stress factor for journalists and producers. Professional identity, on the other hand, functions as a buffer against this strain.

In order to handle this uncertainty, there are, according to McQuail (1969), some frequently used strategies. First, there is specialization, where the broadcaster aims specialized programmes at the interests and needs of known audience groups. Second, there is the increasing professionalization among media employees, which McQuail sees as a problem if it is not simultaneously combined with strong ideals about serving the audience, and an interest in meeting audiences' expectations. A third strategy that originated in a lack of knowledge about audiences is ritualization and routinization, which means a tendency to maintain well-known recipes for what seems to appeal to the audience. Such 'more of the same' thinking is in line with the single-loop learning perspective. It is easy to imitate English or American programme concepts, either regarding the news format or other programme genres. But such attempts to 'play safe' can inhibit creative experimentation in the broadcasting institutions. It hinders the development of qualitatively new programme concepts and images of audiences.

In a situation where a commercial logic is increasing its impact, broadcasting institutions will, as I have suggested, become more concerned with the audience. Such developments will also impact on actors in broadcasting institutions. According to Gallagher (1982), such changes in organizations will have consequences for journalists' and other employees' attitudes, ideals and values. The point is that images that originate in the institution can be experienced and expressed as the actor's professional guidelines. However, new challenges to the institutions can also provide potentials for getting more in-depth knowledge about audiences, beyond perceptions of the audience as market, and numbers. This will again have consequences for the institution.

In order to fulfil democratic ideals, media institutions need to engage audiences. Thus, journalism and media production have to mobilize feelings, to create identification, and to make the material comprehensible. This requires that one has an adequate image of the audiences, in all their nuances. One of the greatest mistakes in communication is to imagine the receiver in stereotypical terms, or to regard the receiver as similar to oneself (for a discussion of this related to news journalism, see Reinton, 1992). Good journalism, at least, requires that one knows whom one is addressing. Furthermore, if broadcasting institutions are to function democratically, the audiences' 'needs' and communication rights must be taken care of (Williams, 1968, among others, discusses this democratization of broadcasting institutions). Since democracy is such a taken-for-granted 'God word', there is also a need to discuss what democratic communication might mean (see Hagen, 1986, 1992c). However, the danger occurs when commercial logic becomes master, overriding democratic concerns.

In the monopoly situation, a public service broadcasting institution like NRK could afford to have single-looped learning in the organization. The organizational norms were more fixed. In the competitive situation, both public service and commercial broadcasting organizations face conflicting norms. NRK needs high ratings to legitimate the licence, while TV2 needs high ratings to sell to advertisers. Both risk being slaves of the ratings tyranny; ratings are uniformly taken as a sign of success, both by the TV institutions themselves and by other media. However, in order to secure organizational survival and organizational development (double-loop learning), broadcasting institutions have to satisfy their audience. But what characterizes the audience? And what will satisfy, fascinate, inform and entertain them? In order to take these questions seriously, broadcasting institutions need new sources of insight about audiences. By enlarging the double loop, the institutions can also be a potential for their agents, as well as a developing organization.

In my view, the more open double loop of media institutions is also insufficient. But as Argyris and Schön (1978) pointed out, it is possible to have organizational learning that is more or less double-looped. Broadcasting institutions may benefit from supplying audience statistics with results and insights from newer audience research, especially reception studies and ethnographic media research.[9] Knowledge from such studies should be continually communicated to journalists and other producers. Increased attention to the audience should imply a real interest in understanding audiences, beyond being categories in audience statistics. Then images of audiences might provide a basis for media production. Better substantiated images of audiences would also modify the dependency on ratings. Hence, such knowledge will probably be liberating for media professionals, rather than functioning like a structural strait-jacket.

In their book *Audience Making*, Ettema and Whitney (1994) raise the question of whether a clearer image of the audience would matter. They refer to research that indicates that a clear 'product image' might have larger consequences for individual producers. However, audience images will reappear in organizational strategies and in interactions within the institution. Thus, audience measurements will probably be on the desk of media planners when deciding whether a particular programme should continue to be produced. For this purpose they will continue procedures – like the TV meter – for 'knowing the audience', or rather knowing what programme the audience will watch. But it should be kept in mind that this construction of the audience – this particular institutional 'making of the audience' – serves the institution's interests and purposes. Thus, TV and other media institutions will not necessarily provide audiences with what they desire. The purpose of 'knowing' the audience is to shape them into predictable markets. Especially for commercial channels, audiences are thought of as the 'coin of exchange'. In the process of catering for the market, the form and content of media output will be shaped.

Conclusion

In this chapter I have discussed the institutional concept of audiences; the institutions' perception or image of the audience, not the actual audiences. It has been common knowledge in rhetorics, from Aristotle onward, that communicators need to know their audience. Audience ratings, based on TV meters – the latest kind of TV audience measurement – are probably TV's main institutional way to 'know' audiences. However, lately there have been increasing attempts, also by the research departments in the broadcasting institutions themselves, to do more qualitative studies of audiences' taste, preferences and reactions, often to specific programmes (e.g. Hake, 1995a, 1995b, 1996).

I think qualitative studies can provide more detailed information about how and why audiences use different media – like TV – and especially what they experience as benefit from this. Docherty et al., in their book on Channel Four's audiences, suggest the following about qualitative audience research:

> The rationale behind such research is that one can strip away layers of superficial responses and begin to peer into the more complex, certainly more subtle, not always consistent construction of the public mind. (1988: 2)

However, it still matters how this knowledge is used and acknowledged within the institutional arrangement and organizational strategies. The point is, as Ettema and Whitney (1994) emphasize, that the institutional interest in actual audiences is to reconstitute them as institutionally effective audiences that have social meaning and economic value in the system. One example is measured audiences that TV channels can sell to advertisers. Another such version is the segmented or target group audiences, who are anticipated to appreciate certain content – and to be potential consumers of accompanying advertised products.

Such institutional, discursive constructs of the audience can be contrasted with the real or social audience (cf. Höijer, this volume). However, qualitative audience research is also an institutional attempt to depict actual audiences, by academic scholars or by researchers in the broadcasting institutions. Examples of such research are focusing on how audiences use and integrate various media into their everyday lives, and what meaning, often contradictory, they attribute to such practices (cf. Hagen, 1992a, 1995, 1996, 1999).

However, the audience also operate with a concept or image of the audience, often an ideal or norm that they judge their own habits against. Höijer (this volume) prefers to call how audiences perceive themselves as audiences 'metacognitions'. One example of such metacognitions are the moral evaluations that viewers make of their media habits, and especially their TV viewing (see, Alasuutari, 1996; Hagen, 1996, 1999). Another such norm is the elevated status attributed to news, often perceived as a social duty (Hagen, 1992a).

The point is that audience images are always inscribed: the institutional according to institutional goals; the academic according to methodological and other scientific (theoretical) discourses; and the audience's image according to cultural codes for good taste and decent lifestyles, that is, according to moral hierarchies in the culture. As Moores reminds us: 'There is no stable entity, which we can isolate and identify as the media audience, no single object that is unproblematically "there" for us to observe and analyze' (1993: 1–2). Thus, while institutions can broaden their concept of the audience through more qualitative research, academics have a challenge in interpreting such audience images, where actual audiences relate themselves to cultural discourses related to specific media, and of audiencehood.

In the multichannel situation, a notion is developing that the licence fee gives audiences a right to expect the broadcasting institution to take their opinion seriously. This notion can be exemplified by the BBC's 'Promise to Viewers and Listeners': 'Viewers and listeners pay for our services and therefore they expect us to take account of their views' (BBC, 1997). Perhaps more broadcasting institutions should learn from this. But the challenge remains: to take proper account of audiences' views, and to let new understandings have implications for institutional practices.

Notes

I would like to express appreciation to Pertti Alasuutari, Dan Y. Jacobsen, Øivind Hagen and Birgitta Höijer for constructive comments on earlier drafts of this chapter.

1. Such feelings were expressed by several of the main executives working in different TV channels during a session called 'The Ratings Tyranny?' at the biannual conference 'Nordiske TV-dager' (Nordic TV Days), Bergen, 1994.
2. I base this part of the argument on the concepts used by Argyris and Schön in their book *Organizational Learning: A Theory of Action Perspective* (1978). These authors build, among others, on Gregory Bateson's theory.
3. This subheading was inspired by the title of a chapter about journalists' relationship to the audience, 'The Missing Link: "Professionalism" and the Audience', in Schlesinger's book *Putting 'Reality' Together* (1987 [1978]).
4. Hansen is one of the most common Norwegian family names.
5. The interviewees consisted of five NRK employees, including two producers/programme directors, two managers with a background in production, and one researcher from NRK's research department.
6. The TV meter measurement was started by the MMI on 1 January 1992 to satisfy NRK's increasing interest in audience measurements. TV2 went on air on 5 September that same year.
7. One example of Norwegian TV2's entertainment productions is the situation comedy *Mot i brøstet* (Bravery) – a very popular slapstick serial with three men living together. Another example is the popular soap opera *Syv søstre* (Seven Sisters), produced with the assistance of Swedish soap opera producers. This soap – taking up numerous taboos in Norwegian society (like homosexuality, immigrants, 'Lebensborn' children – born of German fathers) – has been one of TV2s main attractions on Saturday evenings. Finally, the production *Bot og bedring* (Fines and Improvements) is another humorous serial, where the characters are traffic wardens.
8. This acting chief editor of TV2 was Finn H. Andreassen, interviewed in *Bergens Tidende*, a regional newspaper in Norway (3 May 1995).

9. Elsewhere, I provide an elaborate discussion and examples of reception analysis (Hagen, 1992a, 1993, 1995, 1996, 1998, Hagen and Wasko, 1999) and I also discuss the relationship between reception theory and ethnographic media research (Hagen, 1992b).

References

Alasuutari, P. (1996) 'Television as a Moral Issue', in I. Crawford and S.B. Hafsteinsson (eds), *The Construction of the Viewer: Media Ethnography and the Anthropology of Audiences*. Højberg, Denmark: Intervention Press.

Altheide, D.L. (1977 [1974]) *Creating Reality: How TV News Distorts Events*. London: Sage.

Ang, I. (1991) *Desperately Seeking the Audience*. London: Routledge.

Argyris, C. and Schön, D.A. (1978) *Organizational Learning: A Theory of Action Perspective*. London: Addison-Wesley.

Bakke, M. and Eie, B. (1992) *Sammenhengen mellom programstatestikk og oppslutning om programmer fjernsynet 1991* [. NRKs Forskningsavdeling, 15 February.

Bakke, M. and Futsæter, K.-A. (1991) *NRK fjernsynets dekning av Gulfkrigen: Fakta eller forståelse?* [NRK/Forskningsseksjonen. Notat 91.

Bastiansen, H.G. (1991) 'Nye muligheter for resepsjonsperspektiver i fjernsynsforskningen: det nye seerbrevarkivet i NRK.'[*Om filminnport, seerbrev, kilder og 60-åra*. Levende bilder, Nr 3.

Bauer, R.A. (1964) 'The Communicator and the Audience', in L.A. Dexter and D.M. White (eds), *People, Society, and Mass Communications*. London: Collier-Macmillan.

BBC (1997) BBC Statement of Promises to Viewers and Listeners: 'Our Commitment to You'. http://www.bbc.co.uk/info/promises.htm.

Bondebjerg, I. (1989) 'Oppbruddet fra monopolkulturen: En institusjons- og programhistorisk analyse av dansk tv' *Sekvens – Filmvidenskabelig Årbog*. pp 175–95

Bondebjerg, I. (1990) 'Paternalism, Modernism and Postmodernism: The Changing of Public Service TV', in T. Syvertsen (ed.), *1992 and After: Nordic Television in Transition*. Conference report, Nordiske TV-dager.

Burns, T. (1969) 'Public Service and Private World', in P. Halmos (ed.), *The Sociology of Mass-Media Communicators*. The Sociology Review Monograph No. 13, January.

Burns, T. (1977) *The BBC: Public Institutions and Private World*. London: Macmillan.

Darnton, R. (1975) 'Writing News and Telling Stories', *Dædalus*, 104 (2): 175–95

de Sola Pool, I. and Shulman, I. (1964) 'Newsman's Fantasies, Audiences and Newswriting', in L.A. Dexter and D.M. White (eds), *People, Society, and Mass Communications*. London: Collier-Macmillan.

Docherty, D., Morrison, D.E. and Tracey, M. (1988) *Keeping Faith? Channel Four and its Audience*. London: John Libbey.

Eide, M. (1992) *Nyhetens interesse: Nyhetsjournalistikk mellom tekst og kontekst*. Oslo: Universitetsforlaget.

Elliott, P. (1979) *The Making of a Television Series: A Case Study in the Sociology of Culture*. London: Constable.

Epstein, E.J. (1973) *News from Nowhere: Television and the News*. New York: Random House.

Ettema, J.S. and Whitney, C.D. (1994) 'The Money Arrow: An Introduction to Audiencemaking', in J.S. Ettema and C.D. Whitney (eds), *Audience Making: How the Media Create the Audience*. London: Sage.

Gallagher, M. (1982) 'Negotiations of Control in Media Organizations and Occupations', in M. Gurevitch, T. Bennett, J. Curran, and J. Woollacott (eds), *Culture, Society and the Media*. London: Methuen.

Gans, H. (1980 [1979]) *Deciding What's News: A Study of CBS Evening News, NBC Nightly News, Newsweek and Time*. New York: Vintage Books.

Garnham, N. (1986) 'The Media and the Public Sphere', in P. Golding, G. Murdock and P. Schlesinger (eds), *Communicating Politics: Mass Communications and the Political Process*. Leicester: Leicester University Press.

Gentikow, B. (1997) 'The Viewer's Voice in the Discussion of Quality', in M. Eide, B. Gentikow and K. Helland (eds), *Quality Television*. Department of Media Studies, University of Bergen.

Giddens, A. (1991 [1984]) *The Constitution of Society: Outline of the Theory of Structuration*. Cambridge: Polity Press.

Gitlin, T. (1978) 'Media Sociology: The Dominant Paradigm', *Theory and Society*, 6 (2): 205–51.

Gitlin, T. (1983) *Inside Prime Time*. New York: Pantheon Books.

Golding, P. (1990) 'Political Communication and Citizenship: The Media and Democracy in an Inegalitarian Social Order', in M. Ferguson (ed.), *Public Communication: The New Imperatives. Future Directions for Media Research*. London: Sage.

Gripsrud, J. (1986) 'Commercialism and Television: Notes on a Norwegian (?) Dilemma', *Screen*, 3/4: 88–98.

Gripsrud, J. (1995): *The Dynasty Years: Hollywood Television and Critical Media Studies*. London: Routledge.

Hagen, I. (1986) 'A Theoretical Discussion of the Concept of Democratic/Participatory Communication in Light of the Demands for a "New World Information and Communication Order" (NWICO)'. Master's thesis, University of California, Santa Barbara.

Hagen, I. (1987) *Premisser for et regionalt sendeselskap*. Report written for VEST-TV, a regional TV company, Bergen.

Hagen, I. (1992a) *News Viewing Ideals and Everyday Practices: The Ambivalences of Watching Dagsrevyen*. University of Bergen, Department of Mass Communication, Report No. 15.

Hagen, I. (1992b) *Fjernsynsresepsjon, kvardagsliv og familiesamvær: Ei etnografisk studie av publikums fjernsynssjåing i ein fleirkanalsituasjon* [Television Reception, Everyday Life and Family Interaction: An Ethnographic Study of Audiences Television Viewing in a Multi-Channel Situation]. Project Proposal.

Hagen, I. (1992c) 'Democratic Communication: Media and Social Participation', in J. Wasko and V. Mosco (eds), *Democratic Communications in the Information Society*. Toronto: Garamond Press.

Hagen, I. (1995) *The Morality of TV Viewing: Dilemmas in People's Everyday Lives*. Paper presented to the 12th Nordic Conference for Mass Communication Research. Helsingör, 12–15 August.

Hagen, I. (1996) 'TV-titting som moralsk dilemma', in G. Iversen, S. Kulset and K. Skretting (eds), *'As Time Goes By': Festtidsskrift til Bjørn Sørenssen's 50-årsdag*. Trandheim: Tapir.

Hagen, I. (1998) *Medias Publikum: Frå mottakar til brukar?* Oslo: Ad Notam, Gyldendal.

Hagen, I. (1999) 'Modern Dilemmas: TV Audiences, Time Use and Moral Evaluations'. Paper presented to the 20th Scientific Conference of the International Association for Mass Communication Research (IAMCR), Sydney, Australia, 1996. Under publication in I. Hagen and J. Wasko (eds), *Consuming Audiences? Production and Reception in Media Research*. Hampton Press.

Hagen, I. and Wasko, J. (1999) 'Introduction', in I Hagen and J. Wasko (eds), *Consuming Audiences? Production and Reception in Media Research*. Hampton Press. Under publication.

Hake, K. (1995a) *Åtte & 1/2: Et nærstudium av ungdommers reaksjoner*. NRK Forskningen, Rapport nr 5.

Hake, K. (1995b) *Barne-TV i barneperspektiv: En studie av småbarns opplevelser*. NRK Forskningen, Rapport nr 7.

Hake, K. (1996) *'Baywatch er bare klisjé': Samtaler om fjernsyn med 10- og 14-åringer. En kvalitativ undersøkelse* [. NRK Forskningen, Rapport nr 1.

Helland, K. (1988) 'Constraints in Commercial and Public Service Television Related to the Discussion on a Second Norwegian Television Channel'. MA thesis, Centre for Mass Communication Research, University of Leicester.

Høst, S. (1993), *Dialig mediebruk – en oppdatert oppdatering*. [Daily Media Use – An Updated Updating] Publication No. 41, Møre og Romsdal DH, Volda.

Høst, S. (1998), *Dialig mediebruk* [Daily Media Use] Oslo: Pax Forlag A/S.

Jenson, K.B. (1986) *Making Sense of the News: Towards a theory and an Empirical Model of Reception for the Study of Mass Communication*. Aarhus: Aarhus University Press.

Johnstone, J.W.C., Slawski, E.J. and Bowman, W.W. (1976) *The News People: A Sociological Portrait of American Journalists and Their Work*. London: University of Illinois Press.

Kjørup, S. (1992) 'Faktion – en farlig blanding!' *Mediekultur*, 19: 62–72

Klausen, A.M. (1986) *Med Dagbladet til tabloid: En studie i dilemmaet 'børs og katedral'*. Oslo: Gyldendal Norsk Forlag.

Lundby, K. and Futsæter, K.A. (1993) *Flerkanalsamfunnet: Fra monopol til mangfold*. Oslo: Universitetsforlaget.

Meyrowitz, J. (1985) *No Sense of Place: The Impact of Electronic Media on Social Behavior*. Oxford: Oxford University Press.

McQuail, D. (1969) 'Uncertainty About the Audience and the Organization of Mass Communications', in P. Halmos (ed.), *The Sociology of Mass-Media Communicators*. The Sociology Review Monograph No. 13, January.

McQuail, D. (1987) *Mass Communication Theory: An Introduction*. 2nd edn. Beverly Hills: Sage.

Moores, S. (1993) *Interpreting Audiences: The Ethnography of Media Consumption*. London: Sage.

Murdock, G. (1990) 'Medier, offentlighed og marked' *Mediekultur*, 13: 82–102

NOU (1985) *TV2: Om etablering av en ny permanent riksdekkende fjernsynskanal*. Oslo: Universitetsforlaget.

NOU, (1992) *Mål og midler i pressepolitikken*. Oslo: Statens forvaltningsteneste.

NRK (1996) *NRKs mål og strategi 1996–2000* [NRK's goals and strategies 1996–2000]. NRK, Oslo.

Pittelkow, R. (1986) *TV-Avisen set indefra*. Internal Strategy Document. Copenhagen: Danmarks Radio, Forskningsrapport nr 7b [The TV News Seen From Within].

Puijk, R. (1990) *Virkeligheter i NRK: Programproduksjon i fjernsynets Opplysningsavdeling*. Lillehammer. R. Puijk. Private publication.

Reinton, P.O. (1992) *Undersøkende formidling: Den journalistiske formel.* Oslo: Universitetsforlaget.

Rolland, A. (1999) *Norsk TV-Meterpanel, Årsrapport 1998.* Oslo: MMI

Sande, Ø. (1989) *Nyheter, forståelse og kunnskapskløfter.* Volda: Møre og Romsdal distriktshøgskule, Publikasjon Nr 14.

Schlesinger, P. (1987[1978]) *Putting 'Reality' Together: BBC News.* London: Methuen.

Silvo, I. (1988) *Valta, kentt, ja kertomus* [Power, Field and Narrative]. YLE, Report no. 2.

Siverts, O.B. (1983) 'Nyheter i BT? Endrings- og vedlikeholdsprosesser i Vestlandets storavis'. [News in BT? Change and Stability Processes in the Regional Newspaper of Western Norway]. M.A. Thesis. Department of Social Anthropology, University of Bergen.

Sivertsen, E. (1987) *Det spissformulerte pressebildet.* Arbeidsrapport nr 3, Institutt for massekommunikasjon, Universitetet i Bergen.

Søndergaard, H. (1992) 'Det "Moderniserede" public service-koncept i DR's TV', *Mediekultur,* 17: 45–61.

Syvertsen, T. (1990) 'Kringkasting i 1990-åra: Hvem er mest "public service"?', in U. Carlsson (ed.), *Medier, Månniskor, Samhålle. Nordicom-Nytt/Sverige* 3–4. Göteborg.

Syvertsen, T. (1992a) 'Public Television in Transition: A Comparative and Historical Analysis of the BBC and the NRK'. PhD thesis, Centre of Mass Communication Research, University of Leicester.

Syvertsen, T. (1992b) 'Serving the Public: Public Television in Norway in a New Media Age.' *Media, Culture & Society,* 14. (2): 229–45.

Syvertsen, T. (1997) *Den store TV-krigen: Norsk allmennfjernsyn 1988–96.* Bergen: Fagbokforlaget.

Tuchman, G. (1978) *Making News: A Study in the Construction of Reality.* London: Collier-Macmillan.

Tunstall, J. (1971) *Journalists at Work: Specialist Correspondents: Their News Organizations, News Sources, and Competitor-Colleagues.* London: Constable.

Vaage, O.F. (1996) *Kultur og medievaner: Bruk av kulturtilbud og massemedier i første halvdel av 1990-årene.* Oslo-Kongsvinger: Statistics Norway.

Vaage, O.F. (1999) *Norsk mediebarometer 1995.* Oslo-Kongsvinger: Statistics Norway.

Williams, R. (1968) *Communications.* London: Penguin Books.

Williams, R. (1974) *Television: Technology and Cultural Form.* London: Fontana.

8

THE IMPLIED AUDIENCE IN SOAP OPERA PRODUCTION
Everyday Rhetorical Strategies Among Television Professionals

John Tulloch

In his Introduction to this book, Pertti Alasuutari emphasizes that 'third generation' reception studies needs, on the one hand, to move past an 'obsession' with the 'determinate moments' of encoding/decoding that characterized Stuart Hall's important 'first generation' work, and, on the other hand, to broaden the emphasis on the audience's 'everyday' of 'second generation' 'active audience' studies. 'Third generation' reception analysis should be

> interested in the discourses within which we conceive of our roles as the public and the audience, and how notions of programmes-with-an-audience or mes-sages-with-an-audience are inscribed in both media messages and assessments about news events and about what is going on in the 'world'. The third gener-ation resumes an interest in programmes and programming, but not as texts studied in isolation from their usage as an element of everyday life.

This chapter tries to meet Alasuutari's 'third generation' agenda, retying audiences and programming. But here the everyday life concentrated on is that of the producers of the programmes as they imply their audiences in constructing their texts. The chapter addresses Alasuutari's call for 'questions about the frames within which we conceive of the media and their contents as reality and as representations – or distortions – of reality. And [about] how [. . .] these frames or discourses about the programmes and about viewing and audiences [are] inscribed in the programmes themselves.'

Because a soap opera works especially strongly at the popular ratings edge of television, the frames and discourses dominant in international commercial television are strong. But, as this chapter will demonstrate, other less expected frames – of quality and 'Shakespeare', of an emphasis on current one-parent and step-parent family audiences conceived to be looking for something 'less sentimentalizing than *The Brady Bunch*', of current social issues like unemployment, AIDS and drug cultures – are important frames of popular soap opera too. To avoid an 'obsession with the determining moment' it is just as important to trace the very rich contexts and processes of these frames and discourses in the 'everyday' of television production as it is in television audiences. While inevitably, for heuristic reasons, we must deal with determining moments – with, for example, an actor's or a director's concern that a particular moment of performance 'isn't working' – it is important to situate these moments in their time and space co-ordinates, to understand them in processes of dialogic negotiation between professional and other rhetorics. We need to understand the frames within which these rhetorics are set if, as Alasuutari asks, we are to shed light on 'the big picture' of 'the cultural concerns that surround media use and media messages'.

This chapter does not, as Alasuutari warns, think it can 'outwit the native informant simply because of an outsider's view'. Indeed, the intelligences of television practitioners are the warp and weft of the chapter's analysis. On the other hand, though, we must recognize that our own analytical concern *with* those 'big picture' questions must also be worked through our dialogue with those intelligences, both reflexively positioning them and being positioned by them. Alasuutari is right to point out that the frames we use as analysts, the 'audiencing' frames of television makers, and the frames used by audiences in accounting for and justifying their viewing habits all tell us about 'embedded moralities of everyday life and media use'.

This, as he says, is a sociological perspective which emphasizes a '"discursive" view on talk' which tells us 'most of all, about the discourses within which the media are discussed'. Our particular focus in this chapter – within this broader frame of 'third generation' analysis – is on everyday rhetorical strategies which 'imply' audiences in the television industry. It focuses especially on the frames that professionals use to account for and justify their production habits of 'audiencing'.

As Alasuutari says, the 'third generation is already here'. This chapter has its background in earlier ethnographic work I have conducted in analysing a soap opera's textual positioning of 'youth unemployment' and young people's reading of this television 'realism'; and also other work on science fiction production and audiences. But here the focus is much more specifically on the discursive frames that operate in popular television in attempting to position implied audiences. At the same time, the chapter is determinedly empirical because, while trying to be reflexively theoretical rather than empiricist, I agree with Alasuutari that this is the best way to counter our tendency as researchers to be 'blinded by [our] own fears and concerns', our own particular moral tales.

'Third generation' ethnography

In the late 1980s I conducted ethnographic research at what was at the time Australia's leading prime-time soap opera, *A Country Practice* (*ACP*) (Tulloch and Moran, 1986). If asked why this was 'ethnographic' research, I would argue it was ethnographic in the fairly standard sense that it was attempting to understand holistically the socio-cultural processes, patterns and practices of groups of people in their natural setting. But that sentence itself needs some unpacking and framing:

- 'understanding' here includes an emphasis on subjective reflexivity;
- 'process' includes an emphasis on the competing rhetorics and intertexts that define social situations; and
- 'holistic' emphasizes the understanding of everyday interaction within its broader sociological context of 'discourses within which the media are discussed'.

In this case, the ethnographic study consisted of several months of observation of professional television work practices at a production house (JNP Films) and a television studio (Channel 7, Sydney).

Ethnography attempts to provide a dynamic account of everyday life within a cultural group, describing not only what we do, but also the rhetorics, schemas and mythologies by which we make our actions meaningful. Thus, for example, during the period this book describes as 'second generation' audience studies, ethnography was drawn on to examine the function of media in the everyday life of the audience. The 'third generation' audience study that is the aim of this book needs in addition an ethnography of production, because that is where the implied audience is *practised* (as subjectively reflexive action and as competing rhetorics and intertexts) in the everyday routines of television professionals.

Like 'second generation' audience ethnography, production ethnography must be concerned with human behaviour that occurs within a broader socio-cultural context of time/space co-ordinates. In terms of spatial context, for example, a television production house that is making a 'medical soap opera', like JNP, never implies its audiences in isolation from a larger context, which includes commercial television channels, actual audiences and professional organizations like the Australian Medical Association. In terms of time co-ordinates, implied audiences are constructed sequentially in the context of the rhetorical strategies and intertexts of master plans, forward planning meetings, ratings periods, actors' availability, networking and scheduling demands, the timing of commercial breaks, and so on.

So when an AIDS text is constructed within this particular socio-cultural group, its messages are 'processed' and its audiences are implied according to the rhetorical strategies generated in these broader contexts of space and time. It is, as Elam (1989: 1–26) notes, these rhetorical strategies which put in place (*mise en scène*) textual meaning as understood within production cultures . Ethnography's emphasis on process and the everyday can then be understood in terms of the competing rhetorics and intertexts that define the daily work practice of television professionals. Audiences are implied by way of a 'showing forth' in professional practice of these rhetorics and intertexts in television work practice. This 'showing forth' takes place via both speech acts and routine activity, giving the ethnographer access to what Bakhtin calls 'living utterance'.

As Bakhtin says, 'living utterance, having taken meaning and shape in a particular historical moment in a socially specific environment, cannot fail to brush up against thousands of living dialogic threads [. . .] cannot fail to become an active participant in a social dialogue' (1984: 276). In work on HIV/AIDS interviewing, Hassin has drawn on Bakhtin to argue that 'in dialogue, past and present experiences and divergent ideologies are incorporated into a continually developing, ongoing process in which the speaker negotiates her/his voice' (Hassin, 1994: 394) – as between, in this case for example, the 'dominant ideology' of social outcast and an alternative discourse as responsible agent. Interviewing can thus give access to the 'social dialogue' that marks the multiple subjectivities of an interviewee, whether as a person living with AIDS (PLWA, the subject of Hassin's research), as an individual audience member watching an AIDS text (Tulloch and Lupton, 1997: ch. 10), or as a television professional involved in making that text. Equally, ethnography can give access to the 'thousands of [other] living dialogic threads' within the time/space co-ordinates of a television production. Here *many* 'speakers' negotiate 'voice' through a number of communication modes (writing, set design, lighting, directing, acting, etc.), professional idiolects and time/space determinants.

Production, time/space and intertextuality

The implied audience of a popular television production must always be conceived within commercial frames. But as this section will demonstrate, there will always be other frames for implying audiences too. Soap opera characteristically deals with medical and 'social issue' stories; consequently these will also frame the narratives (e.g. 'how can we warn the young audience about the new risks of needle-sharing?'). To see these implied audiences at work, I have chosen to focus here on a soap opera AIDS story.

By the time of the study, *ACP* had been attracting high ratings for seven years, and was soon to become Australia's longest running drama series. High ratings are, of course, the most central time/space co-ordinates of commercial television. A successful prime-time show must penetrate as many different cultural/demographic spaces as possible in order to aggregate an audience; and it must maintain those ratings over time as other channels throw top-rating programmes against it (at this time, for example, another commercial channel tried programming the very high-rating American situation comedy *The Cosby Show* against *ACP*).

In the view of its executive producer, James Davern, *ACP*'s success as 'the longest running serial in Australia's history' depended on

- *Its demographics*: It was successful in attracting audiences across a broad age-range from teenagers to over-65s by use of age-focused sub-plots and characterization, so that whereas other temporarily successful soap operas which were aimed at a younger audience (*Sons and Daughters*) or older age groups (*Carson's Law*) had been taken off the air, *ACP* continued for over a decade.
- *Its story line*: This satisfied the voracious time demands of commercial 'two hours a week' television by way of its hospital drama ('where stories just walk in the door'); but in addition a pastoral myth of Australian space was incorporated – Davern believed that 'in the subconscious of every Australian there's a yearning for the country. [. . .] I decided to tap into that subconscious by setting the serial in a country town' (Tulloch and Moran, 1986: 28).
- *The budget allocated to writing*: This attracted some of the best film, stage and TV writers in Australia to script its 'serious issues' stories as well as its romances.
- *Its series/serial formula*: Serial romances and ongoing daily events ('soap') were woven through the formula of a weekly two-part ('social issues') series; consequently throughout the industry – for example with set designers, audio directors, floor managers, directors, actors, etc., – *ACP* was seen as 'quality soap', calling for an especially high professionalism.

However, at the time of producing its HIV/AIDS story, 'Sophie', *ACP* was operating under the financial restrictions of the new Christopher Skase management at Channel 7, reducing overtime at the studio. Further, a drop in advertising revenues had, according to script editor Forrest Redlich, necessitated more forward planning in order to produce tighter storylines around the regular characters. The feeling in the production team was that they had to work harder, and be more organized, to continue to keep *ACP*'s market position. So master plans were now tighter, looking annually for 'a birth, a marriage or a death' to produce peak viewing figures in ratings periods. From these peak ratings plans, other stories – both 'romantic/soapy' and 'social issues' – could be hung.

'Sophie' was planned, as is typical of the soap genre, to 'throw a spanner in the works' (Redlich) of *ACP*'s most recent high-rating marriage, between its resident surgeon, Terence Elliot, and the younger doctor, Alex Fraser. As an open-ended genre, television soap opera is constantly destabilizing 'the marriage', which Vladimir Propp described as the plenitude of conventional narratives[1]; and in the case of 'Sophie' this was (as a result of the tighter plotting and master planning) tied in to the next high-rating 'death' as well. Sophie was Terence's (occasionally seen) journalist daughter, a high-class/professional ('Sloane Square') junkie who clashed (because of her habit, and because of their comparable ages) with Alex. 'Q' ratings had established wide audience approval of the Sophie/Terence 'chemistry', so a new story had been forward-planned over six months prior to the writing of 'Sophie'. This new episode was planned to further destabilize the marriage by reintroducing Sophie, now a street-junkie.

However, as part of its 'quality soap' signature, *ACP* regularly took advice from medical and social work 'experts'; and here other time/space co-ordinates became important. Sophie was planned to OD in Sydney's red light district, Kings Cross, after being involved in prostitution to support her habit (this putting-Sophie-at-risk-in-the city narrative would mobilize *ACP*'s familiar pastoral ideology, as Terence goes to the city to restore his daughter to purer country ways). A Kings Cross social worker, Virginia Foster, was consulted, and she converted the narrative into a 'Third Wave' AIDS storyline. Here the time/space co-ordinates of commercial television met those of the medical profession.

Redlich: Heroin aside, we knew that Sophie was going to come back and throw a spanner in the works. Because the audience wants [. . .] to see that kind of stuff happening. So everything's on a master plan. The content of the particular episode comes through research [. . .] but the master plan was already there.[2]

The 'master plan' wove the complex marriage/death/new marriage serial strands tightly around the regular characters (the episode 'Sophie', for example, also had the task of building up the next big romance between teenager Jo and the young doctor, Michael). 'Research' then *accessed* the medical profession's 'Three Waves' discourse, via social worker Virginia Foster.

Foster: We help out the *ACP* team about once a year. [. . .] Sophie had to be written out. [. . .] They were talking about 'maybe the drug addict should die of an overdose', and I said, 'Instead of doing that [. . .] why don't you get rid of her with AIDS because I'm really concerned about the amount of addicts we have in this area who share needles, who prostitute themselves [. . .] and maybe that can get across to other people that [. . .] the disease [. . .] belongs to everybody'. [. . .] *And* she was a female, because despite the educational material and the brochures, I think a lot of people still have in their minds that it's a homosexual disease, and we've really got to get rid of that.

Previously Davern, despite pressure from the Australian Medical Association (with whom the programme had good relations), had resisted doing an HIV story until, as he put it to us, the 'medical profession had got its facts right' about AIDS in the heterosexual community. The Australian series *The Flying Doctors* had already 'done the gay prejudice story', and Davern was waiting for 'a new angle'. 'Expert' discourse's 'Three Waves',

and a social worker's routine daily concern about HIV spreading via prostitution into the general community, gave Davern his new angle. The
different time frames of commercial master plans and medical 'expertise'
coalesced in inscribing their different audiences into the production's
changing texts.

At this point, other texts and idiolects began to operate as Bakhtin's
'living dialogic threads'.

- As a tough, former working-class boy from the Western Suburbs of
  Sydney, Forrest Redlich had established as script editor of *ACP* a particular idiolect of 'balancing stories'. In this case his sense of balance
  was between 'positive' and 'negative stories' about young people. He
  was concerned to show that young people are not only subject to drug
  addiction, but are also prey to other problems, such as structural
  unemployment, being exploited at work by adults, and suffering
  family breakdown. Because Australian mini-series were currently
  attracting high ratings, the producers of *ACP* decided to do a 'mini-
  series' (four-parter) with 'Sophie', instead of the usual two-parter;
  consequently there was more space for Redlich's 'balancing stories'.
  These included (as subplots) a young girl in her first job serving fast
  food who is fired by her employer when she turns 18, but has the
  courage and the ('typical' country) community support to fight for
  her job (her victory thus 'balancing' Sophie's loss); a group of perma-
  nently unemployed young people with an alcohol problem who
  inhabit the country squat where Sophie finally ODs and dies (thus
  indicating that the country is not, after all, so pure); and a father who
  deserts (and blames) his children while looking for his straying wife
  (this story itself paralleling the back-story of Sophie abandoned as a
  child by her father's alcoholism after he 'killed' her young brother
  David through misdiagnosis). So a number of parallel themes of drug
  and alcohol addiction 'balanced', in Redlich's view, the negative
  'young social outcast' ideology of hopeless needle-sharers. These balancing themes embedded addiction in all age groups, in different
  socio-economic conditions, and in country as well as city.
- Writer Tony Morphett then drew on his own alcoholism back-story
  and on stories he had heard at Alcoholics Anonymous to 'bridge'
  Sophie from 'Sloane Square' society addict to Kings Cross street-
  junkie. He recalled a 'respectable' middle-class woman narrating at
  AA her story of secret alcoholism, which continued until she experienced a 'derelict' sitting on a park bench with his bottle. In this
  woman's wakened perspective, the old alcoholic had 'come to terms'
  with his addiction, and so, now, did she.

> I was thinking about this lady as I was thinking about Sophie being sur-
> rounded by people with high income levels. She went to the Cross to score
> and saw a boy shooting up in an alley. And she said, 'I realized that he's

come to terms with it, that he knew what was important.' It was a revelation to her, and so she befriended the boy [. . .] Paul. Paul had been up at a pub, just sold himself for 50 bucks, gone round the corner, bought his little baggy, and shot up in the alley outside the place where he lived because he really didn't want to spend the time going up the stairs. And this to Sophie was the revelation. This was the window into reality. [. . .] This was the moment I was looking for, which turned the middle-class society addict into the street-junkie. It was the embracing of the street-junkie culture.

Via the Alcoholics Anonymous intertext, then, the economy of street needle-sharing entered 'Sophie'.

- Script editor Bill Searle was responsible for timing the script of 'Sophie' under Channel 7's tighter studio regime. Episode 2 was running short, and Searle filled this gap by drawing on one of Davern's ideas (narrated at an earlier script conference) about the need to legalize heroin. Searle himself now wrote an extra 'economy of AIDS' scene. Here, after Terence finds that Sophie is HIV positive, he makes the bemused suggestion that legalizing heroin will break the nexus of the junkie economy, and the hospital matron, Sloane, responds with shock. Terence here is beginning to verbalize Tony Morphett's description of the street economy of needle-sharing as 'about nothing except finding the money [. . .] stealing the money, stealing the stuff to get the money, to get the smack to put into your arm'.

In these ways the *ACP* AIDS story was *transformed* (in Elam's sense of selection and adaptation from various source texts into other written narratives; this contrasts with *transcoding*, which is the process of turning written scripts into multi-camera video). The transforming process was via a series of intertexts mobilized from within the different time/space co-ordinates of commercial television, on the one hand, and of medical 'expertise' in the current history and epidemiology of AIDS, on the other. In a continuous play of utterances and intertexts, new AIDS meanings and narratives were then added to the production agenda as it was 'performed' through its own spaces and times. Moreover, the particular 'balancing stories' that were added in this process of transformation promised in their different ways to challenge what Hassin has described as the dominant ideology of junkies as social outcasts.

Being involved ethnographically with the production then gave me access to the processing of that 'promise' through the later stages of transcodifying the text.

- Some of these utterances stayed on the agenda. For example, the legalizing heroin story (which, however, created studio problems); and also the paralleling of Terence's alcoholism back-story with the father who deserts his children.

- Others were dropped. The teenage alcoholism/rural unemployment story (which would have extended the 'class/culture' debate of 'Sophie') was edited out after recording because of timing pressure and technical problems.
- Still other utterances temporarily were lost during writing. For example, Morphett's handwritten story conference notes for a Kings Cross scene which explicitly paralleled Terence's former alcoholism with Sophie's drug habit were not reproduced in the actual script. But this idea of a parallel was then reinscribed later in the transcoding process, when the music director inserted a bell-tree 'city sting' musical motif in the same scene in order to point up the parallel of Terence and Sophie's addiction.

This process of inclusion and exclusion is not fortuitous; but depends on time/space-embedded competences and values of practice. Myths, memories and other narratives are woven in processually as intertexts (via AA back-stories; via radio, TV and newspaper reports on AIDS' 'Three Waves', on structural unemployment, and on 'McDonaldization'; via *Time Magazine* stories of journalists on drugs and 'the hippy trail'; via 'expert' psychologists' accounts of the 'identities', 'causalities' and 'casualties' of modernity that are supposedly determined by early socialization in the context of marriage breakdown; via conventional pastoral contrasts of city and country). But their survival to-air depends also on professional values of practice and utterance: the masking of main characters' faces, for example, in some of the young unemployed squat scenes as recorded which dissatisfied the director and ostensibly led to their exclusion; or the pastoral contrast of 'country' oboe and 'city' bell-tree brought by the music composer to the show. It is via these utterances (as intertexts) and idiolects that the audiences for 'Sophie' were inscribed in the to-air text.

A processual poetics of production

Our emphasis on a continuous play of utterances and intertexts as new AIDS meanings and narratives were added to the production agenda indicates that we need to rethink television communication in terms of process. 'Process' was, of course, the term given to the version of communication theory that dominated American 'effects' studies, with their particular emphasis, as Alasuutari notes in his Introduction, on the harmful effects of mass media. This tradition has rightly been criticized (by both 'first generation' and 'second generation' reception analysis) for its 'psychologizing' tendency, its belief in a linear process of communication flow, and its assumption of a passive audience.

How, then, can we reintroduce 'process' in 'third generation' studies? I will start by considering one particular scene in the four parts of 'Sophie' which actor Shane Porteous (Terence) had special difficulty with. It was the extra scene between Terence and matron Sloane that script editor Bill Searle had added after timing the early script at rehearsal. Director Leigh Spence also had difficulty with this scene, taking (for him) the unusual step of leaving the control room to change his camera angles on the studio floor.

Searle had been concerned at the time of writing this extra scene that

> there is always the danger that it is going to look tacked on, that it is going to look like a public service advertisement. But having seen it recorded [. . .] I actually felt that it seemed to fit quite nicely, that this was an area of the heroin/AIDS situation that hadn't actually been touched in the whole four hours.

My 'ethnographic' difference from Searle here was that, as well as having seen the scene after recording (during editing), I actually saw it *being* recorded; and this gave me access to the strategies which production personnel adopted to *make* the scene seem less tacked on. But why should seeing these strategies-in-practice give me any extra analytical advantage over simply exploring the final text?

In a useful piece of auto-critique, 'Text Appeal and the Analysis Paralysis', Keir Elam has explored the 'fatal glamour of textuality' (1989: 3) embedded in much of the earlier structuralist work on the semiotics of performance. As he argues, in this earlier semiotics, 'it was unthinkable that one might found a semiotics of anything without first, a priori, positing the existence of [a] fully and autonomously textual object, subject to its own canons of syntactic and semantic coherence, waiting to yield to the expert semiologue his own cherished legibility' (1989: 3).

As with other 'expert' discourses, Elam is pointing here to the need to be reflexive about our own. He quotes a theatre phenomenologist to argue that the problem with his earlier semiotics was that in addressing performance 'as a system of codes [and so as text] it necessarily dissects the perceptual impression theatre makes on the spectator [. . .] Thus the danger of a [semiotic] approach [. . .] is that one is apt to look past the site of our sensory engagement with its empirical objects' (1989: 7).

Since, as I am arguing, production is a continuous time/space play of intertext and utterance, 'spectator' here can be taken to refer to television professionals as themselves 'audiences' for other texts. Elam implicitly criticizes his own earlier work for segmenting the multilayered performance text when he argues that 'we are still too tightly tied to the old structuralist notion of performance as a textual layer structure, as the finished product of the interaction of codes, waiting for the big knife to descend and cut up the slices' (1989: 10).

While Elam's earlier notion of the semiotic density of performance offers a useful map into a production, it clearly does not provide a theory; and I agree with him that a 'decisive and far-reaching change in analytical paradigm and, by the same token, in analytical object' (1989: 11) is needed.

> What we require, in my view, is not so much a textual as a *rhetorical* approach to the theatrical event, concerned no longer with levels but with strategies, and thus less with the product than with the production. (Elam, 1989: 11)

What Elam is getting at here is important; because it *is* concerned with the strategies that Shane Porteous and Leigh Spence adopted *at the site* of their sensory engagement with the empirical objects of performance. A rhetorical approach to the text concerns itself with *strategies of persuasion*, and therefore with the values of practice of the director who changes his camera angles or of the actor who adapts his performance rationale or style. In other words, the analytical advantage of this approach is in the reading of the text at the production/performance 'implied audience' moment rather than at the 'actual audience' level (though this, of course, can benefit by a 'processual poetics' too).

Clearly, this preference for a 'processual poetics of production' rather than with text as 'theoretical object' does call, as Elam says, for 'adequate (preferably direct) access to production material' (1989: 23). And as Elam also says, the processes of transforming and transcodifying a narrative source text can be traced as usefully to 'dramatist or director or designer or actor: what matters are not the sources of the processes but the processes themselves' (1989: 23).

Elam's own interest is with theatre, and particularly with plays that themselves emphazise 'a processualizing of the production' in 'the actual rehearsal methods employed' (1989: 13). My concern here with commercial television takes a different slant, given its inherently naturalistic and 'finished product' conventions. Nevertheless, the emphasis on rhetorics and strategies of persuasion in relation to acting and performance is equally important in the television context – even though it is always necessary to embed them within the global rhetorics and strategies of popular ratings discourse rather than in the 'alternative theatre practice' which interests Elam.

Directing strategies: Leigh Spence and Robert Meillon

As we will see in this section, the global rhetorics of popular television are, while systematic, never homogeneous and uniform. For example, even within one series, directors may differ significantly on which *kind* of global rhetoric – 'public service' or 'commercial' – they work within. As television personnel move backwards and forwards between the different framing extremes (the public service ideal, and the commercial rating) which have marked Western television until recently, they carry with them characteristic values of practice. So even within either one or other of these institutional contexts, different professional idiolects will be in operation – sometimes even within the work of one director in one production.

As a four-parter 'mini-series', 'Sophie' had two directors for its needle-sharing AIDS story, instead of the usual pattern of one director per 'issue'. This gave me the opportunity to contrast different directorial embodiments of the 'memories' and other intertexts circulating in this show. To focus the comparison I will describe two examples in 'Sophie' when the directors, Leigh Spence and Bob Meillon, each changed a camera angle on set.

Spence changed his cameras for Searle's Terence/Sloane scene 'economy of needle-sharing' scene.

> What I originally planned was to work with Terence as foreground. [. . .] A lot of the time it can work if you've got the dominant person foreground, that is where your attention is. [. . .] But I realized [. . .] when I'd recorded it and looked at it back, that the intent of the scene had gone the opposite way. So then I had to rethink it. I kept the same actors' moves, but I realized that you had to see this man much *more* than the way I originally planned it. [. . .] In the visual form that I shot first he was not dominant enough for the information that he was giving. [. . .] It's the eyes you've got to see when those things are happening.

In Meillon's case, his change of camera set-up was in a long Tony Morphett-scripted scene of Terence and Sophie at Kings Cross. In this, Terence finds his street-junkie daughter in her filthy Kings Cross flat, and they retrace together her childhood and his alcoholism. Unusually for a commercial soap opera, the producers had accepted the writer's argument that this 13-minute scene was sufficiently important to span, without cutting to other scenes, the whole time period between two major commercial breaks. Morphett felt that the standard *ACP* convention of 'putting a story aside and doing a scene somewhere else about something totally different [. . .] instead of driving forward with your main story' had implications for the intended audience.

> It's an impact problem. [. . .] You're losing momentum. Now this may, in fact, make *A Country Practice* less threatening viewing. It may be that it creates a sense of audience relief from a heavy story.

Morphett's implied audience here was something of a 'half-way house', replicating Channel 7 programming executives' perception of *ACP* (and indeed of Channel 7 itself) as a 'half-way house' between 'the other commercials' (whose viewers needed 'relief from a heavy story') and the state-funded ABC ('where you are preaching to the converted'). In the case of this Kings Cross scene, the producers also hedged their bets: they kept Morphett's long Terence/Sophie scene intact; but they made the characters themselves travel (into an external park setting with a pretty fountain) in order to give the audience some 'relief' from the 'city-stress' of Sophie's claustrophobic flat.

Meillon's altered camera angle occurred during this scene, when Sophie and Terence have returned from the park to her flat. Sophie reminds

Terence of the death of her young brother, and he swings away to look out of the window. She then speaks – to his back – of his desertion of her as a child.

> *Meillon*: That wasn't a planned shot at all. It just happened. I was going to take that shot as a two-shot *through* the window originally, and then I just happened to look at the monitors while we were rehearsing and it suddenly struck me that it looked much nicer this way. [. . .] It looked like he couldn't face it; he had to keep his back on it. I just liked the idea of one eye turning round but couldn't.

Actor Shane Porteous was the focus of the change of camera angle on each occasion in the case of both directors' scenes I am describing. For Leigh Spence it was 'seeing his two eyes' that counted; for Robert Meillon it was 'the idea of one eye turning round but couldn't'.

But what do these changes in rhetorical strategy by the two directors signify? In the first place, they signify two quite different directing styles. As producer Bruce Best put it, 'you couldn't get two more different directors'.

> Bob Meillon, the director of 'Sophie' 1 and 2, is a pragmatist. [. . .] He's [. . .] very conscious of the limitation of making two hours of television each week, He's been a television director for a very long time, and he has refined the thing so that he can survive in person too. [. . .] He keeps some of himself in reserve all the time, which, if you're a career director, is not such a bad way to go. He keeps things simple. He's an ex-cameraman and his shooting pattern is [. . .] very straightforward. Leigh Spence, the director of 'Sophie' 3 and 4, on the other hand, [. . .] is quite prepared to chop large bits off himself at any time. He has a much more complex directorial style. [. . .] He tends to create mood through use of pictures, whereas Bob [. . .] tends to keep the pictures very simple and lets the drama tell the story.

Behind the personal differences, their different forms of commitment were embodied in two distinctly different institutional backgrounds as television professionals.

> Anybody who's been through the public broadcasting system [. . .] shoots basically the way Leigh does, *plots* his cameras the way Leigh does because that's the way we were all trained. You did everything in advance.

As Shane Porteous observed:

> Bob Meillon comes to rehearsal with blank script. [. . .] Leigh Spence comes to rehearsal with the script already marked with camera shots, in pencil. And Bob will say, 'Right, read it through and then move it', do what you like virtually [. . .] to the more experienced actors. But once we've moved it, he will then start planning on paper the shots that he sees us moving ourselves into. In other words, moving the cameras to catch us at the right moments. Leigh, on the other hand, has already decided on a visual style and pace for that scene, and

has worked out the moves for the characters in advance. So he gives us the moves to fit in with his camera shots, and we respond to that. [. . .] Leigh always gives you reasons for [. . .] making these moves: character reasons, motivation reasons. It's a different thing from finding your own way into it.

Leigh Spence: idiolects of public broadcasting

The difference between Spence's public broadcasting background and Meillon's career path in commercial television (as cameraman then director) led to two quite different rhetorical strategies when it came to directing the actors. While Spence looked for an ensemble of performance *within the picture frame* (and gave his actors their moves and motivations), Meillon liked to establish an ensemble performance *on the rehearsal floor*, thus drawing on his actors' intratextual memories. In this and the following section we will look at how these differences pointed up different emphases of 'dialogic negotiation', with producers and actors of the text.

Leigh Spence told Bruce Best and Bill Searle at the script meeting that

> the style that I wanted to do in 'Sophie' [. . .] was not so much faces, faces. It had to be more in a sort of ensemble playing of it. That means visually you have to block the actors so that you're seeing two or three of them and you're getting *all* the reactions, rather than just getting one reaction, and then somebody else's.

It was for this reason of ensemble visual style that Spence framed the Terence/Sloane 'legalizing heroin' scene the way he did initially, with the two actors both on camera together. Shots of two characters in frame, or often three characters in a triangular relationship, gave spatial depth to Spence's scenes, and, as he said, allowed an 'ensemble playing of it' where the audience saw all the reactions together.

Spence especially foregrounded 'emotion visually'. For example, his camera style for the graveyard sequence after Sophie's death was planned and shot as one continuous steadicam shot. This started from a position high on a ramp from which (taking advantage of an unscheduled pre-breakfast shoot to catch the mist rising in a country churchyard)

> you can look into the valley and see a beautiful morning forming with the stillness of the graveyard [. . .] all in one continuous shot. What I wanted was the audience to get the loneliness of this man, and that's why you go back wide, and slowly just go further and further into his emotion as you come forward [. . .] in almost three minutes of continuous moving around him.

Here Spence directed Katrina Sedgwick (Sophie) to read her last letter (as she became once again the journalist who 'could have been on the front cover of *Time*') in a flat, unemotional voice, because, as he put it: 'I thought, being a journalist, she would read it as a journalist, without emotion, as just a reportage of what she had written'. The emotion of the scene was to be carried neither by her voice nor by Shane Porteous' acting as he reads the letter over her gravestone, but by the camera.

> I thought I could express his emotion visually [. . .] The emotion comes from the camera and Terence's stillness, not showing emotion. I thought I could lead the audience emotionally into it.

'Leading the audience emotionally' via his advance plotting of camera framing and movement was Spence's idiolectal signature as director. He *interpellated* his implied audience by always precise use of space, camera and positioning of actors. For example, rehearsing an OB scene on the veranda at Camelot, he asked Shane Porteous (Terence) and Di Smith (Alex) to move to the corner of the veranda as Terence begins to admit how much he has hurt Alex by bringing Sophie home. On Terence's words, 'And then, having got her away from there, to find I was too late', Spence asked them to move to the very spot on the veranda where they had proposed in an earlier episode. Spence was interpellating (calling up) long-term viewer memory here, creating a subtextual relationship of tension which Terence and the viewer alike are reaching for.

> *Spence*: If people got the connection, they got it, and if they didn't it is not a worry. [. . .] That's what I call working on a subtext. If you can use those sort of things that may trigger someone who *does* remember, they're getting more out of it. [. . .] I do it because of the subtlety.

Spence here deliberately called up *intra*textual (fan) memory by way of planned camera positioning and character moves. With a director so planned and precise in his control of the text, it therefore came as a surprise to see him suddenly leave the control room in the middle of recording the Terence/Sloane scene. Clearly something had intervened to interrupt his normal planned process and his ensemble framing style. By interviewing Spence afterwards, it was possible to ascertain that something in fact *had* changed after he had blocked this scene 'in absolute detail'.

> *Spence*: I thought it was a preachy scene until I heard something on the news a couple of nights before which really pointed that scene up as real to me. [. . .] Because then I realized what he was saying was a lot more important [. . .] than I originally thought. That influenced what I did with the cameras.

What Spence had heard was an item discussing junkie culture and the legalization of heroin. Again we can see how the meanings of 'Sophie' were constructed intertextually. A radio programme, heard between rehearsal and recording, led the director to do what he very seldom did – change his forward camera plotting. What had seemed a preachy scene that Spence was going to pay little attention to suddenly became 'real'; and the director reached immediately for television's convention for representing 'real emotion': close-ups of the 'two eyes'. Bill Searle's 'legalizing heroin' scene was given extra visual pointing by Spence's signalling it visually as (for him) an unusual scene, shot not entirely in ensemble style but with more 'faces, faces'.

In this case the intertextual relation changed the camera style; but in the graveyard scene the camera style actually led to a loss of intertextual reference. This scene, which writer Judy Colquhoun regarded as 'the favourite thing I've written in the last 15 years', embedded Sophie's death in much larger (*Time Magazine*) narratives of 'innocent men mown down in the street', 'famine' and 'sadists in colonels' uniform'. Again the intention was to 'balance' the junkie-as-'social outcast' ideology – on this occasion via the voices of the 'responsible journalist'. However, the producer's own implied audience (and time pressure on the episode during editing) led to Spence's scene (and Colquhoun's favourite words) being cut.

> *Best*: I gave *very specific* briefing on that scene at the director's meeting. I wanted that shot very simply [. . .] because when you've got words which are as moving as the ones that Judy wrote [. . .] there's no point in getting tricksy [with the pictures] because the words themselves are saying everything. [. . .] And with the three minutes ten of screen time [. . .] I had a lot of warning bells ringing. [. . .] I was having trouble right from the word go working out how we were going to convince the audience to hang in. It worried me that it was a little indulgent, the length of it, the style of it.

Power relations are clearly articulated in television production, and the *producer's* implied audience (who, in his view, would find this style 'indulgent') prevailed over the director's.

In the Searle 'legalizing heroin' scene it was a radio intertext which led to a change in visual style during production. In contrast, in Colquhoun's *Time Magazine* graveyard scene it was the producer's utterance (during editing) that the scene as shot was 'a lot closer to radio than television' (because Shane Porteous' face was not emoting) which established a key rhetorical strategy for cutting it. Keeping the audience 'hanging in' is nearly always the most important of commercial television's implied audience rhetorics, and it was the fear of *this* audience switching channel that ultimately determined the producer's decision.

Bob Meillon: 'feeling' for serial memories

In the process of television production, implying audiences is not simply a matter of producer/director negotiation (as in the case of Bruce Best and Leigh Spence). It is also an issue between director and actors. In this section we will look at the way in which a more 'commercial' director negotiates with his actors, and the way in which the latter negotiate their parts via programme and personal memories. It is through these that the actors 'feel' their relationship with their audience (e.g. whether 'too preachy' or whether using programme memory so that 'for the first time viewers have been able to see that Terence can *remember* life with his son David with warmth and affection').

Bob Meillon described his personal style as 'a pretty close concern for the actor'. As Di Smith (Alex) said, 'With Bob you end up coming in with a much firmer idea of what you want to do, and Bob will work with you.' Katrina Sedgwick (Sophie) said that she 'particularly enjoyed the very long scene with Terence' which Tony Morphett had scripted and fought for:

Sedgwick: We moved it ourselves, just whatever felt most natural. [. . .] .And how it felt to us was how we did it. The thing of Terence being at the window and me talking all this stuff to his back. [. . .] Shane and I just did it. And how it felt to us was how they taped it, which was great. [. . .] If he'd been looking at her [. . .] I don't think she would have had the strength to say it to him face-to-face. But because his back was to her she was able to deliver this really very telling piece.

Porteous: I didn't *plan* it a great deal. We moved it in rehearsal. The moves seemed to work. Bob gave us the opening frame in this particular one [. . .] and that's all he gave us and from then on we did it – a combination of following the big print [. . .] and our positioning round the set. The way we were working all the moves just seemed to flow naturally.

It was this kind of 'natural acting' (rather than 'indulgent' directorial style) that the producer was looking for in the graveyard scene. But unlike Spence, in this case Morphett won his argument to keep a long scene, because Best's fears for the audience 'hanging in' were met in part by transferring some of the scene outside, and partly by the 'natural flow' of the acting.

Acting that 'just flows naturally', of course, has to be worked for. Listening to Porteous and Sedgwick describing their acting strategies in this scene brought to my attention two distinct kinds of memory that were being called up to provide the actors with preparatory rhetorics for their performance.

Acting strategies: intratextual memory

Soap operas characteristically weave current 'social issues' themes (like gay relationships, AIDS, teenage suicide, etc.) within their serial 'romance' strands. There are always 'more' of the latter than the former, so controversial issues (like gay sex) can generally first be 'tried out' in less central relationship strands and dropped if proven to be unpopular with significant numbers of viewers. Further, in a series/serial format like *ACP*'s, social issues are bracketed within (usually) single-week two-part series. Thus an actor has little time to construct an acting 'memory' on which to base her or his performance. In contrast, the serial (romance/relationship) strands which are central to soap opera as a genre provide the actor with detailed memories.

The importance of these detailed memories was clear in Shane Porteous' preparation for Bob Meillon's long Terence/Sophie scene. As a long-term actor with *ACP*, Porteous may not always plan ahead his physical moves, but he is meticulous in forward planning his shifts of emotional mood.

> What I enjoyed about that long segment was the range of emotion and topics that we go through in the one scene. They really do connect Sophie and Terence [. . .] and they learn the good bits about each other from that. For the first time viewers have been able to see that Terence *can* remember life with his son David with warmth and affection, and without going through angst. It's only when Sophie actually brings up the time of David's death that he finds it difficult to cope. [. . .] Sophie had already touched on the David theme and [. . .] Terence turned away to try to look anywhere else than [. . .] at Sophie because it was a painful area. He didn't want her to see what he was thinking. Then when she said, 'Am I saying that I'm a junkie because my father left home,' I turned back to her because Terence thought this was getting back to what she wanted to talk about – she had to say 'No, of course not.' But then she said, 'No, when David went away, I went away'. And Terence suddenly realizes what he's done, and again, for the same reason, has to turn away rather than face her, and make an excuse of looking out the window, looking down at the street beneath. Gradually what she's saying – about how she found him slumped in the chair with the whisky bottle beside him – just impinges. He *has* to listen, and he *has* to learn from it [. . .] She reveals that she *saw* he was no longer there then, and *felt* that at the time as a little girl. And so there was the shame, humiliation, Terence realizing that he'd been discovered with his defences down, with his lack of caring hanging out there in the open. [. . .] And eventually the scene ends with the recognition of what he's done and a plea to see if there's anything there with the relationship between them that they *can* save – a little bit of the little girl who was there, a little bit of the father that was left to take home.

The camera style, with far more full-frame close-ups than Meillon normally used, followed the acting here; and Porteous' series of mood changes drew deeply on his intratextual memory of Terence within the history of the show:

> withdrawing into myself as Terence, which has long been a habit of Terence.

> [T]here were more memories of David, because the death of David had been established as Terence's *bête noire* for years.

This performance memory among the regular actors works naturalistically out of the long history of the programme, and it is this that allows the 'career director who's very conscious of the limitations of making two hours of television a week' to work the way he does and get the show in on time. In this way, drawing on performance memory, the regular actors helped the director meet the increasingly tight studio time constraints of the programme.

In contrast, the 'legalizing heroin' scene between Terence and Matron Sloane which Porteous found so hard to act did not have serial memory behind it. Porteous thus only knew where the scene fitted in 'objectively' (but not subjectively) for Terence.

> By that stage there had been some sort of reconciliation between Terence, Alex and Sophie, and he has allowed himself to think about what he has experienced over the last few weeks. He has worked through his personal feelings about this, and is coming up with a more objective judgement, if you like, on what is happening with society in general as far as heroin, or any illegal drugs of addiction, are concerned. And he comes to the conclusion that it should be legalized, that there are no real alternatives [. . .] because it's just not working driving it underground because that's where the crime comes in. That's where corruption goes right through the system, and where the victims are not only victims of addiction, they're victims of law and society. He sort of thinks that through.

But even though he knew 'objectively' what Terence was thinking, Porteous found it hard to act the scene as anything other than 'an aside'. This was because, Porteous said, 'it was a scene that really didn't affect the relationship with Sophie and Alex. It was an aside, if you like, to Matron Sloane.' Consequently, he had not 'planned an attack on that particular scene' as he had with Morphett's long Terence/Sophie discussion. Unlike this latter scene, he had not prepared the 'grading of the changes and the variations in attitude to the other characters'. The result was that the 'legalize heroin' scene, as performed by Porteous (and as initially perceived by Spence) *was* preachy (in terms of acting naturalism), despite the director's reframing.

Given the very tight 'two hours a week' schedule of production, it was the *serial* performances in the programme – the Sophie/Terence/Alex relationships of Forrest Redlich's developing master plans – which got priority over the series (social issues) rhetorics and strategies. Consequently, to flesh out these 'social problem' performances, actors frequently resorted to personal memories.

Acting Strategies: personal memory

The dominant tradition of training for actors in the West is still Stanislavskian naturalism. As the Artistic Director of the Royal Shakespeare Company, Adrian Noble, recently said:

> The British acting tradition [. . .] has absorbed [. . .] Stanislavsky and [. . .] empathy, finding that in you that could inhabit the character, so the character becomes part of you, and you become part of the character. (Noble, 1996, interview).

In the luxury of a high culture production (with plenty of rehearsal time), as in Noble's own 1995/6 direction of *The Cherry Orchard* at the RSC, actors may thus be encouraged to do improvisatory work investigating their childhoods. Kate Duchêne, who played Varya in Noble's *The Cherry Orchard*, said,

> We did lots of exercises like that, which is based on a Stanislavsky method. [. . .] He said ' [. . .] these two chairs are a doorway, when you feel like it just come into a room that you loved as a child'. [. . .] All those exercises about emotional responses to your own and your character's past are Stanislavsky-based (Duchêne, 1996, interview).

In 'two hours a week' television (with just one day of rehearsal time), there is no time for Stanislavskian improvisatory exercises. But actors conventionally reach for their training anyway, and draw on their own personal narratives. Intratextual memory and personal memory are, then, similar-but-different conduits 'to your own and your character's past', of 'the character becoming you, and you becoming the character'.

Katrina Sedgwick, for example, felt that she now knew Sophie much more closely and successfully than in her previous appearance in *ACP*.

> The way I'm approaching the character is 'if *I* had done that'. [. . .] She realizes that the heroin addiction has come through her own experiences. But I think she does blame him for leaving the family, because he had no right to do so. I mean, myself, personally, I've had a situation in my family where my parents divorced when I was very young, and I still harbour resentment to him in all that. [. . .] So certainly, when I abused Terence, I could understand why [. . .] I mean, I don't feel the same sort of anger that she feels towards *her* father, but, yeah, there is quite a lot of me in it because I know what it is like to suddenly not have a parent there. And I can relate to the stepmother thing as well, because my mother got married to a stepfather. And so there's an alien figure coming in and taking away the attention of a single parent.

While not drawing on childhood memory, like Sedgwick, Di Smith also emphazised that her personal experiences had deeply informed her performance.

> Even having seen that long scene [between Terence and Sophie] and how it all worked out and how much we felt for the father/daughter, I still personally believed so strongly that Alex is right. [. . .] She is a totally innocent party, and yet it's affecting her life. [. . .] With AIDS and with heroin that's what happens, as anyone knows, like me, who's had their home robbed by a junkie who needs to sell the video up the pub. [. . .] There is a big personal element in this for me. It was so satisfying to play because a friend of mine touched into the smack area over last Christmas, and came to me and told me. So then you find yourself in the position of saying [. . .] 'Well, why did she tell me? Does she want me to stop her? Or what?' And as with the whole Sophie thing [of robbing Alex] you don't know what to believe. [. . .] My house got robbed about two weeks after she told me. The thought immediately sprung into my mind that it could have been

her. And then I went, 'Oh God, what a horrible thing to think'. That's what I mean – it had nothing to do with me personally, yet it had a profound effect on me personally. Alex's situation is worse, but it's the same thing.

Di Smith here drew on her own personal experience and memory of being touched by the economy of drug addiction. She also drew on her early days as a student. Talking over her scenes with Katrina Sedgwick, Smith became aware that Alex's hard-line attitude to Sophie depended in part on their similarity:

> It's not inconceivable that Alex would have taken to drugs had different things happened to her. [. . .] She went to Sydney University. She travelled overseas. She's not an idiot. She ran around with a lot of wealthy friends, and so I'm sure she would have come across heroin at some stage. I know I have personally. So there's no reason at all why she shouldn't have *at least* the amount of knowledge about the drug as I do. So I gave Alex that, and that underpins her hard-line attitude about the whole thing.

With Shane Porteous too, personal memory played a part in the long Terence/Sophie scene, in addition to his ready recourse to the serial memory of the programme.

> Morphett had Sophie talking about 'remember that house we had in Roseville?' Now in fact I used to live in Roseville and, because I nearly always act in images, I was able to just call up an image of the house that I actually, personally Shane Porteous, lived in in Roseville. I made what Sophie called a study – not in fact a study because I didn't have one, but I had a little veranda that I used to do artwork on out the front of the house – my reference point to that, and imagined that. I knew what door she was coming through to see me sitting in that chair, even though at that time, being very poor, I didn't have anything *like* a leather armchair to sit in. But I [. . .] had a quite strong image of her coming from the bedroom that my actual daughter lived in in those days, walking through the house and seeing me in that thing. So I was able to [. . .] think of *those* images which fitted in so well with what Morphett had written for Sophie to say.

In addition, Porteous used a photograph of his own daughter when Terence is being shown pictures by the Kings Cross social worker of street kids who have ODd and died while still in their early teens. The narratives of personal memory are often very strong and *very* personal in the 'internalized' naturalism of Stanislavskian acting.

Strategies of persuasion

Our rhetorical approach to performance tries to examine the process through which, as Elam puts it, narrative source texts are transformed or transcoded.

(1) In a 'processual poetics' of performance, this emphasis on rhetorical strategies can focus on any point of the production process. It can, for example, look at the way in which a 'quality soap' reading formation channels a writer's transformation of a two-page plot synopsis into 'Sophie' episode 1 by way of rhetorical moves around popular and high cultural intertexts like *The Brady Bunch* and Shakespeare. Tony Morphett drew on *The Brady Bunch* when drawing on his own personal memories as a stepfather to emphasize the 'quality' of *ACP*.

> I have two stepchildren from my wife's first marriage, and my wife has three stepchildren from my first marriage, so I've been through that stepping situation [that Alex faces] a lot. And it's *always* seemed to me that in drama it's been either ignored or sentimentalized in the way that, say, *The Brady Bunch* sentimentalizes it.

Here Morphett tests the 'sentimentalism' of popular culture against the 'reality' embedded in his own memories. In this case Morphett feels his own hard-lived personal narratives and back-stories make 'Sophie' more real (but also therefore more *marketable* to a new generation of what he called 'stepping-syndrome' parents) than the sentimentalizing texts of American popular television. This 'lived experience' is one of his rhetorical markers of 'quality' soap (which is at the same time marketable soap).

On the other hand – but again to justify *ACP* as 'quality soap' – Morphett reached for high culture to support Redlich's 'balancing stories' as well as *ACP*'s 'laughter and tears' formula:

> It's absolutely axiomatic that the subplot ought to be related to, or in parallel in some way, the main plot. [. . .] You can see it working in [. . .] *Othello* where [. . .] you have jealousy played out on all levels.

> Obviously the medical story, the life and death story, tends to be on the heavier side, and then you have the comedy side with the 'rude mechanicals' [. . .] Bob, Cookie and Esmie. But this is a very long-standing tradition. [. . .] The Shakespeare plays with the best comedy in them [. . .] tend to be the tragedies [like] *King Lear*. [. . .] It's always been used by writers [. . .] in the English tradition [. . .] to almost disarm the audience in preparation for the heavy moments.

Morphett's worry, on the one hand, that *ACP*'s commercial tendency for short scenes, and 'cutting away' to comedy, reduces the 'drive' of its serious messages, and his taking comfort, on the other hand, that this formula has a tradition going back to Shakespeare, are part of the dialogic process Hassin describes 'in which the speaker negotiates his/her voice'. Quite clearly, commercial TV professionals like Morphett negotiate this voice by way of implied audiences. Morphett works through this professional writing concern by talking of 'losing momentum' with the audience, on the one hand (a prime mistake in commercial TV), but of creating 'a sense of audience relief', or disarming 'the audience in preparation for the heavy moments' (a prime quality in Shakespeare), on the other. As with the earlier combining of reference to *The Brady Bunch* with his own implied 'stepping-syndrome' audience, intertexts and implied audiences are the 'living dialogic threads' of this negotiation of voice. Watching and interviewing a television writer reveals the way in which being both a 'quality' writer and a 'commercial' writer establishes a dialogic negotiation of voice similar to that described by Hassin in her HIV interviews. In the case of the television writer, both the implied audience which must 'hang in' (i.e. not switch channel) and the implied audience that is opened up to the 'real' stepping syndrome or the 'real' junkie culture negotiate his writing voice.

(2) But as well as this negotiation of subjectivities in any one TV professional (at any one moment of the processual 'flow' of production), Bakhtin's understanding of 'the living utterance' as 'an active participant in a social dialogue' also requires analysis of the 'socially specific environment' – the overall institutional time/space co-ordinates – that the writer works and contends with.

So as well as examining particular points of the process of transformation – from in-house master plans, through the script of 'Sophie', to actors' use of memory in performance, and ultimately to producers' rhetorics of inclusion and exclusion during editing – an analysis of rhetorical strategies needs to focus also on the overall relationship of transformation to transcodification. Here further institutional rhetorics (the 'complex visual signature' of public broadcasting trained directors; the ensemble rehearsal style of a commercial director; the implied audience of a producer who worries whether it will 'hang in' for 'three minutes ten' of 'radio with pictures') call up particular rehearsal, performance, camera and editing styles.

In the end, despite Morphett and others' play between 'serious' and 'soap' audiences, the 'commercial' audience (as implied in Bruce Best's cutting of the funeral scene) does tend to prevail. The 'Sophie' story provided another very simple illustration of this. As social workers involved with 'Sophie' pointed out, Sophie herself was too old to represent the street-junkies 'out there', since these tend to OD much younger (so there is a distinct age disparity between Sophie, as Terence's daughter, and the photograph of actor Shane Porteous' own daughter that the on-screen social worker shows Terence). But commercial considerations were more important: the street-junkie/needle-sharing HIV story was primarily there to 'throw a spanner in the works' of marriage/death ratings-designed master plans. Consequently, the age of Sophie was already pre-determined; so to try to meet the problem of street-junkie age, Sophie was given a younger partner, Paul. But Paul (via the bell-tree music motif, and via his insertion as the city 'villain' in this country pastoral) was constructed, for the most part, within the dominant ideology of needle-sharer as social outcast. Thus the programme itself negotiated its voice: between the 'good' and 'outcast' needle-sharers Sophie and Paul; and to a limited extent within Paul himself (as in one scene Paul narrates his own memory of parental desertion, and thus Redlich's 'balances' are once again invoked).

We have seen that memories are important as strategies of persuasion at several levels; intra-diagetically (as in the case of Paul's memory), and intratextually – both for the audience (Leigh Spence's calling up of fan memory), and for the actor (Bob Meillon's reliance on actors' intense intra-textual and personal memory). Here, too, the 'commercial' (soap-)oriented memory tends to prevail. Actors have no difficulty with this. What they do seem to find difficult is finding working rhetorics which help them embody social issues that lie outside the 'serial' interpersonal relation-ships embodied in the master plans. Actors' memories can and do relate to broader societal issues. But the point is that the serial master plans seldom encourage them to do so; and their resort in that situation tends to be to personalized memories, to 'acting in images', as Shane Porteous puts it. Specific 'social problems' are opened up and closed off in one block (usu-ally in the space of one week; unusually, in the 'mini-series' 'Sophie', over two weeks), while the serial romances continue. Consequently actors' posi-tioning of their characters in a broader social context tends to be episodic – as, in Porteous' 'legalizing heroin' example, 'an aside'.

The conventional competences and values of practice within commer-cial television that lead in this direction are especially evident during editing, when an episode is often under time pressure (as in the case of Best's cutting of the graveyard scene). Another example here was Bob Meillon's preference to cut some of the 'young lovers' (Michael/Jo) hospi-tal material in order to get his episode in on time; only to be told that this subplot was needed because it was seeding the next romance – and the next high-rating 'marriage'. In contrast, there was little or no resistance to Leigh Spence dropping the teenage alcohol subplot. A legitimating rhetor-ical move here was that the teenage alcohol story 'deserves a story to itself'. And sometimes it gets one. But the result is that the social com-plexity of drugs, unemployment and young people is separated out into discrete and temporally distinct narratives, which audiences see far apart, if at all. The possibility for an audience making more complex and layered connections such as Sophie's 'youthful' addiction being read in the context of adult (Terence's) alcoholism, and/or the unemployed youths' alco-holism being read in the context of structural unemployment, tends thus to be lost.

We can see how this operates by drawing again on Elam's analysis of the transformation and transcodification of the narrated source text. He points to canonical procedures via which the narrated locations of the source narrative may be 'shown forth' in the mimetic spaces of drama: by selection and reduction; by identification; by symbolization; by ellipsis.

All of those strategies are present in 'Sophie', where the world of 'Third Wave' AIDS (i.e. the notion of transmission from the 'Second Wave' epi-demic in needle-sharing to the broader heterosexual community):

- is selected and reduced to the pastoral of 'country/city' (rather than, say, to the economy of addiction, whether in country or city);
- is identified as 'risk environments' (Kings Cross), with 'at-risk groups' (street-junkies) and 'risk demonology' (needle-sharing);
- is thus symbolized as the 'menacing' Kings Cross and the 'nice bright' or 'lyrical' country (carried by the varying idiolects of set design, lighting, music and sound which emphasize the dingy, squalid *mise-en-scène* of the city and the 'sun-drenched' but also 'threatened' farmhouses of the country).

Finally, by a process of ellipsis (carried by a range of professional idiolects and channels) the spaces covered in the country–city–country journeys in 'Sophie' are reduced to the 'dramatic conflict' between positive human potential (conveyed by Sophie's attempt once back in the country to return to journalism – represented by Colquhoun's *Time Magazine* letter) and the terminal invasion of the city-as-AIDS (by the 'social outcast' Paul). Thus, in part 4, when Paul journeys to the country to see Sophie (and help her finally OD), he signifies (with his bell-tree sound effect accompaniment) the earlier-narrative spatial closure of the Kings Cross flat, and the later-narrative spatial closure of that other dingy space, the squat, where Sophie will OD and die.

Indication that the 'spaces' of 'Sophie' *were* reduced for some viewers in this way (once the unemployed rural youth who inhabited the squat were edited out) is provided by the fact that the music scorer, Rhys Rees, did not realize that this dingy country squat where Sophie died was not 'back in the city' when he first saw the off-line edit of 'Sophie'. The same was true of many young people to whom we screened 'Sophie' in our audience study (Tulloch and Lupton, 1997: ch. 10) Without the 'unemployed kids' subplot which initially introduced this squat as 'country', the squat's signifiers (heroin, bell-tree, squalor, chiaroscuro) all read 'city'.

The opportunity to embed an 'economy of needle-sharing' reading in city *and* country was thereby lost. In our audience study there was a significant shift (from 29 per cent to 50 per cent for boys, and 21 per cent to 39 per cent for girls) in the 'yes' responses to a 'should heroin be legalized' question in pre- and post-screening questionnaires. But hardly anyone (in over 1,000 senior high school students) focused on the economy of needle-sharing in giving their reasons for this shift in attitude. Although 20 per cent of senior high school students in our audience survey said (in an open-ended question about 'what they particularly liked in the episode') that they liked the realistic view of street life, only 1 per cent said that they liked the 'legalize heroin' aspect, and only 1 per cent tied the problem of street life into socio-economic issues.

Selection and reduction, identification, symbolization and ellipses were all powerful rhetorical strategies in transcodifying space in the to-air text of 'Sophie'. In contrast, Terence's utterance about the legalization of heroin really had little space to construct a diagetic 'out there' (linking with other discourses – of age, class and region – that embedded addiction in its broader culture and economy), or indeed an 'in here' (among the master-planned interpersonal acting spaces of *ACP*). It was, as Porteous said, no more than 'an aside to matron Sloane'. As such its 'rhetoric' was exposed; and because it had little discursive and rhetorical space – textually (via identification and symbolization), intratextually (as actors' character-memory), or extratextually (as either personal memory or, as broader socio-cultural context) – it *was* 'preachy', which was why the director (working through his own radio intertext) changed his camera angles.

Conclusion

Television production works with a whole range of concepts of its audience. As Alasuutari says in the Introduction to this book, 'there isn't really such a thing as the "audience" out there; one must bear in mind that audience is, most of all, a discursive construct produced by a particular analytic gaze'.

Even within the production process, 'audiencing' means many different kinds of 'analytic gaze'. These may be demographic: maintaining audience 'spread' by way of characterization and storylines. They may be grossly quantitative, as in overall ratings; or focused quantitative, such as the 'Q' ratings which brought Sophie and Terence back together. They may be intuitively qualitative, as in the sense of *ACP* (and the channel that screened it) being a 'half-way house' between the ABC and the 'other commercials'. The implied audience is sometimes seen as subject to the 'hypodermic needle' of television (requiring the 'driving forward momentum' of single-minded drama to accept a 'heavy' message). At other times the implied ('stepping-syndrome') audience is seen as ready to switch on if provided with something 'more real' than the 'sentimentalizing' *Brady Bunch*. Sometimes the implied audience is invested with the competencies of a high culture/class habitus, amenable to the 'different layers' of Shakespeare. And at other times again, the implied audience is constituted with 'fan' competences of popular culture, as in Leigh Spence's positioning of Terence and Alex in their betrothal spot.

Further, in the audience-at-risk field, there was Virginia Foster's implied audience (for her Sophie was too old, since the needle-sharing/prostituting kids she dealt with were much younger); and there was also James Davern's implied audience of kids 'about to shoot up once at a party' who might be deterred by watching 'Sophie'.

Intertexts (popular and high cultural texts, AA back-stories, intratextual memories, actors' personal childhood memories, student narratives about heroin, 'stepping-syndrome' stories, social workers' utterance about the 'Three Waves' narrative of AIDS epidemiology, etc.) are used as routine utterances and practices in implying these audiences. These become rhetoric's framing practice, persuasion and identity in the everyday life of television professionals. Through them television professionals negotiate their voices as 'living utterances' and 'active participants in a social dialogue'.

Clearly, ethnographic researchers can never be simply 'neutral' in this process. They also 'speak' within the dialogic debate of the culture they are describing. Observing director Leigh Spence, for example, I was not simply a 'fly on the wall'. When he suddenly left the control room to change his camera angle, I was alerted that this was 'unsymptomatic' by the utterance of producer Bruce Best (when he earlier described Spence's BBC/ABC training and practice). And when I carefully questioned Spence about the 'reason' for this unusual action, I myself was 'spoken' (as in my writing here) by the cultural studies notion of intertextuality.

Similarly, our audience study inevitably (and so as a strategy, centrally and reflexively) spoke with the utterances of the people who made 'Sophie': seeking out methodologies, for example, to 'test' Tony Morphett's question as to whether the HIV/AIDS needle-sharing (and other) messages are conveyed more 'effectively' by narratives that 'cut away' or narratives that do not; or to test James Davern's view that tying the needle-sharing story to a regular, well-liked character like Terence would work more effectively than an impersonal public service advertisement like 'The Grim Reaper'.

But inevitably, also, we structured our audience survey in the light of academic discourse: using as a methodology, for instance, Elam's emphasis on the importance of multi-channelled communication in 'semiotically thick' texts; and also his emphasis on the 'processual' nature of performance (e.g. the shift in communication channel – from writing to music – of Morphett's Sophie/Terence drug-addiction parallel).

We are no more able to escape Bakhtin's 'negotiation of voice' in the practice of research (and its understanding of 'methodology') than in the practice of television production or the practice of being television audiences. 'Third generation' audience analysis needs to be aware of *all* of these layers of 'analytic gaze'.

Notes

1. For a discussion of the 'marriage under threat' in soap opera, see Lovell (1981).

2. All interviews with *ACP* production personnel, except where otherwise indicated, were conducted by John Tulloch during the production study of 'Sophie' in 1988.

References

Bakhtin, M. (1984) *Problems of Dostoevsky's Poetics*, (ed.) C. Emerson. Manchester: Manchester University Press.

Elam, K. (1989) 'Text Appeal and Analysis Paralysis: Towards a Processual Poetics of Dramatic Production', in T. Fitzpatrick (ed.), *Altro Polo: Performance from Product to Process*. Sydney: Frederick May Foundation for Italian Studies, Sydney University.

Hassin, J. (1994) 'Living a Responsible Life: The impact of AIDS on the Social Identity of Intravenous Drug Users', *Social Science of Medicine*, 39 (3): 391–400.

Lovell, T. (1981) 'Ideology and *Coronation Street*', in R. Dyer, C. Geraghty, J. Jordan, T. Lovell, R. Paterson and J. Stewart (eds), *Coronation Street*. London: British Film Institute.

Propp, V. (1968) *Morphology of the Folk Tale*. Austin: University of Texas.

Tulloch J. and Lupton, D. (1997) *Television, AIDS and Risk: A Cultural Studies Approach to Health Communication*. Sydney: Allen & Unwin.

Tulloch, J. and Moran, A. (1986) *A Country Practice: 'Quality Soap'*. Sydney: Allen & Unwin.

9

TO BE AN AUDIENCE

Birgitta Höijer

The focus of this chapter is on people's notions or cognitions of them-selves in their role as television audience. On the basis of research findings it will be shown that we often carry several different audience identities within us. The social and moral dilemmas of television audiencehood will be discussed.

A meta-perspective on audiences

According to McQuail, the term 'audience' is not only shared between media practitioners and theorists, but it has also 'entered into everyday usage, seemingly recognised by the media public as an unambiguous description of themselves' (1994: 283). Not necessarily unambiguous, we all at least recognize that we talk about ourselves as viewers, listeners and readers. We tell our friends that we usually fall asleep when we watch tele-vision or that we only listen to the radio in the car, or that we need to hurry home not to miss a certain programme. And we talk about the audience behaviour of our dear and loved: 'He's a TV slave, always sitting in front of the television' or 'She's not at all interested in sports, so I've bought another television set', or 'The kids want to watch *Cosby* and I usually join them. It's nice and cosy for all of us.' The way we as viewers and listeners perceive ourselves as audience may be labelled metacognitions[1] or simply a meta-perspective on the audience.

This view from the inside partly differs from the concept of audience as some collective entity, implying that a single person is not an audience. Both broadcasting institutions and academic research usually have some abstract collective in mind when studying and theorizing audiences. Public service and commercial television broadcasting institutions, for instance, spend large sums of money to obtain daily audience ratings, that is, aggregated quantitative data. Behind this, we find the logic of regarding audiences as commodity more than as experiencing subjects. Basically it is not the audience which is important, but audience figures (Weibull, 1995). The technique of measuring audiences with people meters sometimes does not even require watching or paying any attention to television. Being present in the room (with the television set on, which is automatically recorded) is sufficient for registering as audience (Gane, 1994). This seems to be in line with Hartley's claim that an audience is nothing but a discursive construction: 'Audiences may be imagined empirically, theoretically, or politically, but in all cases the product is a fiction which serves the needs of the imagining institution' (1987: 125).

Ang (1991) takes a more moderate position, claiming that there are at least two ways of conceptualizing the audience. She emphasizes the difference between the institutional view on the audience as discursive construct and the social world of actual audiences. The latter refers to 'the infinite, contradictory, dispersed and dynamic practices and experiences of television audiencehood enacted by people in their everyday lives' (1991: 13).

From the horizon of people's everyday lives, audiencehood mostly has a concrete personal angle far from conceptualizations of the audience as a mass, as a market, as a lifestyle, or other discursive constructions. People usually think and talk about specific individuals and their interactions with the media, such as about themselves, their mothers and fathers, their children, friends, and so on. People may further refer to small collectives, for instance a specific family or a peer group, which they have personally experienced as an audience or heard about. The personal is, however, embedded in cognitions about cultural norms and ideologies from which people evaluate the audience behaviour of themselves and of others. Everyday cognitions also to a certain extent contain general notions about social categories. People have ideas about abstract collectives as audiences, such as men, women, children, young people or ethnic groups. I will discuss some general notions of this type under the heading 'third-person effects'.

The picture given is also inevitably a discursive construction since we as academics always will study and write our stories about social phenomena through a 'scientific prism'. Whatever subject matter we focus on, our picture will be coloured by the methods, theories and preknowledge we use. But giving voice to the audience via self-reports, in-depth interviews and/or observations in natural social settings are, nevertheless, the closest we can come to actual audiences.

I will illustrate my arguments with utterances about audiencehood taken from a corpus of reception interviews which I have conducted in various studies over several years.

Moral stances

People often judge their own television viewing morally. Television view-ing is seen as a less useful and satisfying leisure activity than other activities (Argyle, 1996; Hagen, 1996). It is considered passive to sit in front of the television, and after an evening's watching people sometimes may have the feeling of having wasted their time. When asked about what tele-vision means to them, people I have interviewed have started by saying quite indifferent things like: 'It's good company when you don't have any-thing else to do'; 'When you're tired it's easier watching television than reading a book'; 'Television doesn't mean very much. But I watch. It's a fix-ation'; or 'I guess I'd miss it if it wasn't there. But it doesn't mean much. Entertainment of course.' A middle-aged prison warden, who spoke about a good deal of television viewing, compared television with a child's dummy, which he attributed a passive role (he had three children himself and his wife took care of other children as well):

> Television doesn't mean very much. It's sitting idle. It's old man's dummy so to speak. You watch television as kids suck their thumbs. Really, it helps to pass the time. It's not even relaxation, because then you may do so many other things.

Interestingly, comforters like children's dummies, thumbs or security blan-kets are ascribed a very important meaning for the child in Winnicott's (1953) theory, but parents often have ambivalent thoughts about them, especially when the child is no longer a baby. The metaphoric utterance about television as an old mans dummy not only underlines passivity and something useless, but also implies that television viewing may be seen as an immature comforting behaviour. People with high levels of education are even more likely to experience television viewing as indolent (Alasuutari, 1992; Hagen, 1996; McQuail, 1994).

The disparagement of television viewing, in a European context, may be a reflection of the collective Lutheran heritage, or other ideological influ-ences for that matter, which says that we should work by the sweat of our brows. We should do our duty. Or it may very well also be part of a uni-versal human wisdom, necessary for the survival of the human species, to highly evaluate the hard-working individual but to look down upon the lazy hedonist. Further, living in postmodern Western societies, we may simply feel a collective shame for having so much leisure time compared with earlier generations – parents and grandparents – who led more stren-uous lives, and had very little time to just sit down. It is hard to feel strenuous when you 'only' watch television.

Not all viewers are 'moralists', however. Jensen et al. (1994) show that there also are 'hedonists' and 'pragmatists', with clearly positive attitudes towards television, among viewers.

Gender roles in the family have an impact on our metacognitions.

Morley shows in his family interviews that women, in particular, feel unproductive as an audience if they do not combine viewing with some domestic activity, for example ironing or other housework: 'I knit because I think I am wasting my time just watching' (1986: 151). The men he interviewed did not express the same compulsion to be productive as an audience. For the husbands, homes were defined in opposition to working places as sites of leisure. For the wives, of which many were housewives, homes were workplaces and there were no natural borderlines between work and leisure. Even women with daily work outside the home mostly have the responsibility for the housework, so that the difference between housewives and women at work may not be so large.

When we communicate about television as a general social phenomenon, we may express a distinct moral standpoint about being a television audience. At a more specific level the picture is more complex. We may conceive ourselves as good or bad viewers in relation to different genres. Sometimes being an audience is associated with feelings of guilt – we ought not to see soaps – other times with feelings of doing our duty as good citizens.

Television genres are evaluated differently, and, as Alasuutari (1992) shows, they can be placed in a value hierarchy. Some genres are considered to be worth more than others. Informative programmes, such as news, documentaries and nature programmes, are placed at the top of the hierarchy, and action series and soap operas are placed at the bottom. This is confirmed by quality ratings, which show much lower quality scores for light entertainment, series and soap operas than for news, current affairs and documentaries. The informative genres are given the highest scores by the audience (Gunter and Wober, 1992).

When asked about what news and fiction on television mean for them, working-class and middle-class viewers whom I have interviewed have expressed the high value of news compared to fiction (Höijer, 1995). You cannot really live without news but, if necessary, it is possible to give up television fiction:

> We need the news because it's about global matters. We have to follow what's going on in the world. (Male viewer)

> The most important thing on television is the news. If I had to choose just one thing on TV I would pick out the news. I can live without fiction. (Male viewer)

> I just have to see the news. It's a must. After all, it might be something serious. The other – fiction – I watch with a smile. It's just casual watching. (Female viewer)

In the last quotation above we also see how genres are connected with viewing ambitions. Some genres can be watched more passively than others. I will return to this under the heading mental effort.

Morley (1986) found that male viewers emphasized the importance of news much more than female, but I found no such gender difference in Sweden. Neither did Hagen (1992) in her study of Norwegian viewers. This probably reflects the fact that women are out at work to a very high degree – almost as high as men – in the Nordic countries as compared to Great Britain. Having a social role as an employee may mean you increase the informational uses as well as the legitimating uses of news (Jensen, 1995).

Alasuutari makes a very important statement when he says about the value hierarchy that it 'reflects a collectively adopted moral code in the sense that it is independent of the programmes the individual watches' (1995: 127). As in other aspects of life, our behaviour is not necessarily in accordance with our ideals or moral stances. Scrutinizing quantitative audience data, Gunter and Wober also note that 'viewers are capable of watching and liking programmes which they themselves say are of low quality' (1992: 80).

As viewers we are usually somewhat omnivorous beings. We watch both news and other factual programmes, different types of fiction and all sorts of entertainment programmes (Findahl, 1991). Barwise and Ehrenberg (1988) conclude that television makes it possible for people to concentrate their viewing around one or two single genres, but most people do not. Instead, they prefer variation. This is not to say that there are no viewers or no demographic groups with more specific preferences. Young people, for instance, watch news and factual programmes less than others, and young and middle-aged women do not watch sports programmes as much as others, and male viewers watch action series more than female viewers, who, in their turn, watch romantic series more (Abrahamsson, 1993). Nevertheless, most of us like to see a little of everything.

The elevation of news viewing

News viewing is ruled by our social ambitions to be informed citizens, and here we may daily practise our responsibilities as citizens (Hagen, 1992; Jensen, 1995). It is 'perceived as a social duty; as part of a citizen's obligation to be informed. In other words, watching the program is perceived as a part of being well-oriented, which is essential to people's constructions of their citizen identities' (Hagen, 1992: 281). Accordingly, news viewing is attributed high importance by the audience. The word 'must' is often used in discourses about news viewing but seldom in relation to fiction viewing (Höijer, 1995). It is, as Jensen says 'an activity which must be attended to before one can "relax" or "go out"' (1995: 79). Not watching the news may even be considered blameworthy: 'I am not a very good news viewer,' said a woman I interviewed. As an audience we seem to have incorporated the ideology of news as a political genre; not necessarily as a resource for

political practice, however, but as a 'daily forum for the viewers' reasser-
tion of their political competence within a representative form of
democracy' (Jensen, 1995: 89).

Social identities in the form of citizen roles are certainly present in our
conceptualizations as news viewers, but it is important not to reduce news
viewing to only social duties. It is quite unbelievable that people choose to
watch news night after night and sometimes several times a day only in
order to perform their social duties. An alternative explanation is to regard
news viewing as ritual behaviour, repeated because it has become a daily
habit (cf. Lull, 1988). This may partly be true. A great deal of our everyday
activities are habits which easily become rituals in the sense that they are
more repressed than conscious choices. Other processes may also be
involved in news viewing. A human being strives to expand his or her
knowledge about the world. Learning to know the world and widen one's
knowledge is a strong prime mover already in us as very small children.
According to Maria Montessori (1987 [1949]), the child is born with a universal conquering mind. Maybe we as adults do not have the same
appetite for knowledge as a child, but we still want to know about things
behind the mountains. We want to confirm and widen our cognitions
about social and political reality, and news viewing may be regarded as a
continuation of the universal conquering mind of the child.[2]

That news viewing is quite complex and may evoke ambivalent feelings
in the audience has been shown by Hagen (1994). I will return to this later.

Mental effort

Salomon (1979) found that American and Israeli children had different
attitudes towards television which resulted in different viewing strategies.
Children in Israel regarded television as a more serious and informative
medium than children in the USA, and as audiences they were prepared to
invest more mental effort in their viewing than American children. We
probably also will find similar differences between adult audiences in
European countries with a long tradition of public service television compared to audiences in the USA where commercial television, with its focus
on entertainment, has dominated.

In the Nordic countries, for instance, with a history of public service television monopoly, broken not until the late eighties, average viewing is very
much lower (a good two hours per day) than in the USA (a good five hours
per day), and television is regarded as a medium to watch fairly attentively
in the evenings. Morning television has not become especially successful and
has quite low audience figures, and even though audiences have found their
way to satellite and commercial channels, the total viewing time has
increased amazingly little. In Great Britain, the amount of actual viewing has
also changed very little despite an increase in number of channels and hours

of broadcasting (Sharot, 1994). Basic viewing habits, embedded in the flow of everyday activities, acquired through socialization and formed during many years of viewing, change only slowly. Young generations will probably be more willing to form new viewing habits, but it takes time.

On the whole, in countries with strong public service television, audiences expect television to provide entertainment as well as information and popular education. They are prepared to invest some mental effort in learning from television. In Sweden on average a good 40 per cent of viewing time is devoted to informative programmes (Höijer, 1995). British audiences devote approximately 30 per cent to 'more demanding programmes' (information, features, news, etc.) and 60 per cent to entertainment programmes (game shows, light drama, sport, etc.). The remaining percentage includes children's and educational programmes (Barwise and Ehrenberg, 1988).

Conceptualizations of mental effort are apparently also part of audiences' specific genre expectations. We conceive of our roles as audiences very differently in relation to different genres, and we usually have no problems with changing roles. For example, we may regard our audience role as more active and mentally demanding in relation to news than in relation to fiction.

A resting-place for the mind

Fiction is so obviously connected with relaxation and entertainment that viewers I have interviewed have said that a good thing about watching fiction is that you can 'relax your brain'. It is something you can 'watch with a smile', or 'just sit idle' doing. In the two extracts below from interviews, we see how very differently people perceive their audience role when they contrast news viewing and fiction viewing (Höijer, 1995):

> You watch fiction and you don't need to think about anything else then. You can relax your brain. When you watch the news you must be more alert and watch more actively. (Female viewer)

> When I watch fiction I just sit idle. It's only entertainment. I don't expect to learn something, being informed or getting knowledge. That's from news and then I need to be more active. (Male viewer)

Some viewers also make it physically much more comfortable for themselves when they watch fiction as compared to watching news. They wrap themselves up in a rug, make themselves cosy on the couch, or place something to eat and drink on the table. Studies also show that audiences more often relax with a cup of coffee when they watch fiction programmes than during news viewing (Gahlin, 1989).

Although we as viewers subjectively experience less mental effort when we watch fiction compared to news, sometimes believing even that we do not need to use our brains at all, interpretation of fiction also implies mental activity, otherwise we would be unable to make sense of fiction programmes. As one viewer said about her fiction viewing, the low level of mental effort is connected to an experience of shutting the door on troubled thoughts:

> It is to empty your head of all the thoughts you have had all day long – you can relax your brain. It's resting your eyes without needing to think. And that's very nice to do now and then – rest your eyes and devote yourself to a world of imagination'. (Female viewer)

To shut the door on troubling thoughts is not done with a conscious mental effort to suppress thoughts. It is something which just happens in the viewing process when we are caught by the narrative. It is experienced as a rest for the mind, which at other times is busy with thoughts about what we need and ought to do, about duties and responsibilities. Other studies confirm such an escapist element especially in audiences' discourses about glamorous popular fiction (Livingstone, 1988; Radway, 1987; Silj, 1988).

We need to distinguish between types of fiction. Social realistic fiction in television, for instance, does invite audiences to think more about themselves. Viewers usually will find connections between the narratives and their own experiences; processes of recognition and identification are activated; and generalizations come to mind (Höijer, 1995, 1996). In audiences' judgements of their own viewing, this is conceived of as a higher level of emotional engagement and stronger elements of learning compared to watching more glamorous and non-realistic popular fiction (Höijer, 1995; Livingstone, 1988). This is in conjunction with Alasuutari's argument that ethical realism is highly valued among Finnish viewers. As an audience, we learn about what life is like for ordinary people, and 'fictional stories should not lead us into believing that life is too easy' (Alasuutari, 1992: 577).

Learning is usually perceived as more demanding than 'just being entertained'. Audiences put the strongest emphasis on learning in relation to news, and they experience themselves being more active as news viewers (see above). 'You take it more seriously,' as a viewer said.

The dilemmas of being an audience for violent news

Audiencehood takes a turn for the worse when we meet pictures of violence in the news, especially of innocent victims of war or other violent events. Exposure to such pictures has increased considerably in television news (Cronström, 1994), and the conjunction between the private and social lives of viewers and reports about inconceivable violence, with the exposure of corpses and wounded and injured victims, gives rise to many dilemmas with conflicting feelings and thoughts.

Sitting in our warm and cosy living rooms we witness brutal events in the world outside, the death and suffering of others. We may only think of pictures we all have seen of the swollen dead bodies in the rivers of Rwanda or of burned corpses, mutilated people and blood pools in Bosnia. Since news viewing is an ordinary and socially desirable practice, we must as viewers handle evidence about the evil as part of this social practice. Studies show how problematic this can be and how audiences develop different strategies to cope with the situation (Höijer, 1994). In audiences' discourses about viewing violent news several dilemmas emerge.[3]

To be able to watch the news at all, the viewer must protect himself or herself by, for instance, fending off the violence: 'If you reacted to all the violence that's shown on the television news you wouldn't stand watching the news.' Not watching the news, however, which is a potential way to avoid shocking violence, is regarded as an undesirable act. Another social dilemma implies a conflict between being upset by the violence in news programmes and performing other social duties of daily life: 'I feel sick and can start crying when I watch the violence. But it's my responsibility to care for my children when I come home since I work long hours. I can't sit in the couch with feelings of suffering for the shape the world is in.'

Furthermore, the uniting of activities and obligations of daily life with conceptions about being a good citizen reacting against violence poses a moral dilemma: 'Most of all I get mad over myself for not doing anything or taking any initiative. It's a matter of priorities. You can't blame it on not having time for it. The little you can do seems just ordinary but we all are busy doing our own businesses.' The dilemma may also imply contradictory feelings between the wish to avoid viewing violence and the wish to acquaint oneself with the violence in order to be informed about what is going on: 'You don't want to watch it but then you have to. Many times I'm telling myself not to watch it. I know it's only going to be about something violent. You're ambivalent but you do watch it after all. It's your duty to know about matters.'

Here again we see how deeply the ideology of enlightenment is rooted in the audience's mind. This is also obvious in a dilemma related to parenthood and thoughts about children and violence in the news: 'You want to protect your children. I really wish the kids never had to watch violent news but at the same time I can't forbid them to watch it. Children have to learn about what is going on.'

To be an audience to the depiction of documentary violence in the news may also imply deeper emotional dilemmas within the individual. Violence is traumatic for everybody since it deals with suffering and death. Hearing about and watching violence may be filled with agony because it awakens mortal fears within ourselves or painful remembrances of the deaths of our relatives. Among immigrants from Latin America, alarming memories of violence against themselves or other people in their countries were brought to the fore when they watched violent news (Pereira-Norrman, 1994). But still they watched news containing violence because they wanted to be informed citizens.[4]

Third-person effects

Studies of self–other perceptions of media impact point out that people use different criteria to make judgements about themselves as an audience and judgements about others (see Gunther and Thorson, 1992). We may, for instance, believe that others are more influenced by mass media texts than we are ourselves. This phenomenon has been called the third-person effect (Davidson, 1983).

In a study about citizens' social worries for the future (Dahlgren and Höijer, 1996), many expressed the view that other people were much more influenced by mass media than they were themselves; for example, the fact that news very much focuses on negative and tragic events and that this creates concern among people – not oneself as an audience member though – and a pessimistic view of society. 'My friends usually turn pale when they watch the news,' as a young man expressed it. 'Weak' groups in society, such as elderly people, women, youths and children, are pointed to as most easily influenced, and questions of violence are often focused on. The two quotations below further illustrate how perspectives of gender may influence our cognitions:

> The media really have a large impact on others. Just look at all the young girls and old ladies who don't dare to be outdoors after five o'clock in the afternoon. It's all through media who create this fear. (Male viewer)

> If the media didn't report about violence it would disappear. Today everything that happens throughout the world is reported about and it is almost only violence. It becomes transmitted in this way. Boys and men become violent. Young folks – it's acceptable to be violent. There is a risk that everybody will arm themselves because they are anxious. (Female viewer)

Third-person effects are often related to opinions about the media, for example opinions about the reporting of violence in the news. In this case they may be used either to justify restrictions or to emphasize the necessity of reporting about violence (Höijer, 1994). One notion is that it is bad for children to see violence, hence showing it must therefore be restricted: 'You don't have to show violence. Children can't handle the violence.' Another notion emphasizes harmful effects on young people. They might commit violent acts themselves, and for this reason violence should be restricted: 'It isn't necessary to show it. The more violence is shown, the more violence we get. Especially the young folks are inspired by it.' But we also find opposite ideas about third-person effects related to violent news. Young people should be exposed to documentary violence in order to learn to understand the real consequences of the violence in society in contrast to the glamorization of violence in fiction: 'It's good for young people to watch what's going on. Otherwise they don't believe it's true'.

Discussion

As we have seen, people have ideas about themselves and others as television audiences. However, it is hard to assess the extent to which the quotations presented above, indicating different cognitions, are constructions of discursive situations, such as interviews which frequently have been used in the studies reported on, or if people in private also think about themselves as audiences in the same way. We must touch upon theories of identity, and, depending on the theoretical perspective, we may have very different views on identity construction (cf., Dickerson, 1996). Some stress the role of language, especially discursive and dialogical practices, while others point to the role of practical activities. Still others see identity primarily as a psychic unit which can be brought to the fore in, for instance, a therapeutic interview.

To a certain extent we do produce different versions of identity in different discursive contexts, but it is also reasonable to assume that we carry within us identities in the form of cognitive self-schemas formed in all kinds of social interaction with the world. Self-schemas may be vague and full of contradictions. Neither is perceiving oneself as an audience member the most prominent in a person's identity construction, whether it occurs in conversations or in the form of inner thoughts or preconscious conceptualizations. And as academic researchers we must admit that our picture of the audience is always coloured by research methods and perspectives. The picture that has been presented here shows that people have some audience identity, partly in the form of collective ideals about being an audience and partly in the form of ideas about one's own and about other people's audiencehood.

Metacognitions on audiencehood are as much stamped by culture and ideologies as are other practices and social roles. According to Billig et al. (1988), everyday thinking has a dilemmatic quality, that is, it contains contradicting themes and conceptualizations. Ordinary life, in work and private, is shaped by social and moral dilemmas. Sometimes we are aware of them, other times not.

The contradictions and dilemmas we find in audiencehood are quite typical of everyday thinking in Western culture, and nothing unique to the social practice of being an audience. We have assimilated cultural norms and ideologies linked to enlightenment and ethics praising productivity and hard work, and they have an impact on our cognitions of human behaviour in general. According to Lakoff and Johnson, we have a conceptual reference point or a cultural basis in our experience for viewing ourselves as 'more UP than DOWN, more FRONT than BACK, more ACTIVE than PASSIVE, more GOOD than BAD' (1980, 132). We use the metaphoric configuration in associating values to social acts. We may see how television viewing becomes problematic in this cultural orientation. We sit down, so we are more down than up and not vice versa, which, historically at least, implies a higher degree of human activity. At an overall level we conceive ourselves as passive when we sit down and just watch television, and this is bad. We are not doing some good. But if we have worked hard during the day, especially with our bodies, we may relax with television and permit ourselves a little entertainment. It is also possible to understand why we find the most ambivalent views on television among people with high education if we consider that professionals sit down when they work. In professionals' minds their bodies need some activity in upright positions and not to be further placed in passive down positions in front of the television screen.

The front–back dimension seems a little harder to apply. Watching television does take place in front of the television set, but metaphorically more important is that we are spectators not involved in the events on the screen. We are not in the forefront ourselves, but rather in the background. The foreground is something taking place on the screen out of our control. We are obliged to take a back seat.

Cognitions of audiencehood in relation to different genres give a somewhat different picture. As news viewers we usually feel ourselves active, but fiction viewing is regarded as a more passive audiencehood. We may further consider ourselves at least a little in the front when we update our world knowledge via daily news compared to fiction, which is primarily associated with pleasure. Accordingly, we also evaluate news and informative genres higher than fiction and entertainment. As news viewers we may even conceive of ourselves as good citizens, but watching soap operas sometimes makes us feel bad. It is a genre that many conceive of as down if we use the metaphoric configuration above, that is, low or lowbrow. This is probably partly formed by public discourses about genres, such as discussions of high and low culture, quality, and so on, and partly by our own direct experiences of genres.

However, neither is news viewing solely a 'good-feeling' activity. There are many ambivalences and dilemmas also in this audiencehood, which can be especially dilemmatic when we watch violent news. We then become passive witnesses to innocent victims of brutal violence. The active news viewer role becomes overpowered by the passive witness role, and as an audience we here come to a critical point.

The active–passive dimension is central, explicitly or implicitly, in different accounts of audiences. It is obviously so in audiences' metacognitions, in audiences' notions of the audience. It is also central in political discourses about democracy and citizenship (Dahlgren, 1995), and in broadcasting ideologies, especially those based on social responsibility models, that is, the public service tradition. Finally, it has been and still is a central dimension in social science and humanistic research on audiences.

Common to all accounts is the ideal that active is better than passive. Social science and humanistic research on audiences argues about who has said that the audience is most active and who said it first. People in general evaluate active audiencehood higher than passive. Public service television in general emphasizes audiences as active citizens who strengthen their social, cultural and political engagements by viewing. Obligations in relation to democracy are, for instance, overarching objectives for most European public service companies (*Diffusion Special*, 1995), which call for active audiences watching news and information programmes (Lund, 1996). Many television companies, irrespective of whether they are commercial or not, strongly underline the value of the active imbued news genre. It is the flagship in programming.

But there are gaps, as in thinking and in human activities in general, between ideals and practices. Audiences practise not only active audiencehood, that is, watch demanding programmes; they also practise what they regard as passive audiencehood to an even greater extent. Public service television increases its output of light entertainment and focuses on audience ratings. Academic research, especially the cultural studies tradition, celebrates all audiencehood as active, and seems unable to make distinctions with regard to active–passive dimensions between any genres or social uses. In my view we should deepen our theoretical and empirical understanding of the concepts of active and passive without falling into the trap that being active is always best for the audience.

Notes

1. For a discussion of the concept of metacognition, see, for example, Jones and Idol (1990).

2. Entertainment and relaxation may also be part of news consumption. This was shown already by Schramm (1949), and has later been confirmed by uses and gratifications studies (e.g. Wenner, 1985).

3. The quotations in the following are from two studies, one with in-depth interviews with a small number of viewers, the other based on telephone interviews with a representative sample of over 500 news viewers (see Höijer, 1994).

4. There are differences between demographically constituted audience groups in their reactions to violent news, and in the strategies they use to handle depictions of realistic violence. One strategy is to harden oneself in order not to become unpleasantly affected by watching violent news. This is a more common reaction among male viewers than among female viewers, and also more common among younger viewers. For female viewers it is harder to stand watching violent news.

They more often shut their eyes, look away or become sad. Such reactions are also more common among the elderly (Höijer, 1994).

References

Abrahamsson, U. B. (1993) 'När kvinnor ser på tv' [When Women Watch Television], in U. Carlsson (ed.), *Nordisk forskning om kvinnor och medier. Nordicom-Sverige*, 3.

Alasuutari, P. (1992) '"I'm Ashamed to Admit it but I have Watched Dallas": The Moral Hierarchy of TV Programmes', *Media, Culture & Society*, 14 (4) 561–82.

Alasuutari, P. (1995) *Researching Culture: Qualitative Method and Cultural Studies.* London: Sage.

Ang, I. (1991) *Desperately Seeking the Audience.* London: Routledge.

Argyle, M. (1996) *The Social Psychology of Leisure.* London: Penguin Books.

Barwise, P. and Ehrenberg, A. (1988) *Television and its Audience.* London: Sage.

Billig, M., Condor, S., Edwards, D., Gane, M., Middleton, D. and Radley, A. (1988) *Ideological Dilemmas: A Social Psychology of Everyday Thinking.* London: Sage.

Cronström, J. (1994) 'The Depiction of Violence and Victims of Violence in Swedish Television Newscasts: A Content Analysis of the Evening News on Public Service and Private Channels'. Paper presented at the International Conference on Violence in the Media, New York 3–4 October.

Dahlgren, P. (1995) *Television and the Public Sphere: Citizenship, Democracy and the Media.* London: Sage.

Dahlgren, P. and Höijer, B. (1996) *Medier, oro och medborgarskap* [The Media, Anxiety and Citizenship]. Stockholm: The Swedish National Board of Psychological Defence, Report No. 141.

Davidson, W.P. (1983) 'The Third-Person Effect in Communication', *Public Opinion Quarterly*, 47: 1–15.

Dickerson, P. (1996) 'Let Me Tell Us Who I Am: The Discursive Construction of Viewer Identity', *European Journal of Communication*, 11 (1): 57–82.

Diffusion Special (1995) 'Media Policy – Council of Europe: The Public Service – A Factor in European Democracy'. Geneva, February.

Findahl, O. (1991) 'Svensk television' [Swedish Television], in U. Carlsson and M. Anselm (eds), *Medie-Sverige 91.* Nordicom-Sverige.

Gahlin, A. (1989) *Tittarsituationen. Om sällskap, bredvidsysslor och uppmärksamhet framför tv:n* [The Viewing Context: On Attention, Companionship and Activities in Front of the Television Screen]. Stockholm: Swedish Broadcasting Corporation, Audience and Programme Research Department, Report No. 16.

Gane, R. (1994) 'Television Audience Measurement Systems in Europe: A Review and Comparison', in R. Kent (ed.), *Measuring Media Audiences.* London: Routledge.

Gunter, B. and Wober, M. (1992) *The Reactive Viewer: A Review of Research on Audience Reaction Measurement.* (Independent Television Commission Research Monographs Series.) London: John Libbey.

Gunther, A.C. and Thorson, E. (1992) 'Perceived Persuasive Effects of Product Commercials and Public Service Announcements: Third-Person Effects in New

Domains', *Communication Research*, 19 (5): 574–96.

Hagen, I. (1992) *News Viewing Ideals and Everyday Practices: The Ambivalences of Watching Dagsrevyen.* University of Bergen, Department of Mass Communication, Report No. 15.

Hagen, I. (1994) 'Expectations and Consumption Patterns in TV News Viewing', *Media, Culture & Society*, 16: 415–28.

Hagen, I. (1996) 'Modern Dilemmas: TV Audiences' Time Use and Moral Evaluation'. Paper presented at the IAMCR Conference in Sydney, Australia, 18–22 August. (Forthcoming in I. Hagen and J. Wasko (eds), *Consuming Audiences: Production and Reception in Media Research.* Hampton Press Inc.

Hartley, J. (1987) 'Invisible Fictions: Television Audiences, Paedocracy, Pleasure', *Textual Practice*, 1: 121–38.

Höijer, B. (1994) *Våldsskildringar i TV-nyheter* [Depictions of Violence on Television News]. University of Stockholm, Department of Journalism, Media and Communication, Report No. 5.

Höijer, B. (1995) *Genreföreställningar och tolkningar av berättande i tv* [Genre Expectations and Interpretations of Television Narration]. University of Stockholm, Department of Journalism, Media and Communication, Report No. 1.

Höijer, B. (1996) 'Audiences' Expectations on and Interpretations of Different Television Genres: A Socio-Cognitive Approach'. Paper presented at the IAMCR Conference in Sydney, Australia, 18–22 August. (Forthcoming in I. Hagen and J. Wasko (eds) *Consuming Audiences: Production and Reception in Media Research* Hampton Press Inc.)

Jensen, K.B. (1995) *The Social Semiotics of Mass Communication.* London: Sage.

Jensen, K.B., Schrøder, K., Stampe, T., Søndergaard, H. and Topsøe-Jensen, J. (1994) 'Super Flow, Channel Flows, and Audience Flows: A Study of Viewers' Reception of Television as Flow', *The Nordicom Review*, 2: 1–13.

Jones, B.F. and Idol, L. (eds) (1990) *Dimensions of Thinking and Cognitive Instruction.* Hillsdale, NJ: Lawrence Erlbaum Associates.

Lakoff, G. and Johnson, M. (1980) *Metaphors We Live By.* Chicago: University of Chicago Press.

Livingstone, S.M. (1988) 'Why People Watch Soap Opera: An Analysis of the Explanations of British Viewers', *European Journal of Communication*, 3 (1): 55–80.

Lull, J. (1988) 'Constructing Rituals of Extension Through Family Television Viewing', in J. Lull (ed.), *World Families Watch Television.* Newbury Park, CA: Sage.

Lund, S. (1996) 'Hva er allmennkringkasting og hvordan kan det måles?' [What is Public Service Broadcasting and How Can It Be Measured?]. in *Public service regnskap 1995*, NRK Forskningen (Norwegian Broadcasting Corporation, Research Department).

McQuail, D. (1994) *Mass Communication Theory: An Introduction.* London: Sage.

Montessori, M. (1987 [1949]) *Barnasinnet: The Absorbent Mind.* Stockholm: MacBook Förlag.

Morley, D. (1986) *Family Television: Cultural Power and Domestic Leisure.* London: Comedia.

Pereira-Norrman, L. (1994) 'Jag vill stoppa våldet: En publikstudie av latinamerikaner i Sverige' [How Immigrants from Latin America Conceive of Violence in the News]. University of Stockholm: Department of Journalism, Media and Communication, (paper).

Radway, J.A. (1987) *Reading the Romance: Women, Patriarchy and Popular Literature.* London: Verso.

Salomon, G. (1979) *Interaction of Media, Cognition and Learning*. San Francisco: Jossey-Bass.

Schramm, W. (1949) 'The Nature of News', *Journalism Quarterly*, 26: 259–69.

Sharot, T. (1994) 'Measuring Television Audiences in the UK', in R. Kent (ed.), *Measuring Media Audiences*. London: Routledge.

Silj, A. (1988) *East of Dallas: The European Challenge to American Television*. London: British Film Institute.

Weibull, L. (1995) 'Mediemätningar i Sverige: Mediebarometerns roll' [Media Measurements in Sweden], in U. Carlsson (ed.), *Mediemätningar: Teori, tolkning, tillämpning. Nordicom-Sverige*, 2.

Wenner, L.A. (1985) 'The Nature of News Gratifications', in K.E. Rosengren, L.A. Wenner and P. Palmgreen (eds), *Media Gratifications Research: Current Perspectives*. Beverly Hills: Sage.

Winnicott, D.W. (1953) 'Transitional Objects and Transitional Phenomena', *The International Journal of Psycho-Analysis*, 34: 89–97.

10

'TO BOLDLY GO . . .'
The 'Third Generation' of Reception Studies

David Morley

The work collected together in this volume is, as its editor, Pertti Alasuutari, suggests in the introduction, most notable for the shift of attention and emphasis it displays in conceiving of 'the media and media messages in a broader sense than just as an encoded text to be then decoded by a particular "interpretive community"'. This focus on the question of 'the cultural community' which inspires the attempt here to map the landmarks of the new 'mediascapes' in which we find ourselves (and the 'metacognitions' we have of them, as Höijer puts it), is very much to be welcomed. In making this move, we are then able to go beyond the evaluation of the effects of any particular media message, the better to investigate, as Alasuutari suggests, the premises which underlie and constitute the discourses through and within which 'the media' (and their 'effects' or 'uses') become an object of research and concern. The emphasis thus shifts, as he observes, to the analysis of discourses on the media and their contents 'as a topic in its own right' rather than 'as a lens through which to peek into individual acts of reception'. Here Alasuutari's argument offers an interesting parallel to Pollock's (1976 [1955]) critique of the very concept of individual opinion. Pollock simply observed that 'the very assumption that there exists the opinion of every individual is dubious', in so far as 'individual opinion, which appears to current opinion research to be the elementary unit, is in fact an extremely derivative, mediated thing' (1976 [1955]: 228, 233). Similarly, Alasuutari rightly insists on moving beyond the investigation of individual instances of media reception in isolation, to focus rather on the discourses through which our very sense of the (different) media, of ourselves as their audience, and of our involvements with them, are constituted.

The slippery slope of intellectual progress

However, some degree of caution is necessary here. Ann Gray rightly warns of the potential dangers confronting any schematic overview of work in this field which attempts to establish too clear and one-directional a storyline. In this case, a meta-narrative of progress, characterized by a series of clear epistemological/methodological 'breaks', would evidently be unhelpful. Happily, the authors here are themselves alert to this danger. Thus, in the Introduction, Alasuutari notes that, in pursuing the question of understanding the discourses of our current media culture '[o]ne does not necessarily abandon ethnographic case studies of audiences and analyses of individual programmes' – rather, one reframes and recontextualizes them in a new way.

If the history of intellectual work can, by definition, only be told retrospectively, it remains none the less important, as Schrøder recognizes, to appreciate the value of previous analytical insights 'in the historical academic context in which they were presented'. Gray offers an illuminating example of this, when she draws on Stuart Hall's retrospective comments on his development of the 'encoding/decoding' model. In them, Hall makes it quite clear that in its initial version, the model was developed for quite specific polemical purposes, with the object of dislodging one particular alternative approach (that of the Leicester Centre for Mass Communications Research under the direction of James Halloran). In this connection, anyone interested in my own take on the historiographical questions at stake in writing the history of research in this field can readily consult the debate between myself and my colleague James Curran (in Curran et al., 1996). Curran's argument there is that what he calls the 'new revisionism' (what is called here the 'second generation' of reception studies) has done nothing more than reinvent the wheel of earlier sociological work in this field, and is therefore involved in an unconsciously circular (if not regressive) rather than linear/progressive movement. In the context of that debate, I was at pains to stress the significant differences and genuine advances made in recent years by the first and second generation scholars involved in the study of media consumption. However, it does not help to overstate these differences. I argued in that debate that the subsequent history of research always creates new precursors for itself – in the sense of making newly visible earlier work which had previously been little regarded. None the less, and notwithstanding the inevitable politics of the writing of history (it could always be written differently and any given history will, no doubt, in time, be rewritten), our understanding of the relation of new work to old is crucial.

My own feeling is that rather than thinking in terms of a linear succession of truths, paradigms or models, each displacing the previous one, in some triumphal progress, we may be better served by a multidimensional model. By this I mean to suggest simply that what is often at stake in intellectual progress is how to build new insights into (or onto) the old, rather than how to entirely replace the old with the new. Perspectives and models are always developed within some particular intellectual context, in relation to the intellectual and political protagonists of that moment. The demands of some given context often require an emphasis on some particular aspect or issue in our research – emphases which, after a time, and in a new context, may well be no longer necessary.

To put the matter in more autobiographical terms, when my own research shifted in emphasis, from the focus on the interpretation of a particular programme in the *Nationwide* (Morley, 1980; Morley and Brunsden, 1998) work to the study of practices of media consumption, in *Family Television* (Morley, 1986), this was not because I no longer believed that the interpretation of programmes mattered. Rather, I was attempting to recontextualize the original analysis of programme interpretations by placing them in the broader frame of the domestic context in which television viewing, as a practice, is routinely conducted. This was not to argue for the supersession of the one concern by the other, but rather to attempt to move towards a model of media consumption capable of dealing simultaneously with the transmission of programmes/contents/ideologies (the vertical dimension of power) and with their inscription in the everyday practices through which media content is incorporated into daily life (the horizontal dimension of ritual and participation). My own view is that it is crucial, as Alasuutari suggests, that, similarly, the transition (if such there be) from a second to a third generation of reception studies should be one in which that emphasis on viewing practices, rather than itself being abandoned, should now be reframed within the new focus on the broader discourses within which media audiences are themselves constructed and inscribed.

Of course, it could simply be that, representing, as I do, work characterized here as belonging to an earlier 'generation' of audience studies, I now offer this more gradualist (or incremental) model of intellectual progress precisely because I feel uneasy about the way in which the 'new generation' of scholars in this field may perhaps entirely displace/decentre my own concerns. To reverse the issue for a moment, I can certainly recall previous moments when I highlighted my own differences with earlier scholars and models more sharply than I subsequently thought helpful. Thus, for example, my polemical comments on 'uses and gratifications' in *The Nationwide Audience* contrast strongly with those made a few years later, in *Family Television*, where I began to develop the outline of the multidimensional model outlined above, and attempted to indicate how elements of the 'uses and gratifications' model could, in fact, usefully be incorporated into what is called here the 'second generation' of work in this field. In now urging the advantages of this 'inclusive' model of intellectual progress, I can only hope that I am doing something more than expressing an unhelpful conservatism, motivated unconsciously by the desire to defend my personal investment in a set of positions and arguments which may well, for the good of the field, genuinely need to be quite transcended!

Methodological byways and journeys to surprising destinations

In this context, the perceptive comments on questions of methodology offered by Kim Schrøder (in this volume) are exemplary, in my view. Rather than staking out any absolutist claim for the essential superiority of any one methodological perspective over all others, Schrøder offers a judiciously pragmatic perspective which gives due weight to both the advantages and 'opportunity costs' of a range of different perspectives. Thus, Schrøder gives due weight to the potential problems of 'anecdotalism' in qualitative media research and to the dangers to which Birgitta Höijer (1990) has rightly noted in relation to the quotations of supposedly 'typical examples' from fieldwork, when the use of one or two particularly vivid 'instances' can sometimes persuade us that they 'represent' a trend of some kind – which we cannot, of course, verify. Schrøder's 'endorsement of Lewis' (1991) call for the need to balance the advantages of 'qualitative depth' in our analyses with those of the 'synthetic organization' of data is a welcome one to me. Likewise, his comments on the way in which qualitative researchers smuggle quasi-quantitative terms ('often', 'many') into their analyses, without proper justification, helpfully echoes those made by Curran (1976) some years ago in defence of quantitative analysis (for another intelligent defence of the potential of quantitative methods, see Lewis, 1997).

Schrøder's is an open-handed approach which I, for one, welcome, sceptical as it is both of the dangers of forms of radical contextualism which would seem to deny the very possibility of generalization, and of 'hard' social science's fetishization of 'representativeness' based on the virtues of large samples. As Schrøder points out, these (larger) 'samples of convenience' are often composed in substantial part of college students, whose main virtue as a 'database' is no more than their ready availability for sampling purposes.

We do need always to be prepared for the possibility that our research trajectories will take us to destinations which we had not anticipated. By way of example, in this connection, we might recall that much cultural studies work in the 1970s followed a structuralist approach to textual analysis, which insisted on the need to analyse a TV programme holistically, rather than dissaggregating it into its constituent parts. On this basis, content analysis approaches to TV texts were dismissed, precisely because of their tendency to 'atomize' their object of study into a series of bits, where, it was argued, the sum of the parts was less than the whole. However, years of ethnographic work in the 1980s have now alerted us to the fact that people often don't watch 'whole programmes': they come into the house, switch the TV on, only pay it intermittent attention, and often surf between and across simultaneous modes of televisual flow, on different channels. At which point, one has to ask whether the structuralist critique of content analysis was as well founded as it once seemed. In which case, scholars of the 'third generation' of audience studies may need to go back to reconsider whether those of the 'first generation' were on the right track at all in their critique of content analysis, or whether today's scholars may need to critically revisit some of the questions which their predecessors imagined themselves to have resolved for certain.

Public morals, responsible viewing and involved citizens

To my mind, what most distinctively characterizes the new work presented in this collection is the recurring focus on the question of the 'moral' dimension of broadcasting and its consumption. This meta-framework connects together a whole set of questions about citizenship, appropriate modes of media consumption and behaviour, and the relative moral value of factual and fictional programming. Clearly, behind these issues lies a particular conception of democracy, the public sphere, and the role of public service broadcasting. In this section I shall concentrate on what is helpfully revealed in this emphasis, and at the same time on how the very clarification of these issues necessarily exposes the particular and problematic premises on which much of this debate rests.

A number of the contributions here focus centrally on the function of the media as a link to the public sphere, and on the implications of a model of citizenship in which it is a responsibility of the good citizen to use the news/factual programming offered by the media to keep him- or herself well informed about 'important matters'. In this perspective, news viewing is a duty (cf. Hagen, 1992, 1994) derived from the romantic ideal of the democratic citizen and from an enlightenment ideology in which, as one of Höijer's respondents observes, however ambivalent you may feel about watching unpleasant things on the news, 'It's your duty to know about matters'. As Hagen puts it, news viewing is 'perceived as a social duty; as part of a citizen's duty to be informed' (1992: 281). It is an 'activity which must be attended to before one can "relax" or "go out"' (Jensen, 1995: 79). It is from this moralistic perspective (as Höijer interestingly observes, with perhaps a specifically Lutheran perspective, in parts of Scandinavia) that the news is then seen as 'the most important thing on television' (respondent quoted by Höijer) – and not watching television news can thus be construed as, in itself, blameworthy, or irresponsible.

As Hagen observes, historically, all of this has taken place in much of Scandinavia within a particular model of public service television (what Bondebjerg [1990] has labelled 'school teachers' television', quoted by

Hagen in this book, page 138), in which the broadcasters have, as a priority, the 'missionary' role of 'educating' their audience within the context of
a normative relationship' based on what Hagen calls a 'fact contract'
between the media and their consumers.

There are, however, substantial difficulties with this model. Many years
ago, even before the widespread prevalence of television, Lazarsfeld and
Merton characterized the problems facing the viewer who attempts to
use the media to become 'well informed', the better to play his or her role
as citizen. They were concerned that exposure to a flood of media information might well 'narcoticize' audiences, rather than motivate them to
action:

> The individual reads accounts of issues and problems and may even discuss
> alternative lines of action. But this rather intellectualised, remote connection
> with organised social action is not activated. The interested and informed citizen
> can congratulate himself on his lofty state of interest and information and forget
> to see that he has abstained from decision and action. In short he takes his sec-
> ondary contact with the world of political reality, his reading and listening and
> thinking, as a vicarious performance. He comes to mistake knowing about prob-
> lems of the day for doing something about them. He is concerned. He is
> informed. And he has all sorts of ideas about what should be done. But after he
> has gotten through his dinner and after he has listened to his favoured radio
> programmes and after he has read his second paper of the day, it is really time
> for bed. In this peculiar respect, mass communication may be included among
> the most respectable and efficient of social narcotics. (Lazarsfeld and Merton,
> 1948, quoted in Morley, 1992: 252)

In a similar way, Brian Groombridge, writing in the early 1970s, pointed to
the fact that, for most people, most of the time, 'the news' has little real significance for them, in so far as it is not clear what, if anything, can be done
with most of the information received from the news. Hence it is very
badly assimilated, if at all. The audience's sense of powerlessness over the
world reported on the news thus frames their fundamental attitude
towards any specific news story/report (see Groombridge, 1972). If the
mode of address of traditional public service news and current affairs programming can be characterized as 'serious, official and impersonal [. . .].
Aimed at producing understanding and belief' (Fiske, quoted in Branston,
1993), then it is clear that the 'believing subject' which it aims to interpel-
late is by no means always available for conscription. One fundamental
question here concerns the relative importance of 'fact' and 'fiction' on
television. The simple fact (sic) is that most people watch fiction on television, most of the time. Notwithstanding this, media studies, in many
places, has long continued to grant special emphasis and importance to the
study of 'serious' factual programming. However, in societies like many of
those in the West, with rapidly declining indices of overall public participation in political affairs (as measured by voting etc.) and increasing
numbers of people excluded or alienated, for one reason or another, from

the process of formal politics, on which 'serious television' focuses, this may well be an inadvisable strategy. To transpose a famous saying of Brecht's, it seems as if, the viewers having failed ('serious') television, some in media studies think that it may be necessary to dissolve the audience and 'elect' another. Of course, the other alternative would be to pay attention to whatever it is that the audience do seem to think is 'real', 'important' and/or 'serious', rather than berate (or ignore) them, when their choices are at odds with our presumptions (for a fuller discussion of these issues, see Morley, forthcoming).

Facts, fictions and morals

Alasuutari, in the Introduction, observes that 'there is a underlying morality which seems to be based on the conviction that watching television has to be somehow useful for the individual'. The premise is that 'merely' watching television, *per se*, is in need of legitimation as a proper activity for an adult citizen. This legitimation is much more easily achieved in the case of factual programming: as Alasuutari also notes in Chapter 5, 'With the exception of the evening news and other current affairs programmes, people seem to feel a compelling need to explain, defend and justify their viewing habits'. Conversely 'whereas people tend to excuse themselves for watching fiction and serials, they perceive watching the news as a civic duty. For not watching the daily news programme is something that has to be accounted for' (Alasuutari, Introduction).

As Alasuutari notes, beyond the premise of the superior moral value of fact over fiction there are also distinctions of value within the realm of fiction itself. Thus, in the latter context, even the viewing of fiction can sometimes be redeemed, as long as it is fiction made within the terms of 'ethical realism' (Alasuutari (1992) suggests for example 'films that portray old country life') which provide 'ethically sound models of life' for the audience; in effect, another form of (moral) education.

What is striking here is the guilt associated with (unredeemed) television viewing in general and, as Höijer puts it, 'how very differently people perceive their audience role when they contrast news viewing and fiction viewing'. Höijer reports her respondents as talking of how '[w]hen you watch the news you must be more alert and watch more actively' whereas '[w]hen [you] watch fiction [you] just sit idle'. The account Höijer goes on to offer of evidence that some viewers also tend to make themselves much more physically comfortable (on the couch, wrapped in a rug, perhaps with refreshments to hand) when watching fiction, as compared to news, only serves to emphasize the 'guilty' nature of the pleasures of the consumption of fiction. Plainly, if the citizen is to do no more than watch TV, he (and much of the point here is that this way of conceptualizing 'active citizenship' is an implicitly masculine model) must at least sit upright in a

hard-back chair, alert and paying full attention to some form of factual programming, so as to increase his stock of knowledge, and thereby become a
better citizen. Evidently, citizens should not be allowed to get comfortable, otherwise their springs of action might perhaps become unbent (in
Hoggart's deathless phrase) and they be quite emasculated. One remem-
bers here the terrible fate of Flaubert's Emma Bovary: a woman quite
ruined by her reading of fiction.

The gender of the real

In his Introduction to this volume, Alasuutari helpfully identifies a number
of the simultaneous changes of emphasis that might be used to distinguish the first and second generations of audience studies. Those changes
can be (retrospectively) understood to have involved a shift from a focus
on factual to fictional media forms; from questions of knowledge to questions of pleasure; from programme contents to media functions; from
conventional to identity politics; and, not least, from matters of class to
matters of race, ethnicity and, central to our purposes here, gender.
    Over the last few years, there has been a notable backlash against the
work of these 'second generation' scholars (myself included), on the part of
those who call for a return to the eternal verities of political economy and
the sociology of mass communications. It has now become the (interestingly Soviet-style) fashion in some quarters to denounce this 'second
generation' of cultural studies work as 'deviationist', that is, (ir)responsible
for redirecting attention away from the 'real' world of parliamentary politics, hard facts, economic truths (and their ideological misrepresentations
by the media) towards the (by contrast) 'unimportant' realm of the domestic functioning of the media and the consumption of fictional pleasures. A
large number of political economists and media sociologists have now
signed up to this critique of what they see as the unfortunate and mis-
guided 'depoliticization' of media studies (for examples, see Corner, 1991,
1995; Ferguson and Golding, 1997; Garnham, 1997; Philo and Miller, 1997).
    In her essay in this volume, Ann Gray captures the spirit of this critique
most elegantly when she picks out Dennis McQuail's (1997: 55) extraordi-
nary use of the words 'flighty and opinionated' to characterize cultural
studies work in this field. As Gray notes, the supposed 'loss of critical
energy' (according to Corner, 1991) involved in, among other things, the
turning of attention to the role of media in the articulation of the public and
private spheres, and the investigation of the deep and complex inscription
of the media in a variety of forms of (necessarily gendered) domesticities,
could only ever be understood as an 'abandonment' of politics within a
quite unreflexive and unhelpfully narrow definition of what 'politics' is. As
Gray rightly observes, in her critique of Corner, his perspective simply
presumes the greater 'reality' and superiority of the 'public knowledge'

project (as he terms it) of media studies over all other issues. I would entirely support Gray when she argues that the definition of 'politics' and the valuation of 'public knowledge' uncritically enshrined in the very premises of Corner et al.'s critique must be understood to be heavily gendered (and 'race'-ed – cf. Husband, 1994; Modood, 1992; Pines, 1992, on the largely unexamined issue of the 'whiteness' of the 'public sphere'). As Gray notes, within this perspective 'the importance of current affairs programming, and of the public knowledge project, is simply taken for granted', as is the implicit (and largely naturalized) hierarchization of the 'power relations therein, which this representation of the field demonstrates'.

In parallel fashion, Joke Hermes demonstrates how the emergence of women newsreaders in Dutch TV can be seen to have provoked a crisis in which the very identity of 'serious journalism' was seen to be at stake, simply because of the association of the feminine with 'non-quality, irrationality, emotionality and the loss of control'. As she notes, drawing on Rebecca Walkowitz's (1997) analysis of the 'Murphy Brown' affair in the USA, it is exactly a 'moment' such as this that 'exposes journalism as other than the "ungendered, objective mediation of truth" [. . .] it sets itself up to be' (see also Hermes, 1997). Perhaps Liesbet van Zoonen puts it most starkly when she notes that the central problem here, which badly needs addressing, is the way that 'the public knowledge project tends to become a new male preserve, concerned with ostensibly gender-neutral issues such as citizenship, but actually neglecting the problematic relation of non-white, non-male citizens to the public sphere' (Van Zoonen, 1994 : 125). And, one might add, thus far at least, the 'public knowledge' project has largely tended to ignore the cultural dimensions of the economic institutions, market mechanisms and legal processes which are, in fact, integral (and indeed crucial) to the effective functioning of this sphere.

It would be a great mistake to concede too much to those who call for a return to the 'eternal verities' of sociology or of political economy, as a way out of the supposed 'dead ends' (cf. Philo and Miller, 1997) into which the second generation of cultural/reception studies work in this field has led us. To do so would be to accept a quite truncated (and unreflexive) definition of what constitutes the 'real' and/or the 'political', built on unexamined premises in relation to the construction of gender, race and ethnic identities. The study of the media's role in the construction (for some people) of the relationship between the private and the public is logically prior to the study of the media's contribution to internal dynamics of that public, 'political' world itself. The sphere of 'political communication' has as its foundation the series of inclusions and exclusions, on the basis of which only the private, domestic experiences of some categories of people are connected or ('mediated') to the sphere of citizenship and its 'moralities'. To use the discourse of this book, here we must be particularly attentive to the processes of 'framing', which constitute the limits (and shape) of the picture we see within the frame of television's 'window of the world'. It makes all the difference in the world if, for some people, that window is wide open, while for others it is double-glazed, to keep out the noise, or perhaps even nailed shut.

If the 'third generation' of reception studies is to fulfil the promise amply demonstrated by the work in this volume, with its welcome attention to the (meta-)discourses within which both media consumption and media scholarship itself are constituted, then it is to issues of this kind that it will need, centrally, to address itself. The 'morality' of television viewing (and its objects) and of the discourses of the public sphere are simply too important to be left to the attentions of fundamentalist political economists and sociologists of mass communications (cf. Geraghty, 1996).

References

Alasuutari, P. (1992) '"I'm ashamed to admit it but I have watched *Dallas*": the moral hierarchy of television programmes', *Media, Culture & Society*, 14 (4): 561–82.

Bjondebjerg, I. (1989) 'Oppbruddet fra monopolkulturen: En institusjons- og programhistorisk analyse av dansk tv' [*Sekvens-Filmvidenskabelig Årbog*.

Branston, G. (1993) 'Infotainment: A Twilight Zone'. Unpublished paper.

Corner, J. (1991) 'Meaning, Genre and Context: The Problematics of "Public Knowledge" in the New Audience Studies', in J. Curran and M. Gurevitch (eds), *Mass Media and Society*. London: Edward Arnold.

Corner, J. (1995) 'Media Studies and the "Knowledge Problem"', *Screen*, 36 (2): 147–55.

Curran, J. (1976) 'Content and Structuralist Analysis of Mass Communication', Open University Course D305, Milton Keynes: Open University Press.

Curran, J., Morley, D. and Walkerdine, V. (eds) (1996) *Cultural Studies and Communications*. London: Edward Arnold.

Ferguson, M. and Golding, P. (eds) (1997) *Cultural Studies in Question*. London: Sage.

Garnham, N. (1997) 'Political Economy and the Practice of Cultural Studies', in M. Ferguson and P. Golding, (eds), *Beyond Cultural Studies*. London: Sage.

Geraghty, C. (1996) 'Feminism and Media Consumption', in J. Curran, D. Morley and V. Walkerdine (eds), *Cultural Studies and Communications*. London: Edward Arnold.

Groombridge, B. (1972) *Television and the People*. Harmondsworth: Penguin Books.

Hagen, I. (1992) '*News Viewing Ideals and Everyday Practices: The Ambivalences of Watching Dagsrevyen'*. University of Bergen, Department of Mass Communication, Report No. 15.

Hagen, I. (1994) 'The Ambivalences of TV News Viewing: Between Ideals and Everyday Practices', *European Journal of Communication*, 9: 193–220.

Hermes, J. (1997) 'Gender and Media Studies: No Woman, No Cry', in J. Corner, P. Schlesinger and R. Silverstone (eds), *International Handbook of Media Research*. London: Routledge.

Hoijer, B. (1990) 'Reliability, Validity and Generalizability. Three Questions for Qualitive Reception Research', *The Nordicom Review*, 1: 15–20.

Husband, C. (1994) 'The Multi-Ethnic Public Sphere'. Paper presented to European Film and TV Studies Conference, London, July.

Jensen, K. (1995) *The Social Semiotics of Mass Communication*. London: Sage.

Lazarsfeld, P. and Merton, R. (1948) 'Mass Communication, Popular Taste and Organised Social Action', in L. Bryson (ed.) *The Communication of Ideas*. New York: Harper.

Lewis, J. (1991) *The Ideological Octopus: An Exploration of Television and Its Audience*. London: Routledge.

Lewis, J. (1997) 'What Counts in Cultural Studies?' in *Media, Culture & Society*, 19(1): 83–97.

McQuail, D. (1997) 'Policy Help Wanted: Willing and Able Culturalists Please Apply', in M. Ferguson and P. Golding, (eds), *Beyond Cultural Studies*. London: Sage.

Modood, T. (1992) *Not Easy Being British: Colour, Culture and Citizenship*. London: Runnymede Trust.

Morley, D. (1980) *The Nationwide Audience*. London: British Film Institute.

Morley, D. (1986) *Family Television*. London: Comedia.

Morley, D. (1992) *Television, Audiences and Cultural Studies*. London: Routledge.

Morley, D. (forthcoming) 'Finding Out About the World from TV: Some Difficulties' in J. Gripsrud (ed.), *Common Knowledge*. London: Routledge.

Morley, D. and Brunsdon, C. (1998) *The Nationwide Television Studies*. London: Routledge.

Philo, G. and Miller, D. (1997) *Cultural Compliance: Dead Ends of Media/Cultural Studies*. Glasgow Media Group Research Paper, December 1997.

Pines, J. (1992) *Black and White in Colour*. London: British Film Institute.

Pollock, F. (1976 [1955]) 'Empirical Research into Public Opinion', in P. Connerton (ed.), *Critical Sociology*. Harmondsworth: Penguin Books.

Van Zoonen, L. (1994) *Feminist Media Studies*. London: Sage.

Walkowitz, R. (1997) 'Reproducing Reality: Murphy Brown and Illegitimate Politics', in C. Brunsdon, J. D'Acci and L. Spigel (eds), *Feminist Television Criticism: A Reader*. Oxford: Oxford University Press.

INDEX